MAKING MONETARY
AND FISCAL POLICY

G. L. BACH

MAKING MONETARY AND FISCAL POLICY

THE BROOKINGS INSTITUTION
Washington, D.C.

THE BROOKINGS INSTITUTION is an independent organization devoted to nonpartisan research, education, and publication in economics, government, foreign policy, and the social sciences generally. Its principal purposes are to aid in the development of sound public policies and to promote public understanding of issues of national importance.

The Institution was founded on December 8, 1927, to merge the activities of the Institute for Government Research, founded in 1916, the Institute of Economics, founded in 1922, and the Robert Brookings Graduate School of Economics and Government, founded in 1924.

The general administration of the Institution is the responsibility of a Board of Trustees charged with maintaining the independence of the staff and fostering the most favorable conditions for creative research and education. The immediate direction of the policies, program, and staff of the Institution is vested in the President, assisted by an advisory committee of the officers and staff.

In publishing a study, the Institution presents it as a competent treatment of a subject worthy of public consideration. The interpretations and conclusions in such publications are those of the author or authors and do not necessarily reflect the views of the other staff members, officers, or trustees of the Brookings Institution.

FOREWORD

THE ACHIEVEMENT of stable economic growth in the United States over the years ahead—with full employment of men and machines—calls for the effective coordination of monetary, fiscal, and other economic policies. But many believe that management of the nation's fiscal and monetary affairs leaves much to be desired. This book examines the problems of achieving coordination, evaluates existing procedures, and suggests ways of improving them.

The study is divided into three parts. The first surveys the goals we seek to attain through the use of monetary, fiscal, and related policies designed to control the level of aggregate demand. It also identifies those officials who are primarily responsible for promoting economic growth and stability and indicates the main areas in which closer coordination among policymakers and their instruments seems essential if the nation's economic goals are to be attained. This part is directed toward readers who are not already well acquainted with the machinery of macroeconomic policy and the tools of the policymakers.

Part Two presents detailed analyses of the procedures used in making and carrying out macroeconomic policies before 1952, during the Eisenhower administration, and in the Kennedy-Johnson years. These case studies are designed to throw light on fundamental issues, providing a background for analysis of the effectiveness of policymaking and for suggestions on ways to improve it. These chapters will be of interest to readers who wish to know how macroeconomic policies were formulated in the past and how today's procedures evolved through experience.

The main argument of the book appears in Part Three, which summarizes the lessons to be learned from a half century of policymaking and recommends changes that might make the process more effective.

Since 1966 the author, G. L. Bach, has been Frank E. Buck professor of economics and public policy at Stanford University. He serves as a special consultant to the Board of Governors of the Federal Reserve System and as a member of the Brookings Institution's associated staff, in which capacity he prepared this study. Mr. Bach acknowledges his debt to a large number of past and present senior government officials for their insights and suggestions, and for their generosity in reviewing the past with him and in looking toward the future.

He is especially grateful to Gardner Ackley, Arthur F. Burns, Daniel H. Brill, C. Douglas Dillon, James S. Duesenberry, Marriner S. Eccles, Henry H. Fowler, Alfred Hayes, Walter W. Heller, John E. Horne, Neil H. Jacoby, Carl Kaysen, William McChesney Martin, Jr., George W. Mitchell, Arthur M. Okun, Don K. Price, Henry S. Reuss, J. L. Robertson, Robert V. Roosa, Raymond J. Saulnier, Charles L. Schultze, Harry Schwartz, Kenneth Scott, Dan Throop Smith, Robert Solomon, Theodore C. Sorensen, Herbert Stein, and James Tobin. The reflections of these outstanding public officials and scholars provided a fascinating journey into fiscal-monetary history.

The author also wishes to thank Christopher L. Bach, David I. Fand, John H. Kareken, Lawrence B. Krause, William R. Moffat, Joseph A. Pechman, George L. Perry, Leonard S. Silk, and Warren L. Smith, who offered valuable suggestions on various stages of the manuscript.

A preliminary version of the book served as the basis for a conference on economic policymaking at Brookings on April 28, 1970. In addition to several of those named above, the participants included Andrew F. Brimmer, Samuel B. Chase, Jr., J. Dewey Daane, Hugh D. Galusha, Jr., Alfred Hayes, Homer Jones, Sherman J. Maisel, Maurice Mann, Frank E. Morris, J. Charles Partee,

Frank W. Schiff, George P. Shultz, Paul A. Volcker, Henry C. Wallich, and Charles J. Zwick. The volume has benefited from the discussion and suggestions made at the conference.

Lorian Marlantes and Lynette Sweet provided able research assistance and secretarial help. Evelyn Fisher checked the manuscript for accuracy, Virginia C. Haaga edited it, and Penelope Stafford prepared the index.

The views expressed in this book are those of the author and do not necessarily reflect the views of the trustees, officers, or other staff members of the Brookings Institution.

KERMIT GORDON
President

August 1970
Washington, D.C.

CONTENTS

MAKING MONETARY AND FISCAL POLICY

1

INTRODUCTION

EFFECTIVE USE of monetary and fiscal policy is necessary if we are to achieve stable economic growth with high-level employment of men and machines over the years ahead. History shows the unfortunate tendency of the largely private enterprise economic system in the United States to swing between recession and inflation, to spurt and then lag in its upward path. And there is little reason to suppose that in the future the system will automatically generate stable growth with high employment unless government monetary and fiscal policies help to keep aggregate money demand growing roughly apace with the economy's capacity to produce.

Monetary policy governs the supply of money and credit, their cost, and their availability. Fiscal policy controls spending, taxing, and borrowing by the government. The two are the major instruments for regulating the level of aggregate demand. Monetary policy is primarily determined by, and executed through, the Federal Reserve System, headed by the Board of Governors and the Federal Open Market Committee. Fiscal policy is determined jointly by several government authorities—the President, his Council of Economic Advisers, the secretary of the treasury, the director of the Office of Management and Budget, and, most important of all, Congress. Thus, responsibility for monetary and fiscal policy is divided among several authorities. Still other agencies have responsibilities that impinge on monetary and fiscal policy decisions.

3

This book analyzes the problem of achieving effective coordination among monetary, fiscal, and other macroeconomic policies to obtain the desired stable growth in aggregate demand. Both history and theory suggest that optimal policymaking arrangements will depend partly on the goals sought and partly on what specific policies are most likely to achieve those goals. Thus, any evaluation of existing policymaking processes must depend partly on the particular monetary and fiscal policies that seem most likely to achieve the desired stable growth in aggregate demand. While the book is concerned primarily with the policymaking *process,* it necessarily involves some evaluation of the effectiveness of alternative monetary and fiscal policies, since different policymaking arrangements will predictably produce different policy combinations.

The analysis leads to the following recommendations:

1. *On fiscal policymaking.* While recent decades have brought the development and widespread acceptance of an analytical base for the use of stabilizing fiscal policy, the practical results have been at best mixed. Economic growth has been more stable since the Second World War than before, and modern fiscal policy deserves part of the credit. But federal taxes and expenditures have also been massively destabilizing at times—for example, during the inflationary boom of 1965–68. These failures have reflected both reluctance on the part of the President to press for needed tax increases or spending cuts and, even more, unwillingness on the part of Congress to follow the dictates of stabilizing fiscal policy.

Given the realities of the U.S. political process, the first need is to modify fiscal policymaking so as to minimize the possibility that governmental actions will be seriously destabilizing; the second is to use tax-expenditure policy positively to counter clearly destabilizing developments in the private and international sectors of the economy. The most critical need is for better coordination between Congress and the administration.

Specifically, fiscal policymaking by the President and Congress should be altered as follows:

a. The *high-employment* budget should normally show a moderate surplus, reflecting the foreseeable shortage of private savings to finance needed housing and other capital expansion over the decade ahead. However, this presumption should be overridden if *serious* disruptive forces develop in the private or international sector. A program should be in readiness for countering such disruptions. Each January the President should routinely propose to Congress with his Economic Report a flat percentage income surtax (positive, negative, or zero) for the year. It should be designed to move the high-employment budget toward restraint or expansion if federal budget pressure is clearly needed to stimulate or restrain the economy. Congress should act promptly on the proposed surtax as a *stabilization* measure, without concern for tax reform or questions of equity. Congressional handling of regular budget proposals and of changes in the tax structure could remain substantially unchanged, to minimize conflict with the traditional tax and expenditure powers of Congress.

Generally, this would mean that the federal government would forego attempts to "fine tune" the economy through frequent discretionary changes in aggregate expenditures or tax rates. But this approach would, of course, retain the powerful effects of built-in fiscal stabilizers and would not necessarily preclude some use of particular fiscal measures, such as the investment tax credit, for stabilization purposes.

b. If (a) is not adopted, the President should be given discretionary power to raise or lower the surtax by as much as 5 percentage points at any time, for a period of six months, subject to congressional veto. Alternatively, the President could be given discretionary power to *raise,* but not to lower, the surtax.

c. The President should emphasize the *high-employment* budget, rather than the unified budget, in his Economic Report and other macroeconomic (stabilization) proposals to Congress and the public, since the high-employment budget provides a more accurate measure of the impact of federal fiscal action on the economy.

2. *On monetary policymaking.* While monetary policymaking is more flexible than fiscal policymaking, the "correct" monetary policy is often in dispute among experts, especially because of long and uncertain lags in its effects on real output, employment, and prices. Given these uncertainties, the appropriate short-term targets to guide monetary policymakers (interest rates, money market conditions, or monetary aggregates) are also in doubt.

As with fiscal policy, a first goal is to minimize the possibility that destabilizing monetary policies will arise from over-reaction to perceived disruptions. For this purpose, a reasonably stable growth in the basic monetary aggregates (the money stock, unborrowed bank reserves, and so on) should be a primary objective of monetary policy, as should a moderate high-employment surplus for fiscal policy. However, since the Federal Reserve may face substantial disruptions from the private sector (for example, fluctuations in inventories and in fixed investments) resulting from shifts in the demand for money, from international disturbances, and from erratic fiscal policy, it should retain its present powers of discretionary action, while recognizing the danger of destabilizing "stop and go" reactions to such disturbances. Interest rate fluctuations are relevant information for monetary policymaking, especially if financial panics threaten, and though the Federal Reserve focuses on the monetary aggregates, it need not completely exclude short-run attention to money market conditions.

3. *On coordination of fiscal and monetary policy.* The President must be fundamentally responsible for administering the nation's macroeconomic policy aimed at achieving national goals. Macroeconomic policies, including monetary policy, should be coordinated through continuing interaction among the major participants in the policy process. To accomplish this end, the President should make use of whatever informal consultative arrangements— a "quadriad," a "troika," or special cabinet-level committees— best fit his style, and should include the Federal Reserve as a major participant in this policymaking.

4. *On Federal Reserve "independence."* The present degree of independence of the Federal Reserve is about right. It should participate actively in top-level macroeconomic policy decisions, expressing where appropriate a strong position against inflationary fiscal and debt policies. Having so participated, it should generally coordinate monetary policy with the administration's macroeconomic policies, reserving for only very important issues its legal right to defy administration policies. The Federal Reserve's partial "independence" permits it to act as a buffer (or inertial force) against the democratic political process, which appears to have a substantial inflationary bias in the United States today.

5. *On the role of the Federal Reserve chairman.* The chairman of the Board of Governors must speak for the Federal Reserve in its contacts and negotiations on major domestic and international

economic affairs. Thus it is essential that the chairman be someone
the President respects and can work with effectively. To assure this
relationship, the term of office of the chairman should be made
roughly coterminous with that of the President.

6. *On presidential and congressional directives.* No further formal directives to the Federal Reserve from the President or Congress are needed. Congress should continue to oversee Federal
Reserve policies closely and should require thorough reports on
policy actions and the reasons for taking them.

7. *On debt policy.* Debt management is at best a minor stabilization instrument. The Treasury, on new and refunding issues,
and the Federal Reserve, through open market operations, can influence the term structure of interest rates, but given the huge volume of other debt in the economy, this effect is generally small
and temporary.

However, most major differences between the Federal Reserve
and the Treasury center on the interest rates to be paid on new
and refunding issues. Understandably the Treasury usually seeks
to minimize interest costs, while the Federal Reserve focuses more
broadly on the need to stabilize the economy. The long period of
tension between the agencies after the Second World War (with
the President generally on the Treasury's side) reflected the Federal Reserve's growing desire for tighter money to fight inflation
and the Treasury's insistence on maintaining low interest rates.

Over all, economic stabilization goals should take precedence
over Treasury financing preferences; debt management policy
should be subsidiary to (Federal Reserve) monetary policy. But
maintaining an "orderly" short-term money market is a proper
subsidiary goal for both monetary and debt policymakers. Coordination of monetary and debt policy should be part of the coordinating process described above.

Three specific recommendations concerning debt management
are appropriate: (a) Congressional interest rate ceilings on all
forms of Treasury debt should be removed; given the funds to be
raised, mandatory rate ceilings do little to restrain inflation and
often force the Treasury into inefficient and more expensive
financing practices to avoid the ceilings. (b) Congress should repeal the formal ceiling on the national debt. The level of the debt
is determined basically by the tax and spending decisions of Con-

gress, and the Treasury has no alternative to borrowing to finance any deficit. The annual "temporary" exemptions to the "permanent" debt ceiling made by Congress involve mainly political record-making. More important, the ceiling sometimes disrupts orderly management of the debt and has driven the administration to subterfuges like "agency issues," which are technically outside the budget. (c) All direct and guaranteed U.S. government financing should be centered in the Treasury instead of being allocated among numerous agencies by program legislation; *or,* as a second-best alternative, a new national credit bank should be established in which all guaranteed and agency issues would be concentrated. This would facilitate the coordination of agency financing with Treasury–Federal Reserve debt policy and would lower the effective interest cost to the government.[1]

8. *On financial institutions.* Federal supervision of financial institutions should be rationalized:

a. All federally insured commercial banks should be made subject to reserve requirements established by the Federal Reserve, and Federal Reserve discount facilities should be extended to them, at least in times of financial disruption.

b. The Federal Reserve's power to provide liquidity to financial institutions in times of crisis through acquiring obligations of other government credit agencies should be extended indefinitely.

c. Federal bank supervision should be concentrated in one agency—the Federal Reserve, the Federal Deposit Insurance Corporation, or a new national bank supervisory agency.

d. Federally imposed interest rate ceilings on deposits and savings and loan shares should be put on a standby basis, or eliminated, as promptly as is feasible.

e. Federal credit and loan-guarantee programs serve many special purposes, and these special purposes dictate a dispersal of responsibilities among several agencies (the Federal Housing Administration, the Veterans Administration, the Department of Agriculture, and so on). However, to coordinate these programs as

1. In principle, agency spending and debt issues to finance it should be part of the federal budget for stabilization purposes, and hence be reflected in the high-employment surplus or deficit. However, this is a complex issue, which is considered at greater length in Chaps. 7 and 8.

far as possible with the government's macroeconomic policies and to reduce inefficiencies, all agency borrowing should be centered in the Treasury Department or in a new national credit bank.

f. The Financial Institutions Supervisory Act of 1966 and the informal committee of representatives of the institutions should be continued, with participating agencies required to consult in making supervisory decisions and (within congressional provisions) determining interest rates to borrowers.

9. *On wage-price policy, direct controls, and structural changes.* Inflation while the economy is significantly below full employment poses a difficult dilemma for macroeconomic policymakers. This dilemma may arise because aggregate demand mounts rapidly, creating wage and price increases in tight markets. It may reflect differential inflationary expectations that lead some buyers and sellers to raise wages and prices in anticipation of rising prices, leaving others behind in the inflationary process. Broadly, it may reflect excess-income claims—income and price demands by workers, businessmen, farmers, retired people, poor people, and many others who believe that society owes them more goods and services than are available at stable prices. Efforts to achieve these larger income shares through markets and through the political process may create strong inflationary pressures before full employment is reached—inflationary pressures that will generate unemployment unless monetary-fiscal policy validates them (and inflation) through expanded aggregate demand. Finally, the dilemma arises because labor, commodity, and money markets are less than perfect—because of immobilities of labor, goods, and money; because of business, union, and governmental monopoly restrictions on resource flows; because of imperfect information on job opportunities; and the like.

In such an economy, aggregate demand policy alone may be unable to achieve high employment and stable prices simultaneously. Restrictive monetary-fiscal policy to check inflation may keep employment below desired levels; expansionary policy to eliminate unemployment may stimulate inflation. Clearly, structural improvements in labor, commodity, and capital markets (to reduce monopoly restrictions, improve information flows, increase labor mobility, and so on) can increase the level of employment obtainable with any level of aggregate demand; and such measures should be given high priority. But as long as some markets are imperfect, the inflation-unemployment dilemma may remain. In essence, the issue of income distribution—how the real national income shall be divided among many claimants—becomes an inescapable part of the problem facing monetary and fiscal policymakers.

Experience since the Second World War suggests that wage-price policies (sometimes called incomes policies) can provide some help in easing the dilemma of excess income claims if excess aggregate demand pressures are absent or only moderate—as they were, for example, during the early 1960s. Some observers argue that in such circumstances other "direct controls," such as interest rate ceilings on deposits and capital controls to direct credit to particular markets, can help to achieve simultaneously a desired allocation of resources and incomes, high employment, and a stable price level. Certainly such circumstances have created strong pressures for direct controls and structural reforms, and they can be expected to continue to do so. But both theory and history warn against relying on wage-price guidelines or controls as primary anti-inflationary tools. These measures may easily lead to over-intervention by the administration in individual wage and price setting.

10. *On international monetary policy.* By law and custom, U.S. international monetary policy is primarily the responsibility of the Treasury, working cooperatively with the Federal Reserve, the Council of Economic Advisers, and the State and Commerce Departments. Coordination among these agencies now operates satisfactorily, but further reform of the international payments and liquidity mechanisms is needed to free domestic monetary policy (and to a lesser extent fiscal policy) from international constraints:

a. Adequate total liquidity for the international system is needed to avoid undue constraints on domestic policy. The introduction of special drawing rights to supplement dollars and gold reserves should ease this problem substantially.

b. Improved international adjustment mechanisms are needed. Widened parity bands, "crawling pegs," or more frequent devaluations and revaluations under the Bretton Woods agreement could ease domestic adjustment problems for the United States and other nations.[2]

c. Improved borrowing facilities for use in confidence crises are needed, preferably through an international organization like the International Monetary Fund or through intercountry agreements.

11. *On Federal Reserve structure and processes.* Changes in the structure of the Federal Reserve are not urgently needed, but the following modifications deserve serious examination in case the over-all structure is reconsidered:

a. All major policy functions should be unified in the Board of Governors, eliminating the Federal Open Market Committee but requiring continuing Board consultation with the presidents of the Federal Reserve Banks.

b. The Board should be reduced in size to five members serving ten-year staggered terms.

c. Special regional and occupational qualifications for Board members should be eliminated.

d. Technical ownership of the Federal Reserve Banks by member banks should be eliminated by retiring the privately held capital stock.

12. *On research.* Adoption of these proposals would significantly improve the ability of the United States to avoid major instability and should further reduce its exposure to minor economic fluctuations. The Achilles' heel of modern macroeconomic policy, however, is our limited and imperfect knowledge of the functioning of the macroeconomy and its major sectors. Only more basic research on monetary, fiscal, and related macrobehavior can provide the foundation needed for effective and reliable macroeconomic policy in the years to come. The potential payoff on investment in such research is high.

2. Elimination of a fixed dollar price for gold would be a more extreme step toward the same goal.

PART ONE

THE POLICY WORLD

2

POLICY GOALS
AND THE POLICYMAKERS

To DEVELOP optimal stabilization policies, it is necessary first to be clear as to what our basic economic policy goals are, who are the important policymakers, and what instruments they have at their disposal.

The Goals of Macroeconomic Policy

The idea of specifically stated national macroeconomic goals and conscious government policy to achieve them is relatively new. Since the development of modern industrial societies, mankind has suffered intermittent inflationary booms, financial panics, and depressions, which have brought unemployment and want to millions. Economists, men of affairs, and ordinary citizens have looked for explanations for these catastrophes and for ways of mitigating or eliminating their grievous effects. But at least until the First World War, the dominant view was that monetary excesses and waves of speculation were largely responsible for inflationary booms and the financial crises they spawned, which were often followed by liquidation and depression. Insofar as there was any conscious government macroeconomic policy, it was, for the most part, to follow roughly the dictates of the gold standard, under which the stock of money should vary in proportion to inflows and outflows of gold from each nation—although deviations from this rule were frequent.

While unemployment and inflation were not to be accepted passively, there was little thought that the government should take an active, continuing role in stabilizing the economy. Establishment in 1913 of the Federal Reserve System—the nation's first real central bank—reflected the widespread concern over financial panics that followed the painful collapse of 1907. The primary goals of the new system were merely to provide an "elastic currency" and to centralize bank reserves so as to reduce the vulnerability of the banking system to financial panics.

In the century preceding the great depression of the 1930s, the prevailing economic doctrine was that the price level was determined by, or at least heavily dependent on, the stock of money (currency and bank deposits) in the hands of the public. This was closely related to the widespread focus on financial panics as *the,* or at least *a,* key to the problems of instability that troubled the economy. Thus, the earliest attempts to state an economic goal toward which public policy should aim centered around stabilization of the price level—avoidance of both inflation and deflation. From 1913 through the 1930s, there were repeated attempts by Congress to prescribe stabilization of the price level as the major goal of the Federal Reserve.[1]

When gold was downgraded in the 1930s from its key position, the question of other guides to monetary policy had to be faced. Even earlier, an unwillingness to submit helplessly to economic instability had led more and more people to press for government action. As Herbert Stein has observed, "Americans who thought about such things in the 1920's did not regard themselves as the accidental beneficiaries of the workings of the invisible hand in a system of laissez-faire. They believed that theirs was an era of deliberate social engineering."[2]

Nonetheless, it remained for the great depression, the ideas of John Maynard Keynes, and the New Deal expansion of government intervention in economic life—followed by massive govern-

1. For a detailed account, see Irving Fisher, *Stable Money: A History of the Movement* (Adelphi, 1934), especially pp. 146–215.

2. Herbert Stein, *The Fiscal Revolution in America* (University of Chicago Press, 1969), p. 7.

ment deficits to finance the Second World War—to mobilize expert and lay opinion behind "full employment" as a widely approved goal of public policy. In the banking reform legislation of 1935, Marriner Eccles, the new chairman of the Federal Reserve Board, urged the House to include a general mandate directing the Board to promote business stability, but his advice was rejected. The thirties, and indeed the Second World War, ended without any clear statement of purpose or goals from Congress. Nor, in spite of growing public acceptance of government action to avoid depression and inflation, was there any congressional statement of basic macroeconomic goals. The nation's prime economic objectives were surely (in the 1930s) to end the depression and (in the 1940s) to support the war effort without serious inflation, but not until 1946 was there a concrete statement of national goals for macroeconomic policy.

THE EMPLOYMENT ACT OF 1946

As the Second World War neared its close, there was widespread concern that peace, with demobilization of more than 10 million men and the end of massive arms spending, would bring widespread unemployment.[3] The devastating impact of the great depression was fresh in everyone's mind. Thus, out of the depression and the Second World War came a widely shared belief that the government could, and should, act to avoid renewed unemployment. In late 1944, 68 percent of all respondents in a survey by *Fortune* magazine believed that "preventing unemployment after the war" was the issue "most important to America."[4] Proposals to avoid depression and unemployment came from many quarters— from government agencies, academic economists, businessmen, labor leaders, and the man in the street.[5] And the climate that pro-

3. For an authoritative, detailed analysis of the forces leading up to the Employment Act of 1946 and its legislative history, see Stephen Bailey, *Congress Makes a Law: The Story Behind the Employment Act of 1946* (Columbia University Press, 1950); also *Twentieth Anniversary of the Employment Act of 1946: An Economic Symposium,* Hearing before the Joint Economic Committee, 89 Cong. 2 sess. (1966).

4. *Fortune,* "The Fortune Survey," Vol. 31 (January 1945), p. 260.

5. An annotated bibliography on plans to avoid postwar unemployment, prepared by the Legislative Reference Service in 1945, covered fifty-six tightly packed pages. (*Bibliography on Full Employment,* Report to the Committee on Banking and Currency, Senate Committee Print, No. 2, 79 Cong. 1 sess. [1945].)

duced the postwar "full-employment" bill was worldwide; by the end of the war, a score of countries and the United Nations had written into their constitutions or statutes clauses concerning full employment or the right of citizens to jobs.

Several major proposals culminated in the Employment Act of 1946. It declared:

> . . . it is the continuing policy and responsibility of the Federal Government to use all practicable means consistent with its needs and obligations . . . to foster and promote free competitive enterprise and the general welfare, conditions under which there will be afforded useful employment opportunities . . . for those able, willing, and seeking to work, and to promote maximum employment, production, and purchasing power.[6]

This declaration has been the cornerstone of U.S. macroeconomic public policy in the postwar years. Through more than two decades of stormy controversy Congress has not amended it either to strengthen its ambiguous language on "maximum employment, production, and purchasing power" (what does "maximum" mean?) or to add other objectives, such as the avoidance of inflation. The act requires the President to submit to Congress an annual Economic Report; and it set up a Council of Economic Advisers to serve the President in implementing the act and a new congressional Joint Committee on the Economic Report (later renamed the Joint Economic Committee) to review the government's economic policy at least annually.

Five major issues have arisen in the interpretation of the Employment Act. Three concern the meaning of the words "maximum employment, production, and purchasing power." The fourth concerns the applicability of the act to the various "independent agencies"—notably the Federal Reserve and later the Federal Home Loan Bank Board (FHLBB). The fifth, and most important, concerns what kind of action by the government is called for.[7]

1. *Maximum employment.* The words "maximum employment, production, and purchasing power" were a final compromise between those who favored and those who feared a guarantee by the federal government of "full employment" for persons able and

6. 60 Stat. 23.

7. These issues are now of primarily historical interest, since each administration and period reinterprets the act and precedent in its own way.

willing to work. The sponsors of the bill could not get the votes to pass the "full employment" language. The term "maximum employment" left it up to future congresses and administrations to define what level of employment is, as a practical matter, the "maximum."

After 1946, 4 percent unemployment was widely considered a practical definition of "maximum employment." As postwar prosperity pushed unemployment down, some suggested 3 percent. But ten years later, because of the persistent slack in the economy, the figure had moved up to 5 percent in much discussion of the act. During the Kennedy administration, however, the figure moved back to 4 percent as an "interim goal" in numerous official statements.[8] Moreover, as will be seen below, the existence of "hidden" unemployment was mentioned in both expert and popular discussion. Reported unemployment is simply that proportion of the labor force (now, all those sixteen years of age or over who are at work or seeking work) that is not employed. But in slack times and even in good times, many marginal workers lose heart and simply do not look for jobs; hence, they are not considered to be in the labor force and are not counted as unemployed.[9]

2. *Economic growth.* Avoidance of unnecessary unemployment in the business cycle sense dominated discussion during the framing of the Employment Act. As the 1950s wore on, however, growing emphasis was placed on the long-term growth rate of total output. Partly this reflected concern because the U.S. growth rate— about 3 percent annually—lagged far behind that of both the USSR and the Western European nations. Partly it reflected a growing recognition that merely assuring full employment might not be enough to keep the real standard of living rising rapidly.

President Eisenhower's Council of Economic Advisers stressed the importance of economic growth.[10] And with the advent of the Kennedy administration, faster growth became an accepted major goal of public policy.[11] Based on experience before the Second World War, 3 to $3\frac{1}{2}$ percent annually was frequently cited as a de-

8. See, for example, *Economic Report of the President, January 1962*, p. 48.

9. The minimum feasible long-run level of unemployment depends heavily on such "structural" factors as labor mobility, training and retraining facilities, information on job vacancies, and the like.

10. See, for example, *Economic Report of the President, January 1957*, Chap. 2.

11. See *Economic Report of the President, January 1962*, Chap. 2.

sirable minimum. But 4 percent became the "interim objective" of the Kennedy administration, reflecting the higher growth rate achieved in the postwar period and the general success of European nations in the postwar years in achieving 5 percent or more. Most statements of Johnson and Nixon administration officials have called for similar growth rates.

The goal of faster economic growth differs significantly from those of high employment and stable prices. The latter two can be sought largely through aggregate demand policy. Faster long-term growth, however, is mainly a problem of supply or productive capacity. While adequate aggregate demand can help assure full use of available capacity, any increase in that capacity depends primarily on new capital investment, technological advance, more workers, and improved worker skills. Thus, although faster long-term growth may be a fundamental national goal, it is somewhat peripheral to this analysis, which focuses on monetary-fiscal policy.

3. *Stable prices.* The "maximum purchasing power" goal in the Employment Act is ambiguous indeed. If it is taken to mean maximum dollar volume of purchasing power, the language is nonsense, for an infinitely high rate of money-issue and inflation would produce the largest dollar volume of purchasing power. If it means maximum purchasing power in *real* terms, the objective appears to be practically identical with "maximum output." Many government officials and observers outside the government have argued that the act must have been intended to specify a stable price level; they generously contend that to read it otherwise strains one's common sense.[12]

Whatever Congress thought in 1946, it is now widely agreed that reasonable stability of the price level (avoidance of both inflation and deflation) is an important objective of macroeconomic policy. The price stability goal has been stated repeatedly by Presidents Eisenhower, Kennedy, and Johnson, by their Councils of Economic Advisers, and by the Federal Reserve Board.[13]

Just what price-level stability means as a practical matter is a

12. See, for example, *The Relationship of Prices to Economic Stability and Growth,* Compendium of Papers Submitted by Panelists Appearing before the Joint Economic Committee, 85 Cong. 2 sess. (1958).

13. *Economic Report of the President, January 1957,* pp. iii–iv; *Economic Report of the President, January 1962,* pp. 7–8; *Economic Report of the President, February 1968,* pp. 19–21 and 63–67; *The Federal Reserve and the Treasury: Answers to Questions from the Commission on Money and Credit* (Prentice-Hall, 1963), p. 21.

subject of considerable dispute. And, as will be seen below, many economists argue that it should be subordinate to the goal of high employment. Nonetheless, avoiding inflation has come to be an accepted major policy goal and was given top billing by the Nixon administration and the Federal Reserve Board in 1969.[14]

4. *Coverage of Employment Act.* The Employment Act states the policy of the "federal government." Does this include the "independent agencies," such as the Federal Reserve and the Federal Home Loan Bank Board (FHLBB)? While some observers at first questioned its applicability, the Federal Reserve Board has repeatedly stated that it is subject to the policy provisions of the Employment Act,[15] and it includes Section 2 of the Employment Act with the Federal Reserve Act in its official publications. The FHLBB has also explicitly recognized the applicability of the Employment Act, though with reservations concerning possible conflicts between its provisions and those in housing legislation.[16] As a practical matter, there is no doubt as to the general coverage of the Employment Act, but there is a great deal of uncertainty about economic policy where (as in the case of the FHLBB) conflicts arise with the more specific goals set for individual agencies.

5. *Implications for action.* Section 2 of the Employment Act of 1946 is heavily laden with constraints and provisos. The federal government declares its policy to be "to use all practicable means consistent with its needs and obligations and other essential considerations of national policy"; it is to proceed "in a manner calculated to foster and promote free competitive enterprise and the general welfare"; and the whole statement rests under a cloud of uncertainty as to whether the final clause, "and to promote maximum employment, production, and purchasing power," is subject to all the reservations specified by the preceding clause, or is to be read as directly following the injunction to "use all practicable means." Either reading makes equal sense, but the strength of the directive differs substantially under the two interpretations.

14. Difficult decisions must be made if action to reduce unemployment generates inflation, and vice versa. This problem is examined in Chaps. 7 and 8.

15. See, for example, William McChesney Martin, Jr., in *Monetary Policy and the Management of the Public Debt,* Hearings before the Subcommittee on General Credit Control and Debt Management of the Joint Committee on the Economic Report, 82 Cong. 2 sess. (1952), p. 78.

16. *Report of the Federal Home Loan Bank Board for the Year Ending December 31, 1967,* pp. 50–51.

In fact, however, this ambiguity seems not to have mattered much. Two decades have brought widespread acceptance of the spirit of the act, both inside the government and out, whatever the letter of the law. This is evidenced by a long series of Economic Reports of the President, by many statements by congressmen and high government officials, and by sweeping acceptance of the spirit of the act by observers outside the government—from newspaper writers to corporation presidents.

BALANCE-OF-PAYMENTS EQUILIBRIUM

No word about the international balance of payments appears in the Employment Act. This is not surprising, since the act was written in 1946, when the United States had two-thirds of the world's monetary gold stock. But ten years later a persistent U.S. balance-of-payments deficit and the related gold drain began to attract attention. By 1960 concern for the restoration of balance-of-payments equilibrium had become a major constraint on U.S. domestic macroeconomic policy.

Just what would constitute equilibrium in the U.S. balance of payments is a debatable question, which will be discussed at length in later chapters. When U.S. payments abroad (for imports and through capital transfers) exceed payments received, foreigners accumulate an increased stock of U.S. dollars. They can hold these dollars in bank deposits or short-term investments in the United States, or, until recently, they could (through their central banks) ask for U.S. gold in exchange for their dollars.[17] This was the type of payments disequilibrium that the United States faced through the 1950s and 1960s; as a result, foreigners accumulated over $30 billion of liquid U.S. dollar holdings, and the United States paid out about $14 billion in gold, a cumulative payments deficit of nearly $45 billion.

As the U.S. gold stock dwindled in the 1960s, officials felt increasing pressure to reduce, if not to eliminate entirely, the U.S. payments deficit. Thus, in the 1960s international payments considerations became a significant constraint on our freedom to use expansive domestic macroeconomic policy aimed at "maximum em-

---

17. Since early 1968, as will be seen below, except for central banks, the ability of foreigners to obtain U.S. gold for dollars has been substantially eliminated.

ployment, production, and purchasing power." In the judgment of many conservatives, equilibrium in the international payments balance is itself a major goal of macroeconomic policy, as important as high employment, faster growth, and stable prices.[18]

RELATED GOALS

In a complex democratic society there are many economic goals. Nearly every piece of economic legislation has one or more, and various branches of the government develop explicit or implicit economic goals of their own. For example, assistance in financing middle- and low-income housing has been the goal of numerous congressional acts, and several federal agencies (such as the Federal Housing Administration and the Federal Home Loan Bank Board) have this as a prime, though not a sole, objective; they view the housing industry and the financial institutions serving it as their special constituency. Even more important for this study, the Federal Reserve Board, like central banks abroad, feels a special concern for the financial markets, and stability in those markets is a primary policy objective. The financial collapse of 1907 stimulated establishment of the Federal Reserve System. The great financial collapse of 1929–33 dominated thinking about monetary policy for many years. Moreover, central banks everywhere consider it their responsibility to facilitate, within reasonable bounds, Treasury financing of the national debt at a moderate cost. In recent years this support for Treasury financing has been termed "even keeling" of the market.

These special objectives impinge to a greater or less degree on the pursuit of the broader macroeconomic objectives in the Employment Act. In the case of the individual federal agencies concerned, their particular constituencies often reflect more pressing goals, as a practical matter, than the broader but more amorphous macro objectives. This conflict, which often arises out of particular situations, frequently leads to policy measures that seem inappropriate in the light of the nation's macro goals. Special goals—often

18. As is discussed below, there is considerable dispute over just what constitutes "equilibrium" in the balance of payments. The issue is considerably more complex than merely attaining "balance" in payment flows. Different concepts of balance (notably in the "liquidity" versus the "official settlements" definitions) give significantly different statistical results. Nor does it necessarily follow that "balance" under either concept is a desirable, or equilibrium, position.

clarified and articulated by particular constituencies that speak with a loud and effective voice—may predominate over broader, unrepresented macro goals. Such conflicts of goals arise repeatedly in the chapters ahead.

POLICY OBJECTIVES

Despite the ambiguities of the Employment Act and the somewhat disorderly way in which in practice the United States formulates its economic goals, since 1946 a surprisingly wide consensus has developed as to the major objectives of macroeconomic policy —in the White House, in the Council of Economic Advisers, in relevant congressional committees, among economists, and even among the general public. High-level employment, a reasonably stable price level, a satisfactory rate of growth in total output, and, to a lesser extent, equilibrium in the balance of payments are the goals cited over and over—all within the constraint that substantial freedom of economic choice be maintained for individuals and for businesses. If the reports of the Council of Economic Advisers are used as a test, the triad of high employment, growth, and price stability was established as early as the first Eisenhower administration. They have recurred more and more explicitly with the passing years. Equilibrium of external payments appeared in the late 1950s as a separate goal, or a major constraint on domestic policy; and it has persisted since then.

Different specific interpretations of the Employment Act reflect reality in the United States. The act sets no specific target figures for any of the goals. Nor are any likely to be set by Congress, which had trouble enough agreeing on even the ambiguous language now in the act. But so it is with much legislation. To look only to formal legislation for national economic objectives is to miss much of the substance of the democratic process. Public policy is defined as much in congressional committee hearings as it is in the often ambiguous words that appear in the statutes. At least a half dozen major committees in the House and Senate (for example, Ways and Means, Appropriations, Banking and Currency, and Finance) deal continuously with central issues of macroeconomic policy. Many others deal with macroeconomic policy peripherally —for example, in farm or housing legislation. In the voluminous reports of these committees and in their legislative proposals, the operational definition of many economic goals is to be found, just as it is in the public and private statements and acts of the President and his chief administrative officials.

The Policymakers

The Constitution allocates to Congress the power to legislate, and to the President and the executive branch the power to execute this legislation. Thus, in a fundamental sense, Congress holds the power to make macroeconomic policy, through broad directives or through detailed specifications, to be implemented by the executive branch. In some areas, such as monetary policy, Congress has seen fit to delegate its powers almost entirely to an "independent" agency or commission like the Federal Reserve. In others, such as tax policy, it clings firmly to the power to legislate in detail. But even where Congress delegates its legislative power, it can at any time revoke this delegation and undertake directly the policymaking involved.

CONGRESS

The process of congressional policymaking varies greatly from time to time and issue to issue. Most of the critical work of legislation goes on behind the scenes, in committees and subcommittees and in off-the-record negotiations among individuals and interest groups in Congress. On major policy issues, the entire Congress may inform itself thoroughly, and Congress as a whole actually makes the law. In most cases, however, given the immense complexity of the issues Congress faces, only the committees immediately concerned, plus perhaps a few other especially interested congressmen, are intimately involved with the development of the legislation that comes from the committee onto the floor of either house. For the most part, committee recommendations are accepted by both houses, though sometimes with substantial modifications. The individual congressman has no choice but to rely heavily on the expertise of his fellows who are on the committees handling any particular legislation. Only on major issues can he afford to take the time to inform himself thoroughly on the details of the legislation and its merits.

On macroeconomic policy issues, nine congressional committees

—four in the House and four in the Senate, plus one joint committee—occupy strategic positions. Both the Senate and the House have appropriations committees, through which all appropriations must clear. Thus, these committees, headed by congressional veterans of long standing, have enormous power over the amount and direction of federal spending. In turn, the appropriations committees have many subcommittees, each responsible for some portion of the federal budget. Washington veterans know and often fear the power of the chairmen of these subcommittees (thirteen in the House alone). Each is a lord ruling over his fiefdom, jealous of his prerogatives. Many of these men are virtually unknown outside Congress, except by the interest groups they affect and by news reporters. Some have made a lifetime career of expertise in the particular sector of expenditures over which they preside. Regardless of what the President and the Council of Economic Advisers may say about the national economy and fiscal policy, the subcommittee is concerned about the welfare of the groups and interests in its own domain—the military, farmers, atomic energy, education, housing. The largely independent actions of thirteen subcommittees cannot easily be guided by one national fiscal policy, governed by the need to control aggregate government spending in relation to aggregate tax receipts.

Equally important are the two committees that handle tax matters—the House Ways and Means Committee and the Senate Finance Committee. Here, too, individuals with many years of seniority have gained the important chairmanships, and they wield great power to expedite or block particular pieces of revenue legislation. The key position of Representative Wilbur Mills, longtime chairman of the House Ways and Means Committee, which must originate all tax legislation, is well known. Without his support, tax legislation has virtually no chance of getting to the floor of the House and hence into law; with his support, few tax bills reported out of the House Ways and Means Committee have failed of enactment. These four committees thus occupy strategic positions in the making of federal fiscal policy—the levying of taxes and the approval of federal spending.

The President each year presents an overview of federal expenditures and taxes in relation to the health of the total economy, and periodically recommends major tax or spending changes aimed at stimulating or damping the economy. But the broad view tends to be lost in the complex appropriations process. Even presidential tax proposals generally move slowly; months and even years elapse before a divided, bickering Congress finally acts on complex major tax bills, while economists and administration officials wring their hands in frustration.

Both the Senate and the House have Banking and Currency Committees, which are also prestigious committees with sweeping powers on the economic front. They have direct responsibility for all monetary and banking legislation and thus occupy critical positions in relation to monetary policy. They are also concerned with a host of related issues, such as regulation of financial institutions, housing legislation and mortgage credit, and the Treasury's handling of the federal debt.

Interposed between the legislative committees and final enactment of bills are the House and Senate Rules Committees, whose chairmen wield the greatest power of all in determining what legislation can go on to the floor of their respective houses for action. The entire House or Senate can require that legislation be brought to the floor without the approval of its Rules Committee, but this happens only rarely.

In addition, the Employment Act of 1946 established what is now the Joint Economic Committee of Congress. This is a nonlegislative committee, but it has exercised considerable influence. It is directed by the Employment Act to consider the annual Economic Report of the President on the state of the economy, and it does so in detail. Moreover, it has steadily widened its sphere of consideration to include a variety of economic issues—inflation and depression, international economic affairs, gold, economic growth, fiscal policy, and many others.

The JEC does not have as much prestige as do the legislative committees. Its chairman has often been an "intellectual" among members of Congress, and its influence has depended in considerable part on the chairman and his few leading colleagues. Reflecting this status, the committee has increasingly provided a broad forum for consideration of both macro- and microeconomic issues. It brings to its hearings a wide range of government officials, academic economists, businessmen, and labor leaders. Its deliberations are widely reported by the news media. Perhaps most important, these hearings serve as a major educational experience for the congressmen who sit on the committee. Many of them have benefited substantially by "going to school" through the Joint Economic Committee.

To consider only the legislative activities of Congress would be to miss a major part of the picture. The various committees maintain a continuing surveillance over the administrative branch of the government and the so-called independent agencies. For example, the banking and currency committees and their subcommittees have held literally hundreds of hearings on Federal Reserve policy and operations. The subjects of their investigations have ranged from the role of money and monetary institutions in our economy to trivia, such as how much entertainers at staff parties at Federal Reserve Banks have been paid. Representative Wright Patman of Texas, a long-time foe of banking interests and critic of the Federal Reserve, has devoted thirty years of his life to surveillance of the System and its operations. The exchanges at committee hearings between him and the chairmen of the Federal Reserve Board can by now be predicted in advance, since they have been over the same ground so many times since the 1930s.

Congressional committee investigations are a major channel for policymaking as well as for checking on policy implementation. Much legislation is broad and sweeping in language. This is notably true in the area of monetary policy, less so in the area of fiscal policy, since Congress has been jealous of its prerogatives to control in detail both expenditures and taxes. The hearings of a subcommittee on financial institutions of a Banking and Currency Committee may not get many headlines, but they will be followed with avid interest by savings and loan associations throughout the country and by the federal agencies concerned with financial policy, such as the Federal Reserve, the Federal Home Loan Bank Board, the Office of the Comptroller of the Currency, and the Federal Deposit Insurance Corporation.

THE PRESIDENT AND THE EXECUTIVE BRANCH

The President can exert great power over macroeconomic policy. He is responsible for executing the laws enacted by Congress, and he heads the huge executive branch of the government—a sprawling hierarchy of departments and agencies, many of which are given broad powers and responsibilities by law. He exerts substantial influence over the so-called independent agencies and commissions, which are actually only partly independent and are to a considerable extent in the President's domain.

Even more important, over the past century the President has become the leader of his party and of the entire government in proposing and pressing for legislation. Thus, although he moves only within a restricted range in administering the spending and tax laws enacted by Congress, the President and his office have become the nation's principal analyst of the need for fiscal expansion or for restraint in the economy and its foremost proponent of legislation to meet these needs.

The *Office of Management and Budget* (a new agency which absorbed the Bureau of the Budget in 1970) is the President's right hand on expenditure policy. Each year it organizes the spending plans of the entire federal government and molds these into a coherent budget, which the President presents to Congress. It also oversees the expenditures involved in the budget. Thus, unless Congress specifically goes beyond the budgetary plans of the President, the office's position is a commanding one, since no regular federal agency obtains funds except through the budget. The director of the Office of Management and Budget probably sees the President more frequently than does any other top government official. The office works closely with the various agencies and with committees of Congress.[19]

The *Treasury Department* is responsible, under the President, for raising the funds authorized to be spent by Congress, partly through taxes that Congress enacts and partly through borrowing when taxes are not sufficient to cover expenditures. Tax legislation is traditionally detailed, and the role of the Treasury in tax administration is essentially the straightforward one of administering the law. This is in contrast to expenditure policy, where the President and the Budget Bureau have some leeway as to rates of spending within the dollar totals authorized by Congress. But the Treasury's voice in proposing new taxes and adjustments of tax rates to meet the needs of the economy is a central one. The secretary of the treasury normally acts as the President's representative on tax

19. Arthur Smithies, in *The Budgetary Process in the United States* (McGraw-Hill, 1955), provides a complete account of the federal budget process.

issues, and the Treasury has the major role in preparing new tax bills that the President wants to present to Congress. Treasury experts, together with the experts of the tax committees in Congress, map out the detailed provisions of tax legislation.

Also, by law and tradition, the Treasury has been responsible for U.S. international monetary policy. The law gives the Treasury control over gold and foreign exchange operations and over U.S. representatives on international financial agencies. The secretary of the treasury, more than the secretary of state, speaks for the United States on international monetary issues. On such matters, the Treasury works closely with the Council of Economic Advisers, the State Department, the Federal Reserve Board, and other agencies, as well as with special assistants to the President. But even though many voices are involved in setting the government's international monetary policy, it is generally agreed that the government must have a single foreign economic policy, not a series of different ones advocated by different agencies. In the last analysis, the Treasury speaks for the U.S. government and the President on these issues. Thus, the secretary of the treasury has substantial power in formulating and carrying out international monetary policy.

The Council of Economic Advisers is part of the Executive Office of the President. It heads no department and has no formal constituency. Its role depends heavily on the relationship to the President of the chairman and other council members. Under the Employment Act of 1946, it is directed to assist the President in implementing the objectives of that act, but the President has wide discretion in his use of the council.

Since 1950, the council has become increasingly important as economic analyst and adviser to presidents. Fundamentally, it is responsible for overseeing the state of the economy, for continually checking on the appropriateness of government policies for stable economic growth, and for working intimately with the President and other parts of the executive branch in developing overall legislative policy in the economic field. Some council chairmen have worked closely with congressional committees; others have remained more in the background as presidential advisers. But for macroeconomic policy, the council is now perhaps the President's most important single advisory group. It is *his* council and more specifically *his* part of the government than are the regular executive branch departments.

As will become evident in later chapters, every President has had his own behind-the-scenes White House assistants who act as his personal eyes and ears on domestic or international economic issues. These special assistants have no formal power. But in fact they can exert great influence, because they have direct access to the President and because usually they understand most clearly the President's position on the issues at stake. Gabriel Hauge under President Eisenhower, Carl Kaysen and Theodore Sorensen under President Kennedy, and Francis Bator under President Johnson, names often little known to the general public, have been near the center of decision making on domestic and international economic policy issues.

These are the central agencies in the executive branch, working for and with the President on domestic and international economic policy. But there are a host of others that play important roles on particular issues. Where wage-price policies are involved, the secretaries of labor and commerce and their staffs have influence. On questions of domestic credit policy, the so-called credit and lending agencies, such as the Federal Housing Administration and the Farm Credit Administration, are centrally involved. Even departments like Defense, State, and Agriculture often play important roles in formulating macroeconomic policy. National defense policy and macroeconomic policy are interwoven at many points. International political decisions may have sweeping implications for domestic economic policy. Farm price supports, farm credit activities, and so on, may be important forces affecting the over-all level of economic activity.

Thus, the process of macroeconomic policy formation within the executive branch is complex. The over-all fiscal position of the government is the result of all its expenditures and taxes. In a political democracy, many individuals and groups are involved on important issues, and, as elsewhere in economic life, each looks out for his own interest and his own constituency, while being concerned at the same time for the over-all welfare of the nation.

The potential power of the President is great, yet it is far from complete. He proposes, and Congress disposes. Even his own agencies come to have constituencies and goals of their own; the Commerce Department speaks for business, the Labor Department for labor, the Defense Department for the defense complex, the Department of Housing and Urban Development for the cities, and so on. Often they disagree. The pressures they feel may conflict with the President's own goals. How much power the President actually has depends on the effectiveness with which he marshals the powers of his office—by leading and coalescing public opinion, by influencing important congressmen, and by leading his own executive officers. Formal "powers" are no guarantee of power. Many a new president has discovered to his dismay that he may make decisions, yet nothing happens. Fundamentally, the President is the leader of the government and the nation, but he can exercise that leadership only through persuasion. As Richard Neustadt has perceptively observed:

The essence of a President's persuasive task with congressmen and everybody else, *is to induce them to believe that what he wants of them is what their own appraisal of their own responsibilities requires them to do in their interest, not his.* Because men may differ in their views on public policy, because differences in outlook stem from differences in duty . . . that task is bound to be more like collective bargaining than like a reasoned argument among philosopher kings.[20]

INDEPENDENT AGENCIES AND COMMISSIONS

Beginning with the Interstate Commerce Commission in 1887, Congress has established a series of "independent" regulatory commissions to administer regulatory rules or principles established by legislation. These commissions are "independent" in the sense that they are outside the regular executive branch of the government and thus do not answer directly to the President in the same way that cabinet officers do. In each case the regulatory responsi-

---

20. *Presidential Power: The Politics of Leadership* (John Wiley, 1960), p. 46. Neustadt also relates the following anecdote:

"In the early summer of 1952, before the heat of the campaign, President Truman used to contemplate the problems of the General-become-President should Eisenhower win the forthcoming election. 'He'll sit here,' Truman would remark (tapping his desk for emphasis), 'and he'll say, "Do this! Do that!" *And nothing will happen.* Poor Ike—it won't be a bit like the Army. He'll find it very frustrating.' Eisenhower evidently found it so. 'In the face of the continuing dissidence and disunity, the President sometimes simply exploded with exasperation,' wrote Robert Donovan in comment on the early months of Eisenhower's first term." (*Ibid.,* p. 9.) Eisenhower was not the first, nor the last, President to learn this lesson.

bility is delegated to a multimember board or commission. This recognizes the quasi-judicial role of the commissions, which both administer the law and pass on the actions of individuals or businesses under the act. Commissioners are typically given long terms of office, presumably to remove them somewhat from the day-to-day pressures of the political process that bear on Congress, the President, and the rest of the executive branch. In many cases, bipartisan appointments are required by law. Normally it is expected that the President will not try to remove commissioners who do not agree with his policies, although the exact conditions under which he may do so are legally somewhat hazy.[21]

The Federal Reserve System. Establishment of the Federal Reserve System in 1913 represented a compromise among competing approaches to central banking. Believing that monetary control and regulatory responsibilities should be kept apart from the day-to-day pressures of partisan politics, Congress made the Federal Reserve substantially independent of the President and other executive agencies.

It is important to recognize that there was no thought in 1913 of establishing a central bank to make monetary policy in the modern sense, directed primarily at stabilizing the growth in aggregate spending. Since adherence to the gold standard and to sound commercial banking practices were relied on to determine the proper amount and use of currency and bank credit, little attention was given to the possible need for a unified national monetary policy.[22]

---

21. The standard reference on the independent regulatory agencies and commissions is Robert E. Cushman, *The Independent Regulatory Commissions* (Oxford University Press, 1941). See also *Task Force Report on Regulatory Commissions*, Prepared for the Commission on Organization of the Executive Branch of the Government [Hoover Commission] (1949); and Samuel Krislov and L. D. Musolf (eds.), *The Politics of Regulation: A Reader* (Houghton Mifflin, 1964).

22. Representative Carter Glass of Virginia, who sponsored the Federal Reserve Act in Congress and before the public, and who for over three decades thereafter played a leading congressional role in all legislation concerning the System, records his picture of this period in *An Adventure in Constructive Finance* (Doubleday, Page, 1927). Lloyd W. Mints, *History of Banking Theory in Great Britain and the United States* (University of Chicago Press, 1945), especially in Chaps. 11 and 12, provides the best account of the development of banking theory underlying the Federal Reserve Act. Authoritative accounts of the background of the act are provided by H. Parker Willis in *The Federal Reserve System: Legislation, Organization, and Operation* (Ronald, 1923) and by Paul M. Warburg in *The Federal Reserve System: Its Origin and Growth* (Macmillan, 1930).

The massive financial and economic collapse of the early 1930s, however, demonstrated that the Federal Reserve was unable, or unwilling, to preserve financial stability in the economy. The gold standard as an automatic regulator of the money supply lost much of its glamour, both here and abroad. The public and the experts were convinced of the need for strong central action to open the banks in 1933, to keep them open, and to reverse the disastrous credit deflation. Thus, the Banking Acts of 1933 and 1935 made two major changes in the Federal Reserve System. First, the Federal Reserve authorities were given important new powers aimed at more effective control over the total amount of bank credit and the uses to which it could be put. Second, more complete control over Federal Reserve policy was vested in the presidentially appointed Board of Governors in Washington, and less in the twelve regional Federal Reserve Banks.

The Federal Reserve now plays a central role in macroeconomic policymaking. Congress has delegated to it responsibility for controlling the amount of money (currency and bank deposits) in the United States and for regulating the behavior of member commercial banks. The Federal Reserve Board (consisting now of seven members appointed by the President, with the advice and consent of the Senate, for staggered fourteen-year terms) holds the ultimate power in the System. However, the twelve regional Federal Reserve Banks can exert substantial influence. They furnish five members of the twelve-member Federal Open Market Committee (five of the bank presidents, plus the seven board members). The FOMC controls Federal Reserve open market operations—the purchase and sale of government securities in the open market. It thus regulates the supply of reserves available to commercial banks, on which they make their loans and investments.

The Federal Reserve Board also has the power to change the reserve requirements, which determine the amount of credit that banks can extend against any given amount of reserves. Moreover the twelve regional Federal Reserve Banks may, subject to the approval of the Board, change their rediscount rates—the interest rates at which commercial banks can borrow from them. And finally, the Board exercises numerous direct controls over the banking system and other financial transactions—notably over margin requirements, which specify the amount of cash that must be paid down on the purchase of common stocks, and over maximum interest rates that commercial banks may pay on their time deposits.

Exactly who makes monetary policy in this complex organization is difficult to pinpoint. The chairman of the Federal Reserve Board is the chief official of the System and to a large extent is the one who speaks for it. But formal actions are taken by majority vote of the Board and of the FOMC, so six other Board members and the twelve Federal Reserve Bank presidents have important formal responsibilities. How much these individuals are influenced by various interest groups, such as the commercial banks, has been a matter of dispute. Since the Federal Reserve has no clear policy mandate from Congress, its officials have wide discretion, and Federal Reserve policy has frequently been the subject of intense controversy. Indeed, the interrelationships among the Federal Reserve, the executive branch, Congress, and the public, will be a primary focus of the later analytical chapters in this book.[23]

Other "independent" agencies. Congress has established a number of other banking and financial regulatory agencies, most of them with some degree of independence from the executive branch of the government and from the day-to-day pressures of Congress itself. While these are of minor importance in macroeconomic policymaking compared with the Federal Reserve and the executive agencies, several have played important roles on particular occasions.

The Federal Deposit Insurance Corporation (FDIC) and the comptroller of the currency have substantial regulatory powers over commercial banks, roughly parallel to those exercised by the Federal Reserve over its member banks. The FDIC is a semi-independent, rather than a regular executive agency. The comptroller of the currency occupies an ill-defined position in the U.S. Treasury, somewhat independent of the secretary of the treasury. As will be seen below, inadequate coordination of bank regulatory policies among the Federal Reserve, the FDIC, and the comptroller of the currency has sometimes posed serious problems for finan-

23. For a more detailed picture of the organizational structure and operations of the Federal Reserve System, see G. L. Bach, *Federal Reserve Policy-Making* (Knopf, 1950), and Board of Governors of the Federal Reserve System, *The Federal Reserve System: Its Purposes and Functions,* 5th ed. (1967).

cial stability. But all the officials concerned are appointed by the President, with the advice and consent of the Senate, and are specifically subject to regulation by Congress, which established their agencies.

The Federal Home Loan Bank Board (FHLBB) has regulatory functions over savings and loan associations somewhat parallel to those of the commercial banking agencies mentioned above.[24] The board views itself as primarily responsible, under the legislation, for the financial flows that make possible residential construction in the United States. Thus, its constituency is different from that of the other financial agencies mentioned. This invites interagency policy conflicts—as, for example, in 1966 and 1969, when an inflationary economy called for monetary-fiscal restraint but the housing industry needed stimulation.

Another group of special agencies, more closely woven into the executive structure of the government, are the so-called lending and credit agencies. The Farm Credit Administration, for example, extends large amounts of credit authorized by Congress to aid farmers. Similarly, the Federal Housing Administration, the Veterans Administration, and other executive agencies have lending powers that directly affect financial markets. These agencies are required by law to consult with the Treasury in setting interest rates and other terms when they issue securities to obtain funds, and as a practical matter they operate under the control of the President.

PUBLIC-INTEREST GROUPS AND CONSTITUENCIES

Behind this array of government policymakers and administrators is the American public. Careful observers have long recognized that the democratic process in such a huge society does not, and cannot, mean a rule by majority vote on every issue. At best, the people at large elect a President, a Vice President, and congressmen (plus state and local officials) every two, four, or six years. They vote for an individual and for his general political and

24. The FHLBB has three members, appointed for four-year terms by the President with the advice and consent of the Senate. While the board emphasizes its position as an agency of Congress rather than as a member of the executive branch, in fact it has worked closely with the executive agencies and de facto is subject to the President's policies.

Direct regulation of, or influence over, wages and prices has been used intermittently when aggregate demand exceeded potential aggregate supply, with resulting inflation. For example, in 1962 the President's Council of Economic Advisers suggested "wage-price guideposts," spelling out the wage and price increases that would be consistent with a roughly stable price level at high employment. These guideposts have been cited frequently by the President, by council members, and by other government officials in opposing inflationary wage and price increases. Such moral suasion, or "jawboning," has apparently had limited effect. However, the guideposts and related direct attempts to check rising wages and prices sometimes have served as supplementary, albeit limited, instruments of macroeconomic policy.

DEBT MANAGEMENT

Changes in the size of the public debt are the direct result of surpluses or deficits in the federal budget. When the government runs a deficit, the debt must be increased accordingly to provide the extra funds the government wants to spend. The Treasury, which is primarily responsible for managing the public debt, may exert some influence over aggregate demand and financial markets by changing the composition of the debt. For example, if the Treasury borrows at short term on bills or certificates, it tends to raise short-term interest rates relative to long-term. Conversely, if it borrows on long-term bonds, it tends to raise long-term interest rates relative to short-term. Similarly, Federal Reserve officials can influence the structure of interest rates through the maturity dates of the securities they buy or sell in open market operations.

Changes in the term structure of rates, as the relationship among rates on securities maturing at various dates is called, may exert some influence on the composition of demand in the private sector of the economy. However, market interest rates are determined by the total supply of, and demand for, the funds in question; thus, government action is only one of many factors affecting interest rates. There is some question whether, barring dramatic actions, government debt policy can significantly affect the term structure of interest rates more than temporarily. And there is further doubt whether changes in the structure of interest rates normally exert much effect on aggregate spending and hence on aggregate employment and output.

INTERNATIONAL MONETARY POLICY

Under the Bretton Woods agreement of 1945, Congress agreed that the United States would maintain the value of the dollar internationally in a stable relationship to gold.

Other major currencies have been tied to the dollar at fixed rates. These fixed exchange rates have become a cornerstone of U.S. international monetary policy; and since the Second World War the U.S. dollar has become the foundation of the international monetary system. The dollar is now a "reserve currency," used much like gold by other nations as part of their basic international monetary reserves.

Given these fixed exchange rates, a deficit in the U.S. balance of payments is likely to result in an outflow of international monetary reserves from the United States to other nations, in the form of gold or dollars. Conversely, a surplus in the U.S. balance of payments is likely to lead to an inflow of gold or a reduction in foreign holdings of U.S. dollars. Under the traditional gold standard, these gold flows would normally be expected to produce corresponding decreases or increases in the U.S. money stock. But neither the United States nor other major nations are now willing to see their national money supplies or levels of economic activity governed exclusively by international gold flows. Instead, independent national monetary and fiscal policies are used to achieve domestic stabilization, preferably in a way that is consistent with equilibrium in the international balance of payments at the fixed exchange rates.

Thus, the U.S. policy of fixed exchange rates means that changes in our international balance of payments may put pressure on domestic monetary and fiscal authorities to stimulate or restrain the economy in order to maintain a reasonable international reserve position. If U.S. international monetary policy rests on fixed exchange rates, clearly there may be conflicts with its fiscal and monetary policies that are aimed directly at domestic stabilization.

One approach to international monetary policy would be to shift to a "floating" exchange rate, permitting the dollar price of gold to vary and exchange rates to fluctuate with supply and demand, rather than holding them fixed through government stabilization measures.[31] This action would basically alter the world's international monetary arrangements and, though it is advocated by many academic economists, has little or no support among government officials and leaders in the financial community. However, the possibility of freeing exchange rates to vary within a narrow range, or to "crawl" up or down over time, is now being seriously considered by many officials and private experts.

Under prevailing law and the Bretton Woods agreement, the President, the Treasury, and Congress have the option of "devaluing" or "revaluing" the dollar from time to time—that is, of changing the number of dollars the United States offers to exchange for gold. Such changes are permitted under particular circumstances by the Bretton Woods agreement but have been viewed by most officials as an undesirable instrument of U.S. international monetary policy. If floating or crawling rates, or periodic devaluation or revaluation of the dollar in relation to gold is ruled out, the government has left, as instruments of international monetary policy, mainly capital controls and other direct restrictions on international flows of goods and services. These measures were widely used during the 1930s, were generally discarded during the 1950s to restore free international movement of goods and capital, and have been reestablished on a limited scale since 1960 as the U.S. balance-of-payments deficit has persisted.

31. The United States could not unilaterally "float" the dollar, since other countries peg their currencies to the dollar; the United States stabilizes the official dollar price of gold.

3

THE NEED FOR COORDINATION

SIMULTANEOUS ATTAINMENT of multiple social goals through macroeconomic policy is a complex and difficult undertaking. Sometimes, as in the great depression of the 1930s, policy prescription is easy. Massive unemployment and slow growth clearly call for expansionary monetary and fiscal policies; with massive unemployment, inflation is no problem, and the balance of payments is generally favorable on both trade and capital accounts. But in prosperous times, when the economy is operating near full employment of men and machines (as in the years 1965–69), maintaining the optimal policy mix to achieve simultaneously all the desired goals becomes a precarious undertaking. For example, an expansionary fiscal policy to fight recession may conflict with a restrictive monetary policy aimed at reducing a deficit in the balance of payments. Or expansionary monetary and fiscal policies to increase aggregate demand may encounter rising prices before satisfactorily high employment is achieved.

Since the Second World War, economists have suggested approaches to determining the optimal combination of policies when goals conflict. In 1955 Paul Samuelson, in an influential statement before the Joint Committee on the Economic Report, argued that an economy can simultaneously have full employment, the rate of capital formation that it wants, and the income redistribution desired on ethical grounds, by applying aggregate fiscal policy to the iirst goal, monetary policy to the second, and changes in the tax structure to the third.[1] A decade later Robert Mundell demonstrated further that, by using an optimal combination of monetary and fiscal policy, a nation could have both internal and external stability, even under a system of fixed exchange rates.[2] Other economists have examined carefully the kinds of policy mixes that might reconcile conflicting policy goals under differing circumstances—for example, when the trade and capital accounts of the balance of payments point in opposite directions.

In principle, to achieve multiple policy goals, a nation must have at least an equivalent number of policy instruments, so that one can be allocated to the achievement of each goal. For example, four goals of macroeconomic policy are widely accepted—high employment, rapid economic growth, a reasonably stable price level, and rough equilibrium in the international balance of payments. To achieve these goals, U.S. government policymakers have four possible major instruments, or groups of instruments—monetary policy, fiscal policy, exchange rate policy, and direct intervention (wage-price policy, ceilings on interest rates, controls over international capital movements, and so on). Thus an optimal mix might be fiscal policy for the employment objective (through regulation of aggregate demand), monetary policy for the growth objective (through control of interest rates), exchange rate policy for the international payments objective (through varying exchange rates), and direct controls for the price-level objective (through wage-price, or incomes, policy, and direct intervention in markets).

Unless the government is prepared to use all four of these in-

1. "The New Look in Tax and Fiscal Policy," in *Federal Tax Policy for Economic Growth and Stability,* Papers Submitted by Panelists Appearing before the Subcommittee on Tax Policy, 84 Cong. 1 sess. (1955), pp. 229–34.

2. "The Appropriate Use of Monetary and Fiscal Policy for Internal and External Stability," *International Monetary Fund Staff Papers,* Vol. 9 (March 1962), pp. 70–77. But Mundell assumed that there would be no international retaliation against U.S. domestic policies that affected the trade of other nations—which seems highly unlikely. David J. Ott and Attiat F. Ott, in "Monetary and Fiscal Policy: Goals and the Choice of Instruments," *Quarterly Journal of Economics,* Vol. 82 (May 1968), pp. 313–25, demonstrate that the Mundell proposal for combining monetary and fiscal policy to achieve internal and external stability will not necessarily give optimal results when imports are a function of the separate private and public components of aggregate demand.

struments, it may be unable to achieve the four separate policy goals simultaneously. Indeed, even coordinated use of the four separate policy instruments could not guarantee successful achievement of the four goals stated. Use of any of the policy instruments to achieve one goal may produce unwanted side-effects on the other three goals. For example, the much discussed Kennedy-Johnson tax cut of 1964 was designed to increase the public's disposable income and aggregate demand and thereby to move the economy closer to full employment. This presumably also speeded the rate of economic growth (desirable) but worsened the U.S. balance of payments on trade account by increasing U.S. imports and decreasing U.S. exports (undesirable). There was a still further side-effect on the balance of payments. By increasing the amount of government borrowing required to finance government expenditures in the face of lower tax rates, without offsetting monetary actions, the tax cut raised interest rates and thereby stimulated a capital flow to the United States. Comparable side-effects of macroeconomic policies are the rule, not the exception. Sometimes the side-effects are desirable, sometimes undesirable.

Coordination of macroeconomic policies is thus imperative if the desired goals are to be achieved. This is true especially as between monetary and fiscal policies. High employment might be pursued through expansionary fiscal policy alone. But without a cooperative monetary policy, growing aggregate demand would increase the demand for money, thus raising interest rates and partially negating the expansionary effects of fiscal policy. Similarly, expansionary monetary policy that raises aggregate demand will automatically raise government tax receipts, which, other things being equal, will partly counteract the expansionary monetary policy.

So it is with the interactions among other policy instruments. The undesired side-effects of one policy measure may be too strong for other policy instruments to overcome. Consideration of the probable side-effects of each policy instrument emphasizes the difficulty that even a fully coordinated government program to achieve macroeconomic goals must face. If the recent U.S. policy of forswearing the use of two of the four policy instruments (wage-price policy and exchange rate adjustments) is continued, there is serious doubt whether the four goals of macroeconomic policy can be achieved simultaneously.

A still more serious problem arises when one instrument is used improperly and the remaining instruments must overcome the unwanted results of the first. In 1966, for example, expansionary fiscal policy based on rising Vietnam war outlays fed an accelerating inflation. Monetary policy thus had to assume the full responsibility for fighting inflation, in the face not only of a buoyant private economy but of a destabilizing fiscal policy as well. Similarly, in the spring and summer of 1969, undue reliance was placed on monetary measures.

The episodes of 1966 and 1969 illustrate still other side-effects of monetary policy when it must be used forcefully against inflation. For technical reasons, which are discussed in Chapters 6 and 7, the effects of tight money were focused especially on housing construction and to a lesser extent on states, municipalities, and new small businesses. Large, well established firms are the banks' best customers, and they are the last to be turned away as credit tightens. Homebuilders are generally less preferred borrowers. The "credit crunch" of 1966 caused housing starts to fall from a rate of about 1.5 million to 800,000 annually in nine months. Savings and loan associations faced savings withdrawals as funds were shifted to higher interest uses, threatening some with failure and dramatically reducing the flow of savings from that source into housing. Clearly these overly drastic results would have been less necessary had fiscal policy been restrictive, or even neutral, instead of highly expansionary. The full burden of stabilization was forced onto monetary policy. The results were predictably drastic and uneven.

The lesson is clear. Unless monetary, fiscal, and other macroeconomic policies are coordinated, the outlook for high employment and stable economic growth is uncertain indeed.

The Channels of Monetary and Fiscal Policy

To understand the problem of achieving coordinated macroeconomic policy, one must know the channels through which monetary and fiscal policies work and interact. Economists do not agree on the exact linkages between monetary and fiscal policies, on the one hand, and their ultimate effects on employment, output, and prices, on the other. Yet without some picture of these channels and the time lags involved in their use and impact, it is difficult to judge the effects of various policy combinations. In the following analysis and proposals, an eclectic economic model is implicit. Both monetary and fiscal policies have direct and indirect effects that are important and complex. Thus, simple statements about the total effects of any change in monetary or fiscal policy, or the time needed for these effects to be felt, are seldom possible.

In nontechnical terms, the use of *monetary policy* (open market operations, reserve requirements, and discount rates) directly affects the reserve positions of commercial banks and interest rates (yields) on securities. These in turn affect spending on goods and services through three channels: (1) Interest rates influence investment in business plant and equipment, housing, state and local construction, and consumer durable goods. (2) Changed rates of return on securities and other assets influence the total wealth position and the portfolio balances of households, and hence their consumption. For example, rising stock market prices increase the perceived wealth of households and hence their spending. (3) Credit rationing by lenders (particularly financial institutions) affects investment, especially in the housing market.

These changes in investment and consumption spending in turn have multiplier effects as the additional income generated is respent throughout the economy. The multiplier effects feed back on the entire system and induce further "accelerator" effects (that is, they induce further investment spending). The time lags involved vary according to the initial conditions of the economy—the level of unemployment, prices, inventories, and excess reserves. Monetary policy effects are substantial in most circumstances, and they extend over months—even years if indirect effects are considered. Under many conditions, half of the total direct and indirect effects take two or more years before they are felt, and half of even the direct effects may take two or three quarters, or more.[3]

Interest rates play an important part in the process. Monetary policy can affect the interest rates on market securities almost in-

3. Frank de Leeuw and Edward M. Gramlich, in "The Channels of Monetary Policy: A Further Report on the Federal Reserve-MIT Econometric Model," *Federal Reserve Bulletin*, Vol. 55 (June 1969), pp. 472–91, outline a model of the financial system which approximates that assumed here.

stantaneously; for example, open market purchases drive bill prices up and yields down. But the stimulative effect of higher bank reserves and lower interest rates then helps to induce more spending, higher incomes, and an increased demand for credit; this income effect partially offsets the first-round depressive effect on interest rates. Moreover, if the economy is near full employment, these higher incomes are likely to induce inflation; and inflation, if continued, affects the expectations of both lenders and borrowers, so that both increasingly incorporate an "inflation allowance" in their interest rate bargaining. Market interest rates thus tend to rise by roughly the expected rate of inflation. Thus, the long-run effects of open market purchases during a period of inflation may be to *raise* interest rates, even though, in the short run, an increase in reserves leads to lower interest rates.

There are many different interest rates, which are the prices paid for different kinds of credit borrowed for different periods of time, as well as for the direct use of money (demand deposits and currency). Thus, market interest rates reflect supply and demand conditions in a wide variety of markets. Credit is supplied from many sources; banks (the source of demand deposits) typically provide less than half the total amount of credit borrowed each year, and the Federal Reserve provides only a small fraction. Thus, Federal Reserve monetary policy directly affects only one segment of the total of credit markets and only a few of the many interest rates paid by borrowers. Table 1 shows the principal domestic borrowers and suppliers of credit (including money) in two recent but quite different years—1966 and 1968.

If the relationships among these credit flows and the interest rates associated with them were stable, Federal Reserve control over bank reserves or the money stock still might be an effective control over borrowing and real expenditure and employment. But they are not stable. Thus, most economists doubt that one simple, direct causal relationship exists among bank reserves, the money stock, and real output, employment, and prices—though bank reserves and money appear clearly to be one major force influencing these ultimate variables.

Fiscal policy directly affects employment, output, and incomes through federal government spending and taxing. The effect of government spending on income and output is partly immediate,

TABLE I

Funds Borrowed by, and Advanced to, Domestic Nonfinancial Sectors, by Principal Borrowers and Suppliers, 1966 and 1968

(*Dollar amounts in billions*)

Borrowers and suppliers	1966		1968	
Borrowers				
Private domestic nonfinance				
Short-term debt				
Households	$ 8.3		$15.5	
Businesses	13.6		13.0	
State and local governments	0.4		0.3	
Long-term obligations				
Households	11.0		15.4	
Businesses	22.5		24.6	
State and local governments	6.4		10.9	
Subtotal	——	$62.0	——	$79.7
Federal government (net)		0.6		11.8
Total borrowed		$62.6		$91.4
Suppliers				
Private domestic nonfinance				
Households	10.7		1.7	
Businesses	3.2		7.7	
State and local governments	6.2		7.7	
Subtotal	——	20.1	——	17.0
Financial institutions (net)				
Banks	17.3		38.6	
Nonbank savings institutions	8.7		15.1	
Other	14.6		15.5	
Subtotal	——	40.6	——	69.2
Rest of the world (net)		−1.6		1.6
Federal Reserve		3.5		3.7
Total advanced		$62.6		$91.4
Federal Reserve funds supplied, as a percent of total		*5.6*		*4.0*
Bank funds supplied, as a percent of total		*27.6*		*42.1*

Source: Based on flow-of-funds data from Board of Governors of the Federal Reserve System. Figures are rounded and may not add to totals.

partly lagged. The effect of tax changes may be rapid (for example, when tax withholding rates change the disposable incomes of families), or delayed (for example, when tax changes alter profit expectations of businesses and the availability of cash flows to finance investments). "Permanent" changes in taxes and government spending generally have stronger effects than do temporary ones. As with monetary policy, changes in private spending induced through changes in fiscal policy have further multiplier effects, which in turn have accelerator effects, inducing still further spending. As with monetary policy, the total direct and indirect effects cover a long time span, though the average time lag for fiscal policy is apparently somewhat shorter than that for monetary policy, and its initial impacts are quite different. As indirect effects take over, the difference in timing of effects lessens rapidly.[4]

As will be explained later, the high-employment budget surplus provides a useful intermediate indicator of the net impact of federal fiscal policy on the real variables in the economy. The level of free reserves and of short-term interest rates on the one hand, and the rates of growth of bank reserves and the money stock on the other, provide alternative intermediate indicators of the impact of monetary policy. Both sets of financial measures have some validity; monetary policy acts through multiple channels. But it is important to remember that most credit markets are dominated by private supplies and demands and that interest rates become increasingly misleading as indicators of the stance of monetary policy when inflation is expected. This is because market interest rates then include both the "real" interest rate *and* a hard-to-measure inflation allowance. The inflation allowance reflects both increasing demands for credit when inflation is expected and allowance for expected inflation by lenders. "Real" interest rates may thus be much lower than "money" (actually paid) rates. In such periods, growth in bank reserves and in the money stock are more reliable indicators of the impact of monetary policy on the real economy, because they are less distorted by variable inflation allowance. In

---

4. For a more detailed treatment, which roughly approximates the fiscal model used here, see Albert Ando and Franco Modigliani, "Econometric Analysis of Stabilization Policies," in American Economic Association, *Papers and Proceedings of the Eighty-First Annual Meeting, 1968 (American Economic Review,* Vol. 59, May 1969), pp. 296–314.

noninflationary periods, substantial divergence among the different indicators is less likely, and both sets may be valuable for determining policy.[5]

The details of these fiscal-monetary models are not critical to most of the analysis that follows. Many of the main conclusions are the same as would follow from different macro models. But in planning coordinated macroeconomic policies it is essential to recognize that linkage channels are complex and that time lags are often long. Prima facie, it might appear that, to stabilize the economy, maximum flexibility in the use of all macro policy tools would be optimal, so that policymakers could continuously adjust their instruments individually and in combination. However, given the differences in linkages and lags for different macro instruments, such flexible "coordination" by discretionary authorities—each focusing on different intermediate target variables—would not necessarily give optimal results. Indeed, these uncertain linkages and lags suggest substantial difficulties for any discretionary policies aimed at "fine-tuning" the economy.

The principal test of how effectively macroeconomic policies are coordinated is how closely employment and prices approach their desired paths. It is important to recognize that coordination per se is of little value unless the end result is better than would follow from independent policy decisions. Coordinating policies by giving control to one policymaker would do more harm than good if that policymaker turned out to be wrong. Coordination of macro policies, therefore, is a necessary, but not sufficient, condition for achieving optimal over-all macro policy.

The Meaning of Policy Coordination

The general case for coordinated macroeconomic policies is clear; but "coordination" needs to be defined more precisely.

1. Coordination may mean parallel expansionary and restrictive movements in monetary, fiscal, and related policies.[6] For example, monetary and fiscal policy moved together in 1955–56 but not in 1966, when fiscal policy was expansionary but monetary policy

5. The issue of which indicators are most useful during inflation is a complex one. It is considered more thoroughly in Chap. 8.

6. Figures 2 and 4 (on pp. 105 and 147) provide a basis for checking the effectiveness of coordination by this definition.

tightened sharply. But this is clearly an unacceptable definition for evaluating policy effectiveness. Wise policymaking may call for changes in the policy mix. For example, in 1966 monetary policy was tightened primarily to offset an overexpansive budget policy.

2. Coordination may mean exchange of information and joint discussion of issues by the policymakers concerned, though not necessarily agreement on the policies to be followed. By this definition, for example, monetary and fiscal policy were clearly coordinated in 1969, when extensive discussion led to tightening on both monetary and fiscal fronts. But they were also coordinated in 1956 and late 1965, when, in spite of interagency discussions, the Federal Reserve raised the discount rate against the expressed wishes of the Treasury.

3. Coordination may mean discussion *and* agreement on the actions to be taken by the various policymakers concerned. Clearly this is the strongest test of coordination and the most satisfactory of the three for present purposes. By this definition, monetary and fiscal policy were coordinated in 1969 but *not* in 1965, since in 1965 policy discussions did not produce agreement on the combined monetary-fiscal policies to be followed. This is the definition used throughout this book unless a different one is specified.

Some Special Problems

Three particularly troublesome goal conflicts deserve special preliminary attention, for repeatedly in recent history they have plagued policymakers who were trying to achieve coordinated macroeconomic policy.

INFLATION VERSUS UNEMPLOYMENT

Macroeconomic policymakers have frequently faced the dilemma that increasing aggregate demand in order to reduce unemployment appears to generate price rises before full employment is reached. Thus, many economists believe that the achievement of "full" employment is impossible unless some inflation is accepted, and, indeed, that inflation may help reduce unemployment.

A decade ago, A. W. Phillips, a British economist, found that over the past century stable wage costs per unit of output and stable consumer prices seemed to be achievable in the United Kingdom only when the unemployment rate was 5 percent or more. The lower the rate of unemployment, the higher was the rate of increase in wages and prices.[7] Several American economists have conducted similar investigations in the United States and reported results roughly consistent with those of Phillips.

Several reasons have been advanced for this inflation-unemployment dilemma. As aggregate demand expands, some sectors of the economy reach full employment before others; wage costs and prices begin to rise in those sectors, thus raising the average of all prices before general full employment is reached. This might be called the "bottlenecks" explanation. Closely related is the "sectoral" explanation, which argues that prices in particular industries may be bid up with rising demand, but that downward wage and price rigidities prevent offsetting price reductions elsewhere.

Other observers stress the market power of large unions and oligopolistic firms, which seek to advance their own incomes by pushing up wages and prices before full employment is reached. This is sometimes called the "cost-push" or "sellers'" explanation.

Still others stress market forces, quite aside from increased monopoly powers. In a period of rising aggregate demand, employers try to attract workers away from one another, thus bidding up wage rates. Higher wage offers may be used also to attract additional workers into the labor force—housewives, students, and retired persons. The ability of workers to obtain large wage increases is greater in prosperous times, when employers are especially anxious to avoid strikes. Profits are usually higher and inventories lower in such periods, so employers are in a weaker position to resist wage demands. When wages rise, for whatever reason, they tend to increase wage costs per unit of output, and hence prices, except insofar as they are offset by rising productivity. As a practical matter, "demand-pull," "cost-push," and "sectoral" inflationary forces often interact, and all may play partly "causal" and partly "response" roles.

Still another group of investigators agrees that a Phillips trade-off exists in the short run, but argues that in the long run there is

7. A. W. Phillips, "The Relation Between Unemployment and the Rate of Change of Money Wage Rates in the United Kingdom, 1861–1957," *Economica*, Vol. 25 (November 1958), pp. 283–99.

no unemployment-inflation trade-off. They argue that the _basic_ (long-run equilibrium) level of unemployment is determined by the relation among real wage rates, labor productivity, and product selling prices. In inflation, selling prices usually rise faster than do wage rates, thus reducing the real wage rates received by workers; this leads to higher employment. But wage earners (and others, especially lenders) soon become aware of their losses due to inflation and act to restore their pre-inflation real wages and interest returns. When the pre-inflation relationships between costs and product prices is reestablished (that is, when inflation has become fully anticipated), the original level of unemployment will have been reestablished (omitting for the moment changes in productivity). Thus, it is only by continuing to speed up inflation that the monetary authorities can increase employment (by reducing real wages). As soon as the public comes to anticipate the existing rate of inflation, real wages, real interest rates, and unemployment will tend to return to their pre-inflation levels. Except temporarily, policymakers cannot buy higher employment by accepting inflation.[8]

Thus the nature, indeed the very existence, of a Phillips type of trade-off between inflation and unemployment is not clear. Surely there is no one simple, stable "Phillips curve" relating unemployment to wage rates and prices. Two leading investigators have warned:

> Our final caution is that we [the authors] have been astounded by how many very different Phillips curves can be constructed on reasonable assumptions from the same body of data. The nature of the relationship between wage changes and unemployment is highly sensitive to the exact choice of the other variables that enter the regression and to the forms of all the variables. For this reason, the

8. See, for example, Milton Friedman, "The Role of Monetary Policy," *American Economic Review*, Vol. 58 (March 1968), pp. 1–17, and Edmund S. Phelps, "Money-Wage Dynamics and Labor-Market Equilibrium," *Journal of Political Economy*, Vol. 76 (July/August 1968, Pt. 2), pp. 678–711. The validity of this analysis is hard to test on empirical grounds, since the United States has seldom had long periods of increasing price inflation. Thus, it depends largely on theoretical analysis. In some other countries (for example, Brazil and Chile) where inflation has been long-standing and often accelerating, experience has been consistent with the proposition that inflation buys higher employment only when the rate of inflation is increasing beyond the anticipation of the public. But Europe offers counter-examples of milder inflation.

authors of Phillips curves would do well to label them conspicuously *"Unstable! Apply with extreme care."* (Italics in original.)[9]

But all agree that, *in the short run,* rapidly rising aggregate demand is likely to generate wage and price increases well before "full" employment is reached throughout the economy. Whether reductions in unemployment that are more than temporary can be achieved through an inflationary expansion in aggregate demand is far less clear. *If* indeed full employment cannot be reached in the U.S. economy without some inflation, this country faces a painful trade-off between goals or a need to find new policy instruments to supplement monetary-fiscal policy. The unemployment-inflation dilemma seems very real to many macroeconomic policymakers, as will be seen in the chapters that follow. Direct wage and price controls, wage-price guideposts, and national "incomes policies," in addition to monetary-fiscal policies, have been urged by some as the only feasible solution to the unemployment-inflation dilemma.

THE EXPECTATIONS DILEMMA

A related expectations dilemma has intermittently troubled policymakers. For example, in the period 1955–57 and again more strongly in 1967–69, there were firm and widely held expectations of inflation and continuing prosperity. Households, workers, and businessmen anticipated continued inflation and good times. This reflected partly the inflationary trend of more than two decades, partly increasing confidence that major depressions were a thing of the past.

These widespread expectations made the task of macroeconomic policymaking very difficult. Gradual restraint on the growth of aggregate demand (to damp inflation without generating unemployment) deterred private investment and consumption spending less than was expected, apparently because many households and inves-

9. Albert Rees and Mary T. Hamilton, "The Wage-Price-Productivity Perplex," *Journal of Political Economy,* Vol. 75 (February 1967), p. 70. For a summary of the issues, see also "The Relation Between Prices and Employment: Two Views," Federal Reserve Bank of St. Louis, *Review,* Vol. 51 (March 1969), pp. 15–21; Ronald G. Bodkin, *The Wage-Price-Productivity Nexus* (University of Pennsylvania Press, 1966), pp. 143–51; and George L. Perry, *Unemployment, Money Wage Rates, and Inflation* (The M.I.T. Press, 1966).

tors simply did not believe that a recession would be forced on the economy. Especially in the years 1967–69, inflationary expectations were so strong that business investment plans seemed substantially impervious to anything less than a major shock through monetary-fiscal restraint. When businessmen thought construction costs would rise rapidly in the future, to postpone investment because of high interest rates seemed irrational. Consumers continued to buy in anticipation of further price rises. Unions demanded large wage increases and got them, since businessmen were unwilling to pay the costs of strong resistance to union strike threats when raising prices seemed a feasible way out. Only in late 1969 did the impact of tight money begin to shake these expectations.

Macroeconomic policy may be to some extent a victim of its own success and of the Keynesian revolution's doctrine that serious depressions can (and will) be banished forever. A depression-proof economy may be fundamentally unstable in an upward direction; expectations of inflationary prosperity may so cumulate that they cannot be checked without at least periodic major shocks of restraint and enforced recession. Insufficient evidence is available to be sure whether this is an actual, or only a theoretical, policy dilemma. But it is real enough to pose a major problem for monetary and fiscal policymakers who are trying to achieve a prosperous, noninflationary economy without the use of wage-price policies.[10]

DOMESTIC VERSUS INTERNATIONAL GOALS

Macroeconomic policymakers may face a third major policy dilemma—the need to choose between domestic and international goals, so long as exchange rates between the United States and other countries remain fixed. Some economists argue that monetary-fiscal policies that insure high employment and a satisfactory growth rate will make money so easy and aggregate demand so large that they will almost certainly lead to unacceptable balance-of-payments deficits. Capital will flow out, and U.S. imports of goods and services will rise rapidly relative to exports. If this is so,

10. For a pessimistic evaluation, see Hyman P. Minsky, "Financial Crisis, Financial Systems, and the Performance of the Economy," in Irwin Friend and others, *Private Capital Markets*, Prepared for the Commission on Money and Credit (Prentice-Hall, 1964).

the United States can have high employment and rapid growth, but only with disequilibrium in its balance of payments; or it can have balance-of-payments equilibrium but only by accepting slower growth and a lower level of employment than is desired; or it must use a third policy instrument, like exchange rate flexibility or direct controls, to help reconcile domestic stabilization and international equilibrium.[11]

This domestic-international dilemma is further complicated by the fact that the U.S. payments position on trade and capital movement accounts may diverge. Conventional economic theory has long suggested that a balance-of-payments deficit calls for monetary-fiscal restriction at home to reduce imports and encourage exports. But during much of the 1960s, the continuing U.S. payments deficit reflected a large *surplus* on trade account, together with an even larger deficit on capital account. Given the strong export position of the United States and (until 1965) underemployment at home, domestic monetary-fiscal restraint to eliminate the payments deficit would have made little sense. It would have made domestic unemployment even worse. More recently, since 1965, when inflationary "full" employment has characterized the U.S. economy, restrictive monetary policy makes sense domestically. But the resulting higher interest rates may be partially self-defeating because they attract capital from abroad, which partially or completely offsets the domestic restrictive effects of tight money. As with the dilemmas arising from simultaneous unemployment and inflation and from the inflationary expectations that accompany prosperity, reconciling domestic and international goals calls for close coordination among the nation's macroeconomic policymakers.

11. Precisely what constitutes balance-of-payments "equilibrium" is a matter of dispute. See Chap. 6.

PART TWO

THE EVOLUTION
OF POLICYMAKING

4

THE PRE-1952 POLICY PROCESS

MACROECONOMIC STABILIZATION POLICY as we know it today is a product of the past fifty years, especially the past thirty.[1] For at least two centuries, economists, businessmen, and bankers have been concerned about the relationship among central banks, note issue, and prices; on this subject, the works of Ricardo and Thornton in the early 1800s give modern analysis a surprisingly ancient ring. But the Federal Reserve System was not established in the United States until 1913. Not until the great depression of the 1930s was it widely agreed that the federal government and the central bank should take strong, positive measures to return a depressed economy to a high level of employment and to promote stable economic growth.

Chapters 4–6 review briefly a series of episodes in macroeconomic policy formation. These episodes were chosen to suggest some of the major issues involved in attaining effective coordination of macroeconomic policies, mainly monetary and fiscal. They are drawn largely from the years since the great depression, since this period has provided most of our experience with active stabilization policy. The account makes no pretense of being complete; rather it offers an illustrative sample of events and problems.

Chapter 7 then summarizes what seem to be the principal les-

1. This chapter is of largely historical interest. Some readers may wish to skip directly to Chap. 5 or 7.

sons of stabilization experience. Chapter 8 provides a more complete analysis of the recommendations for change that are summarized in Chapter 1.

The Federal Reserve and Monetary Policy, 1913–33

Before the 1930s, macroeconomic policy was, for all practical purposes, monetary policy. Consequently there was no major problem of coordinating macroeconomic policies among different government units. However, several of the problems that have plagued the United States in the postwar years are apparent in the early history of the Federal Reserve System.

The Federal Reserve Act of 1913 directed the authorities "to furnish an elastic currency" (to be provided through newly authorized Federal Reserve notes) and "to afford means of discounting commercial paper" (a mechanism through which the commercial banks could obtain liquidity in the form of Federal Reserve notes in periods of currency withdrawals).[2] Two criteria for determining the amount of money to be created or retired by the Federal Reserve were implicit. First, a gold standard rule was incorporated in the gold reserve requirements for Federal Reserve liabilities. Second, a "real bills" theory of banking suggested that the amount of money issued should be determined by the "real" needs of business, as these needs expanded or contracted.

Thus, the new Federal Reserve was not perceived as having any substantial discretionary authority over the amount of money it would issue. The act gave Federal Reserve authorities no direct guidance on what is now considered to be monetary policy. The development of monetary policy as a conscious device for regulating the stock of money and the cost and availability of credit did not appear until the 1920s. Indeed, when the act was passed, there was strong, explicit opposition to any suggestion that Congress might be establishing a "central bank," particularly one controlled by the large private banks.[3]

2. The full title of the Federal Reserve Act is: "An Act to provide for the establishment of Federal reserve banks, to furnish an elastic currency, to afford means of rediscounting commercial paper, to establish a more effective supervision of banking in the United States, and for other purposes."

3. Both Carter Glass and Robert Owen, chairmen of the Senate and House Banking and Currency Committees, respectively, protested against private banker

The most bitter controversies over the new Federal Reserve System centered around the issues of public versus private (banker) control and the "independence" of the Federal Reserve from government (especially Treasury) control. Both the Aldrich commission volumes and the congressional hearings on the proposed Federal Reserve Act are full of indications of fear of "the money trust." There is little doubt that Congress wanted to develop a clear alternative to economic dominance by private bankers, which was widely feared.

The result was an elaborate compromise under which twelve Federal Reserve Banks were established in different parts of the country, with a central Federal Reserve Board in Washington. The regional Federal Reserve Banks were to be owned by commercial banks, which would elect the majority of their boards of directors. These twelve Reserve Banks would issue currency and carry out the rediscount function. They would, however, be "supervised" by the Federal Reserve Board in Washington, which was to be appointed by the President with the advice and consent of the Senate, and which would include the secretary of the treasury and comptroller of the currency as members ex officio. Congress also gave the Treasury substantial powers to issue coin and currency.

The Federal Reserve was barely established when the First World War broke out. Its early years, therefore, were dominated by the need to aid the Treasury in financing the war by providing reserves for a huge expansion of bank credit. Heavy gold inflows rapidly built up the Federal Reserve's own reserves. A rapid expansion in holdings of U.S. bonds by the commercial banks shifted the composition of bank assets away from commercial paper, on which the "real bills" doctrine of currency control was based.

---

control over the banking system and note issue through the Federal Reserve. See, for example, *Changes in the Banking and Currency System of the United States*, H. Rept. 69, 63 Cong. 1 sess. (1913), pp. 10–11; and *Banking and Currency*, S. Rept. 133, 63 Cong. 1 sess. (1913), p. 6. These statements were in part arguments against the so-called "Aldrich bill," which reflected the recommendations of the National Monetary Commission, organized by Congress in 1908, under the chairmanship of Senator Nelson W. Aldrich, to investigate the problem of financial crises and possible reform of the monetary and banking system. The Aldrich bill provided for centralized control of banking and currency through a National Reserve Association with fifteen regional branches.

These events were to change radically the nature of central banking and monetary policy in the United States.

During the 1920s, major controversies swirled around the new Federal Reserve System. First, the Federal Reserve authorities soon faced the problem of deciding on guides for the use of discount rate policy and, later, open market operations. What was to have been a substantially automatic mechanism for producing the right amount of money turned out to be far from automatic. Immediately after the First World War, an inflationary boom, followed by a precipitous collapse in 1920, forced the Reserve Banks to face the question of whether, and when, to raise or lower rediscount rates. The automatic gold standard, as it was restored in most of the Western world by the mid-1920s, called for expansion of the nation's money stock, which the Federal Reserve authorities believed might produce undesirable inflation. Thus, although such action was questionable under gold standard mores, the Reserve Banks began to offset gold inflows through open market sales of government bonds. Open market operations, unmentioned in the Federal Reserve Act, gradually became the System's major policy tool. Increasingly, Federal Reserve authorities faced the issue of discretionary monetary policy—the need for decisions by men rather than by rules or automatic mechanisms.

Second, and even more controversial, were the related issues of Federal Reserve "independence," the distribution of power within the System, and public versus private control.

As early as 1914, the attorney general ruled that the Federal Reserve Board was a government establishment independent of the Treasury, not a division of the Treasury.[4] But in fact this left the issue far from settled. The secretary of the treasury was ex officio chairman of the Federal Reserve Board, and the Treasury's needs for assistance in selling war bonds to the public and the banks were persistent. During the First World War the Federal Reserve objected to the low interest rates proposed by the Treasury for its securities and to the large amount borrowed, arguing that more of the funds needed should be raised by taxes. As has been the case so many times since, the Federal Reserve–Treasury difference was compromised, with general Federal Reserve support for Treasury bonds.

4. See the *First Annual Report of the Federal Reserve Board for the Period Ending December 31, 1914,* pp. 54–57.

After the war, both inflation and sharp recession contributed to the controversy. In 1922, Benjamin Strong, governor of the New York Federal Reserve Bank and perhaps the dominant figure in the System, wrote that the Federal Reserve System is a "creature of Congress" that certainly could not negate policy sanctioned by Congress, or override the policy of the secretary of the treasury. What it could do was (1) express its views frankly to the secretary and then (2) accept his decision and carry out the plans he proposed. It is interesting to note that during this period the Treasury dealt with the Federal Reserve Banks directly, rather than through the Federal Reserve Board in Washington. Most other Federal Reserve officials, however, argued that Federal Reserve policy should be more independent of the Treasury's needs.[5]

From the outset, the President of the United States maintained a hands-off attitude toward the Federal Reserve. As early as 1915, the Federal Reserve was split by dissension over the issue of whether the number of Reserve Banks should be reduced from twelve to eight; several of the Reserve Banks seemed unable to show a profit and pay their way in the System. The issue was taken to President Wilson, who clearly had the power under wartime legislation to change the structure of the System. However, he decided not to intervene, because he did not want to be "accused of trying to bring political pressure to bear" on the actions of the Board. The President's position was strongly approved by Carter Glass, "the father of the Federal Reserve Act." Glass wrote: "The President held to the obviously proper view that commercial credits and banking processes were matters which should be as far removed from all sinister influences as one pole is from the other. It was to insure just this thing that the Federal Reserve System was devised."[6]

In 1927, when a similar issue arose, President Coolidge stated on several occasions that the Federal Reserve Board was independent of the Treasury and beyond the scope of the executive; interestingly enough, Secretary of Commerce Hoover at that time objected strongly to Federal Reserve policy, which he considered overly buoyant; but he received little support from other high-

5. Lester V. Chandler, *Benjamin Strong, Central Banker* (Brookings Institution, 1958), pp. 120–21.

6. Quoted in A. Jerome Clifford, *The Independence of the Federal Reserve System* (University of Pennsylvania Press, 1965), p. 93.

ranking members of the executive branch. However, top Federal Reserve officials recognized early that presidential nonintervention was not an unmixed blessing. Carter Glass noted that nonintervention was not the best policy if it meant no contact with the President. What he hoped for was not just the respect of the President but also his understanding and cooperation.

Federal Reserve relations with Congress were even less clearly defined. Congressional committees persistently inquired into Federal Reserve decisions and operations. As early as 1921 there was a major inquiry as to whether the Federal Reserve System should receive a large share of the blame for the deflation of 1920–21. Congress appointed a special committee to investigate the causes of the collapse and to check the integrity, honesty, and competence of Federal Reserve officials. The result of the investigation, as of most others in the years to follow, was a congressional report that supported the independence of the Federal Reserve System. Indeed, the congressmen criticized the Federal Reserve for not standing more firmly against the Treasury, and found no dishonesty and no knavery on the part of the bankers.[7]

From the outset the governors of the twelve Federal Reserve Banks tried to establish their authority, working individually and through a newly established "Governors Conference." This conference met independently, made recommendations for legislation directly to Congress, and was clearly reluctant to take orders from the Washington Board. Within the conference, the New York Federal Reserve Bank rapidly assumed a dominant position. This reflected the dominant position of the New York money market and the fact that the Treasury dealt directly with the New York Reserve Bank on its money market needs, rather than through the Federal Reserve Board.

In March 1923 the Board finally asserted its jurisdiction over open market operations by the Federal Reserve Banks. It dissolved the governors' committee on open market operations and then reappointed the same committee to carry on its work under principles and regulations determined by the Board. Governors of the Reserve Banks reacted vigorously—especially Governor Benjamin

7. See *The Agricultural Crisis and Its Causes*, Report of the Joint Commission of Agricultural Inquiry, 67 Cong. 1 sess. (1921).

Strong in New York and Boston Governor W. P. G. Harding, who had previously been a member of the Board.[8]

To a considerable extent, the Board succeeded in establishing its jurisdiction over open market operations and discount rate changes. It was an uneasy truce, however, and in 1927 disagreement flared again over board actions that many officials of the banks felt were unduly expansionary in a time of general prosperity. The Chicago Bank refused to lower its discount rate from 4 to 3½ percent as suggested by the Board; and the Board finally, by a four to three vote, ordered that the Chicago discount rate be fixed at 3½ percent. In the showdown the Board won. But it had many critics—in the financial community, in the Treasury, and in Congress. The secretary of the treasury, three members of the Board, and Senator Carter Glass all vigorously denounced the Board's action, questioning its legality and denying its prudence. Glass called it "utterly capricious."[9]

The issue was further confounded by widespread rumors that Governor Strong at the New York Bank was in constant touch with the heads of the European central banks, especially with Governor Montagu Norman of the Bank of England. These international banking connections had a sinister overtone for many Americans. Criticism of alleged control by the international money trust was focused on both the New York Bank and the System as a whole, although the Board in Washington also took a somewhat dim view of the relations between Strong and Governor Norman.

It is clear that Strong and Norman did work closely together through much of the 1920s, and that their views carried much weight on international monetary issues. Chandler reports, however, that:

. . . Most, if not all, the central bankers acted with the knowledge

8. Strong, who was ill at the time, later wrote: "The Federal Reserve Board had no right to discharge the committee and wouldn't have done so had I had a crack at them. . . . I'd see them damned before I'd be dismissed by that timid bunch." Chandler, *Benjamin Strong*, p. 228.

9. For detailed accounts of the differences, see A. Jerome Clifford, *The Independence of the Federal Reserve System* (University of Pennsylvania Press, 1965), pp. 118–21; and Andrew Brimmer (a Board member), "Federal Reserve Discount Policy in Perspective," an address to Robert Morris Associates (Oct. 28, 1968).

and approval of their governments. Though they were, in varying degrees, "independent" central bankers, they were in constant consultation with their finance ministers and even higher government officials. They knew the attitudes of their governments, and their governments knew in at least general terms what the central banks were doing and planning to do. Both governments and central bankers thought it natural that heavy responsibility and broad discretion should be delegated to central banks. In that period most governments had no desire to deal directly with international monetary matters. They were unwilling to make large international loans or grants of their money, to take the initiative in calling international monetary conferences, or even to cooperate directly with other governments in monetary stabilization. It then seemed quite appropriate that the initiative should be left to central banks, which already had both broad responsibilities and expertness in the monetary field.[10]

Thus, the development of personal relations between Strong and the heads of the other central banks reflected a growing custom for central banks to deal mainly with other central banks, not with foreign governments, on such matters as stabilization of exchange rates, gold flows, and the like.[11]

The struggle for power between the Board and the Reserve Banks was enlivened through the 1920s by widespread arguments that the banks were dominated by their privately elected boards of directors and thus represented the private money interests, while the Federal Reserve Board was predominantly a public body, including ex officio the secretary of the treasury and the comptroller of the currency. In addition, the first governor of the Board had been assistant secretary of the treasury and could be presumed to continue his allegiance to the secretary. To some extent, therefore, the Federal Reserve was divided into two factions—one group clearly representing the government (the public), the other seen largely as trustees for the private commercial banks.

During the late 1920s, these conflicts intensified. There was a

10. Chandler, *Benjamin Strong*, p. 249.
11. Chandler quotes a letter of Dec. 10, 1920, from Herbert Hoover to Strong: "It is far better that these problems be solved by the process of business and individual initiative than that they be attempted by our Government. The resort to direct loans by our Government to foreign governments to promote commerce can only lead to a dozen vicious ends. . . . Our experience in war shows that foreign governments which are borrowing our money on easy terms cannot expend it with the economy of private individuals and it results in vast waste. Our Government cannot haggle in the market to exact the securities and returns appropriate to varied risk that merchants and banks can and will exact." (*Ibid.*, p. 251.)

continuing clash between the Board and the Federal Reserve Banks over growing speculation in the security markets. The banks, especially the New York Bank, applied in vain for increases in their discount rates to halt the speculative boom in 1929, while the Board favored persuasion and credit rationing at the discount window. Indecision and lack of forceful leadership characterized the System in 1928 and 1929, as it did in the following years.[12]

The Banking Acts of 1933 and 1935

The massive economic contraction of 1929–33 brought a parallel liquidation of bank assets, and with it a reduction of the nation's money stock by over one-third. In retrospect the Federal Reserve's monetary policy, or lack of policy, was a disaster. In 1931, there was evidence that the economic decline was ending and an upturn was beginning. But drains on the U.S. gold stock alarmed Federal Reserve officials, and they raised the discount rate in spite of widespread unemployment. The result was a return to contraction, and the depression worsened rapidly, culminating in a wave of bank failures and the nationwide "bank holiday" of March 1933.

The downward slide makes a fascinating tale, but the immediate subject is the reasons for the Federal Reserve's behavior. There appear to have been two. First, the conventional wisdom of the times looked to a balanced budget, protection of the gold stan-

---

12. Detailed accounts of the establishment of the Federal Reserve and its early decades are provided by Milton Friedman and Anna J. Schwartz in *A Monetary History of the United States, 1867–1960* (Princeton University Press for National Bureau of Economic Research, 1963), Chaps. 5–6; and Clifford, *Independence of the Federal Reserve System*, Chaps. 2–4. For a criticism of the "real bills" banking theory underlying the act, see Lloyd W. Mints, *A History of Banking Theory in Great Britain and the United States* (University of Chicago Press, 1945). Firsthand accounts of events of this period can be found in: Carter Glass, *An Adventure in Constructive Finance* (Doubleday, Page, 1927); W. P. G. Harding, *The Formative Period of the Federal Reserve System* (Houghton Mifflin, 1925); and H. Parker Willis, *The Federal Reserve System: Legislation, Organization, and Operation* (Ronald Press, 1923). Analytical accounts of Federal Reserve policy during these years are provided by Charles O. Hardy, *Credit Policies of the Federal Reserve System* (Brookings Institution, 1932), and S. E. Harris, *Twenty Years of Federal Reserve Policy* (Harvard University Press, 1933). Elmus R. Wicker, in *Federal Reserve Monetary Policy, 1917–1933* (Random, 1966), stresses especially the importance of gold and related international monetary factors in determining Federal Reserve policy during the 1920s and early 1930s.

dard, and a return to "sound" finance as key objectives. The Reserve's actions judged in the light of those times were understandable. Few leading economists or financiers recommended radically different policies before 1932, though some did, as the depression wore on. Second, the death of Benjamin Strong in 1928 left the Reserve System without a leader. The New York Reserve Bank, under Strong's leadership, had long dominated the nation's monetary affairs, both domestically and internationally. With Strong's death and the shift of authority from New York to Washington, the Federal Reserve Board was ill equipped to accept the challenge. It lacked leadership and was weak and divided. The actions required to prevent monetary collapse did not call for precise analysis or dramatic intellectual breakthroughs. They called for courage to apply the most important lesson of monetary history: that the first task of a central bank is to provide liquidity when banks are under great financial pressure. Strong, had he lived, might have led the System in aggressive action to check the liquidity crisis of the early 1930s. George Harrison, his successor as governor of the New York Bank, either could not or would not.[13]

The unwillingness of President Franklin D. Roosevelt, his advisers, or the general public to tolerate the collapse of the banking system led to prompt action in 1933 to restore the nation's monetary structure and to guard against a repetition. The Banking Acts of 1933 and 1935 reorganized the Federal Reserve, shifting the locus of power from the twelve Reserve Banks to a newly constituted Board of Governors in Washington. They placed authority for

13. Chandler writes: "Strong's death left the System with no center of enterprising and acceptable leadership. The Federal Reserve Board was determined that the New York Bank should no longer play that role. But the Board itself could not play the role in an enterprising way. It was still weak and divided despite the substitution of Young for Crissinger in 1927. Moreover, most of the other Reserve Banks, as well as that in New York, were reluctant to follow the leadership of the Board, partly because of the Board's personnel, partly because they still thought of it as primarily a supervisory and review body. Thus it was easy for the System to slide into indecision and deadlock." (*Benjamin Strong*, p. 465.)

Although the open market committee took some steps following the renewed downturn in 1932, the actions were generally weak and indecisive. As late as Jan. 20, 1933, Governor Harrison of the New York Federal Reserve Bank told Hamlin, a member of the Board, that "a majority of the governors really favored a complete reversal of open market policy by letting government securities run off." (Charles S. Hamlin, Hamlin Papers, Manuscript Division, Library of Congress, Diary, Vol. 22, p. 61, as cited in Friedman and Schwartz, *Monetary History of the United States,* p. 415.)

open market operations in a new, twelve-member Federal Open Market Committee, consisting of all seven Federal Reserve Board members and five of the Reserve Bank presidents. They gave new powers to the Board to change reserve requirements of member banks and to place ceilings on rates of interest payable by commercial banks on time deposits. They clarified the ultimate authority of the Board over changes in discount rates. Perhaps most important of all, the acts introduced federal insurance of bank deposits; and they removed from the Board both the secretary of the treasury and the comptroller of the currency, making it an entirely presidentially appointed body, with no ex officio members.[14]

Simultaneously, the Gold Reserve Act of 1934 took the United States off the traditional gold standard. The price of gold was raised from $20.67 to $35 an ounce; and the President was given discretion to vary this price in terms of dollars and to vary international exchange rates involving the dollar. The Thomas amendment to the Agricultural Adjustment Act of 1933 gave the Treasury the power to issue up to $3 billion of new currency as needed to offset the deflation. Parallel legislation gave authority to the Federal Reserve to impose margin requirements on stock market transactions.

Together these measures dramatically altered the monetary control structure of the United States. They almost produced a forerunner of the Employment Act of 1946. Marriner Eccles, Roosevelt's appointee as chairman of the reconstituted Federal Reserve Board, with the support of Congressman Henry B. Steagall, advocated a congressional directive to the new Board "to exercise such powers as it possesses in such manner as to promote conditions conducive to business stability and to mitigate by its influence unstabilizing fluctuations in the general level of production, trade, prices, and employment so far as may be possible within the scope of monetary action and credit administration."[15] However, the language did not survive congressional hearings.

14. Senator Carter Glass, who had earlier been secretary of the treasury himself, insisted that in the new legislation the secretary of the treasury be dropped as an ex officio member. "When I was Secretary of the Treasury," Glass said, "[I] had considerable influence with the action of the Board, and I have suspected that frequently since the Secretary of the Treasury has had too much influence upon the Board, and I do not think he ought to be there." (Quoted in Marriner S. Eccles, *Beckoning Frontiers: Public and Personal Recollections* [Knopf, 1951], p. 216.)

15. Eccles, *Beckoning Frontiers,* p. 228.

Monetary, Fiscal, and Debt Policy in the 1930s

The birth of modern fiscal policy in the 1930s was slow and disordered. Although John Maynard Keynes's proposal that the federal budget be used to fight unemployment circulated in Washington as early as 1933, his *General Theory of Employment, Interest, and Money* did not appear until 1936, and there is little evidence that anyone in authority in Washington accepted the general Keynesian analysis on budget deficits until the renewed recession of 1937. The federal government ran deficits—but in spite of itself, not because government officials wanted it that way. Try as he would, President Roosevelt could not balance the federal budget.[16]

Thus, the New Deal in its early years placed heavy emphasis on monetary expansion. Devaluation of the dollar, the Thomas amendment, and expansion of Federal Reserve powers were all steps in that direction. As it happened, a rapid expansion in bank reserves and the money supply was generated by a large inflow of gold from Europe, in search of a safer haven. Thus, monetary expansion came largely without positive Federal Reserve action.

Chairman Eccles found the path toward coordinated action with the Treasury a rocky one. The Banking Act of 1935 stated that Federal Reserve open market directives were to be issued with the approval of the secretary of the treasury. And, as was noted above, the "Thomas amendment" gave the Treasury new powers to issue up to $3 billion of currency without gold backing. Moreover, debt management was the Treasury's responsibility. The rapidly growing government debt thus increasingly limited the Federal Reserve's freedom to restrain inflationary pressures. The Treasury wanted to do its financing at low rates of interest. Memories of the disastrous 1929–33 collapse strengthened the belief that government bonds should sell at or above par.

In 1935 and 1936 these issues came to the attention of the public. Excess reserves of member banks were large and growing rapidly as gold flowed in. Fear of inflation pressed Federal Reserve officials to sell bonds in order to absorb bank reserves. But this ac-

16. For a detailed account of the development of fiscal policy during the 1930s, see Herbert Stein, *The Fiscal Revolution in America* (University of Chicago Press, 1969), Chaps. 3–7.

tion would obviously have weakened Treasury bond prices. Eccles argued that excess reserves were so large that the Federal Reserve was "out of touch with the market" and that they could be reduced substantially without seriously impairing the ability of banks to make desirable loans and investments. Extended negotiations between Eccles and Secretary of the Treasury Morgenthau failed to produce agreement. The Treasury used funds from its trust accounts to support bond prices when the Federal Reserve did not do so. But the Treasury trust funds were not inexhaustible, and the bitter Treasury–Federal Reserve disagreement was, in effect, taken to President Roosevelt.

The outcome was a mixed strategy. The Federal Reserve would tighten excess reserves, but without any substantial decline in Treasury bond prices. Reserve requirements were raised by 50 percent in 1936; a few months later they were again raised by 50 percent. Although this eliminated a large amount of excess reserves, there was little decline in bond prices.

At the same time, a new gold "sterilization" policy was inaugurated. The Treasury Stabilization Fund purchased and transferred to the Treasury the net increases in gold. The Stabilization Fund paid for these purchases with dollars acquired by the Treasury through the sale of ninety-day bills in the market. The Treasury, in turn, issued no gold certificates for this addition to the gold supply, so there was no increase in the stock of money or in excess bank reserves. This gold sterilization plan clearly represented an intrusion by the Treasury into traditional central banking responsibilities, and Federal Reserve officials agreed to it only under pressure from the White House.

The sterilized gold was soon to emerge as a Treasury weapon in Federal Reserve–Treasury disputes. When in 1937 the Federal Reserve again proposed raising reserve requirements, the Treasury threatened to release the sterilized gold into the monetary system to offset the Federal Reserve's restrictive measures. After bitter disagreement, again before President Roosevelt, Secretary Morgenthau agreed to withhold the desterilization action if the Federal Reserve would agree to stabilize the price of government securities through open market operations. To ensure that the understanding would be carried out, Morgenthau attended the next meeting of the Federal Open Market Committee and at President Roosevelt's suggestion, made a forceful statement that if the Federal Reserve did not stabilize the bond market, the government would do so itself. Morgenthau said, "I'm not threatening, I'm just making a statement."[17]

The episodes of 1936–37 meant a loss of prestige for the Federal Reserve and made clear the odds involved in a Treasury–Federal Reserve clash. There were offsetting gains, however. Chairman Eccles's increased involvement in White House discussions on general economic issues strengthened the hand of the Federal Reserve in over-all economic policy negotiations. Increasingly Eccles became an advocate of expansionary public spending programs. He strongly supported the President's proposals in this direction. Moreover, he led the support for the President's proposed "undistributed profits tax" in 1936. This position was not popular, but it won him the President's affection. When, after the sharp downturn in 1937, experts began to support the use of fiscal policy—deficit-financed government spending—rather than monetary policy to check the new recession, Eccles was one of the leaders.[18]

There is little doubt that the Federal Reserve's de facto influence in setting over-all government stabilization policy was increased substantially by Eccles's influence with the President, even though he was on less close personal terms with him than was Secretary Morgenthau. But Eccles's competitive position was often made clear when conflicts were taken to the President for resolution. When Eccles and Morgenthau were deadlocked on fiscal matters, the chairman increasingly turned to direct contacts with key members of Congress. His vigorous support of Keynesian economics continued to generate friction between him and the more conservative gentleman-farmer Morgenthau. Within the Federal Reserve, policymaking was increasingly dominated by Eccles.

President Roosevelt made clear that he expected the Federal Reserve to coordinate its policies with the over-all recovery program of the government. At the same time he acknowledged that the Federal Reserve authorities were also directly responsible to Congress. In dedicating the new Federal Reserve building in Washing-

17. Clifford, *Independence of the Federal Reserve System,* p. 157.

18. In his memoirs, Eccles notes with pride his leading role in the establishment of an active federal fiscal policy. See *Beckoning Frontiers,* Part V.

ton in 1937, he said: "To this public body [the Federal Reserve Board] Congress has entrusted broad powers which enable it to affect the volume and the cost of money, thus exerting a powerful influence upon . . . agriculture, trade and industry. . . . Much as they may contribute to the country's progress, monetary powers possess no peculiar magic. They are not omnipotent. To be effective in performing their function, they must be closely coordinated with the other major powers and policies of government which influence the country's economic life."[19]

The sharp downturn of 1937–38 and continued depression in 1938–39 underscored another problem in coordinating federal stabilization policies. While both the Federal Reserve and the White House moved strongly to stimulate expansion in 1938–39, the Federal Deposit Insurance Corporation and the office of the comptroller of the currency, which are quasi-independent agencies responsible for supervising insured banks and national banks, respectively, were apparently tightening their bank examination standards. This involved classifying dubious loans as "slow," and generally restrained the banks from making loans that might prove marginal in the eyes of bank examiners, in spite of the government's efforts to stimulate economic expansion. Facing this situation, Eccles advocated new steps to coordinate bank supervisory policy with Federal Reserve monetary and federal fiscal policies. He complained bitterly about the restrictive implications of the bank examination policies of the other agencies.

Again, Eccles was in conflict with Secretary Morgenthau, under whom the comptroller operated. Eccles took his case to Congress and to the White House against strong opposition from financial traditionalists who saw bank examination as something apart from countercyclical monetary policy. Eccles reports in his memoirs that he finally told the President he would not continue as Federal Reserve chairman unless steps could be taken to eliminate what he saw as a disgraceful lack of coordination among the bank supervisory agencies.[20] While the President agreed to support Eccles's views, the outbreak of the Second World War diverted attention from these issues before action was taken. How far bank supervi-

19. *Federal Reserve Bulletin*, Vol. 23 (November 1937), p. 1062.
20. Eccles, *Beckoning Frontiers*, pp. 278–79.

sion policy should be the handmaiden of monetary policy remained an unsettled issue, to recur in later years.[21]

Eccles also pressed strongly for coordination of federal housing policy with easy money policies in the recession of 1937–38. Again he moved outside the traditional boundaries of monetary policy, advocating aggressive measures to expand federal financial aid to the depressed housing industry. The Wagner-Steagall housing bill of 1937 authorized a $500 million federal expenditure, through the Federal Housing Administration (FHA), over a period of three years. But to Eccles this was merely a drop in the bucket, and he played a leading role in expanding FHA loans and easing requirements for federal assistance to the industry.

The formal responsibilities of the Federal Reserve remained unchanged after 1935, but Eccles's direct involvement in expanding federal counter-recession activities increasingly blurred the lines separating the Federal Reserve from the executive branch of the government. The close involvement of the Federal Reserve in other recovery measures was no accident. The same needs for coordinated action were to arise again when aggressive government stabilization measures were needed.

The Second World War and the Accord of 1951

The outbreak of war in 1939 found money cheap, bank reserves plentiful, a large current federal deficit, and more than 9 million workers unemployed. Increasing federal deficits and heavy private borrowing, together with a more rapid turnover of private funds during the rearmament boom, soon swelled the national product to unprecedented levels. But the existence of a huge reservoir of unemployed workers prevented sharp inflation, and a large excess of reserves eliminated any need for concern over how private or government bank borrowing might be financed. In this period, Federal Reserve and Treasury officials agreed, with perhaps more pa-

---

21. The Federal Reserve urged a general reorganization of bank supervisory agencies in its *Annual Report* for 1938, but counterpressures were strong from the other supervisory agencies and from bankers who argued that bank supervisory policy should not become a "political tool," tied to the government's monetary-fiscal policy.

triotic fervor than foresight, that there must be no shortage of money to buy the weapons of war and that Treasury borrowing would be at a fixed rate of 2½ percent on long-term bonds, with a corresponding rate pattern of about ⅜ of 1 percent on ninety-day bills and ⅞ of 1 percent on nine-month notes.

By 1942 unemployment had substantially vanished; inflation was an obvious reality. Nevertheless, only about 40 percent of total war spending was financed by taxes. While it was universally agreed that the other 60 percent should be financed by borrowing personal and business savings, in the end nearly $100 billion of new money was created during the war by borrowing from the banking system. At first, the excess reserves that had built up in the 1930s were adequate to finance commercial bank lending. But soon the Federal Reserve had to buy new government securities heavily (a total of some $25 billion during the war) to create new excess reserves on the basis of which the commercial banks could in turn buy larger amounts of government securities, thus in turn creating new deposit credits for the Treasury. The Federal Reserve provided additional reserves to the commercial banks to assure the "success" of every Treasury war-loan drive, though with increasing protests against sales practices that permitted easy bond acquisitions by commercial banks between drives.

In the postwar period, the Federal Reserve moved slowly to establish a more independent position vis-à-vis the Treasury. In its *Annual Report* for 1945, the Board reaffirmed its policy of cooperating with the Treasury in the bond price support program, though it pressed for gradual rate increases on short-term Treasury bills. As an alternative to flexible interest rates on government bonds, the Board asked Congress for new powers over the investments and reserves of commercial banks. But substantial friction developed between Eccles and the new secretary of the treasury, John Snyder. By the late 1940s, Eccles and other Federal Reserve authorities openly charged that the Federal Reserve was being made an "engine of inflation" by the bond support policy; Treasury bonds were as good as excess reserves for the banks. They argued that such a price support policy was no longer justified since the Treasury no longer had new-money problems and since inflation was rampant. Treasury officials, on the other hand, continued to cite as reasons for continuing the easy-money policy (1) the need to maintain confidence in the government's credit, (2) the advantages of low interest cost on the debt, and (3) the doubtful anti-inflation powers of tight money.

After the Second World War it became increasingly clear that Eccles, as chief spokesman for the Federal Reserve, had lost influence at the White House. In 1948 President Truman did not reappoint Eccles as chairman of the Board and was increasingly influenced by Secretary Snyder, an old personal friend.[22] The new Federal Reserve chairman, Thomas B. McCabe, was a conciliator, apparently intent on working cooperatively with the Treasury as well as on providing sound monetary policy.

As the controversy grew, Senator Paul Douglas, himself a distinguished economist, headed a major investigation of the Federal Reserve System in 1949, centered on the charge that the System had become an "engine of inflation" and was improperly subservient to the Treasury.[23] The hearings called attention again to the Federal Reserve's inability to restrain credit expansion as long as U.S. bonds held by commercial banks could readily be converted into cash reserves with no risk of loss. They emphasized too the many interactions between Treasury-administration fiscal and debt policies on the one hand and Federal Reserve monetary policy on the other. They focused on the issue of Federal Reserve independence to use anti-inflationary monetary policy in the face of large Treasury debt refunding requirements.[24]

22. Eccles reports in *Beckoning Frontiers* that Truman's unwillingness to reappoint him reflected not a difference on policy issues but the strong antagonism to Eccles of the Giannini family because of Eccles's role in bringing antitrust proceedings against the Transamerica Corporation. (See pp. 434–56.)

23. *Monetary, Credit, and Fiscal Policies*, Hearings before the Subcommittee on Monetary, Credit, and Fiscal Policies of the Joint Committee on the Economic Report, 81 Cong. 1 sess. (1950); *Monetary, Credit, and Fiscal Policies*, Report of the Subcommittee on Monetary, Credit, and Fiscal Policies of the Joint Committee on the Economic Report, 81 Cong. 2 sess, (1950).

24. Although the President's Council of Economic Advisers was established by the Employment Act of 1946, there is little evidence that it played a significant role in the major disputes over macroeconomic policy prior to the Eisenhower administration. Edwin G. Nourse, first chairman of the Council, stayed in the background as an adviser to President Truman. His successor, Leon Keyserling, was an outspoken advocate of the Treasury (low-interest rate) position, but he apparently did not exercise much influence in the controversy, either in the executive branch or in Congress.

After extensive hearings, the committee recommended that "flexible and vigorous monetary policy" should be used in coordination with fiscal and other policies to achieve the objectives of the Employment Act of 1946. It recommended further the establishment of a new coordinating council in the federal government, including the secretary of the treasury, the chairman of the Federal Reserve Board, the director of the budget, and the chairman of the Council of Economic Advisers as chairman. The new council was to be purely consultative, however, and would have no formal power over the agencies represented. Plans for moving rapidly toward a more flexible monetary policy were discussed thoroughly, but were not strongly supported by most witnesses.[25]

In January and February 1951, the behind-the-scenes differences between the Federal Reserve and the Treasury flared into open conflict. Extended negotiations on short-term and long-term Treasury security rates produced growing friction. On January 18 Secretary Snyder announced, apparently without the agreement of the Federal Reserve Board, that ". . . the Treasury Department has concluded, after a joint conference with President Truman and Chairman McCabe . . . that the refunding and new money issues will be financed within the pattern of that [the 2½ percent] rate."[26]

Several Federal Reserve Board members, especially Eccles, believed that the statement was a planned maneuver to further commit Federal Reserve officials to the 2½ percent rate, in the hope that they would hesitate to proclaim an open Federal Reserve–Treasury split by disputing the announcement. In any case, within a few days the Federal Reserve dissent was openly known, and a

25. Two leading economists, Professors John H. Williams of Harvard and Jacob Viner of the University of Chicago, stressed the need for close informal consultation—among substantially equal participants—if monetary, fiscal, and debt policy were to be effectively coordinated. (*Papers and Proceedings of the Forty-Eighth Annual Meeting of the American Economic Association, 1935* [*American Economic Review*, Vol. 26, March 1936].) Viner wrote, in "Recent Legislation and the Banking Situation" (pp. 106–19), that the Federal Reserve's relationship to the President and the Treasury should be "more a question of the relative strength of personalities than of the legal definition of lines of authority. . . . Harmonization of the activities of the two sets of authorities must be through exchange of views between agencies which meet as equals rather than by making one agency merely the instrumentality of the other." See also Williams's paper, "The Banking Act of 1935," pp. 95–105.
26. Clifford, *Independence of the Federal Reserve System*, p. 240.

strong anti-Treasury reaction appeared in the financial press and in Congress.

Then on January 31, in an unprecedented move that was presumably encouraged by Secretary Snyder, President Truman summoned the entire Federal Open Market Committee (FOMC) to the White House for a talk about current monetary developments. No President had ever before summoned the Federal Reserve Board or the FOMC in order to influence or even to discuss its policy actions, and this move was viewed with alarm by many observers. After the meeting, the White House and the Treasury issued statements to the press that the Federal Reserve authorities had agreed to continue to support Treasury bonds at par.

Federal Reserve officials were surprised, some outraged, at this action, for they felt that they had made no such commitment. The discussion had been very general, with no specific reference to the long-term interest rate. They debated at length what to do next, but came to no definite conclusion. In this delicate situation, Eccles, without consulting other Board members, released to the press the next day the full official and confidential Federal Reserve "minutes" of the White House meeting. These minutes flatly disputed the Treasury–White House announcements and denied any such Federal Reserve commitment to continue supporting Treasury bonds at par. The denial was front-page news.

In a very tense atmosphere, the Federal Reserve Board then formally wrote to the President suggesting that Federal Reserve–Treasury negotiations be resumed on an official basis to resolve the differences. President Truman's answer was to appoint a committee consisting of Chairman McCabe, Secretary Snyder, Charles E. Wilson, and Leon Keyserling to reconsider the problem and work out an acceptable compromise solution.

In fact, Assistant Secretary of the Treasury William McChesney Martin, Jr. (later to become chairman of the Federal Reserve Board), and top Federal Reserve officials took the initiative in working out an "accord," which was announced publicly on March 4, without the intervention of the President's formal committee. This accord provided that the Treasury would offer a new *nonmarketable* long-term security at 2¾ percent, thus not openly breaching the 2½ percent rate on marketable issues. But it also provided that the Federal Reserve need not continue its support of the existing pattern of market rates. Soon thereafter the Federal Reserve carefully but firmly pulled the market price pegs from under marketable Treasury issues. Flexible monetary policy was reestablished, but with a clear understanding that the Treasury and the Federal Reserve were jointly responsible for continuing active consultation.[27]

By mid-summer 1951 both Chairman McCabe and ex-Chairman Eccles had announced their resignations from the Federal Reserve Board (in accordance with previous plans, they said). William McChesney Martin, Jr., the chief architect of the accord, was appointed chairman of the board of governors, a post he was to hold for nearly two decades.[28]

But the furor had not died down. The Joint Committee on the Economic Report established a special Subcommittee on General Credit Control and Debt Management, with Congressman Wright Patman as chairman, to investigate the entire situation. Senator Douglas repeated his argument for Federal Reserve independence and for the dominance of monetary policy over debt management. Extensive testimony was presented by the Treasury and the Federal Reserve and by a host of experts outside the government. Support for movement toward a more flexible monetary policy and away from the price-fixing of government bonds was widely expressed.

The committee report urged coordination of monetary and fiscal policy to achieve the basic objectives of stabilization as spelled out in the Employment Act of 1946. It recommended again establishment of a National Monetary and Credit Council, headed by the chairman of the Council of Economic Advisers and including the secretary of the treasury, the chairman of the board of governors, and the heads of the other principal federal agencies that make and guarantee loans. Again the language specified that the council "should be purely consultative and advisory, and it should not have

27. For more detailed accounts of the events leading up to the accord, see Eccles, *Beckoning Frontiers,* pp. 479–99; Stein, *Fiscal Revolution,* Chap. 10; and Clifford, *Independence of the Federal Reserve System,* Chap. VIII.

28. Interestingly, in view of his dominant role since 1951, Martin's original appointment was almost accidental. Although Martin was Snyder's choice for the post, the President and other advisers preferred Harry McDonald, chairman of the Securities and Exchange Commission. At the last minute, it was discovered that McDonald was ineligible because there was already a governor on the Board from his Federal Reserve district. Martin's name was thus substituted at the last minute.

directive power over its members."[29] A new congressional directive to the Federal Reserve and the Treasury on monetary and debt management policies was considered, but none was agreed on.

Senator Douglas's role throughout the controversy is of special interest. He was a strong supporter of Federal Reserve independence and of flexible monetary policy. He stressed the need for a clear directive from Congress to the Federal Reserve and challenged the "common responsibility" theory of Treasury–Federal Reserve relations. He urged that the Federal Reserve be given clear responsibility and directives for monetary policy and authority to carry them out. Repeatedly he argued that "good fences make good neighbors," in supporting a clear division of responsibility and authority between the Federal Reserve and the Treasury.[30] But most witnesses emphasized the need to coordinate monetary and fiscal policy and to share the responsibility for an over-all stabilization policy between the administration and the Federal Reserve.

The Douglas and Patman subcommittees represented a milestone in U.S. economic stabilization policy. The position of the Douglas subcommittee was: "Money is important after all. Restore monetary policy." But the theme of the Patman subcommittee investigation was: "Yes—but how can we really make monetary policy work in a world of vast public debts and huge government expenditures?" Broadly speaking, the hearings revealed agreement among experts on fiscal and monetary policy that:

1. Joint use of both fiscal and monetary policy is probably necessary for effective government action against economic instability, and primary reliance should be placed on these tools rather than on direct controls over prices, wages, materials, and so on.

2. Fluctuations in the quantity of money are an important factor in booms and depressions, though it is not clear just how important money is relative to other variables.

3. The record of monetary policy in mitigating economic insta-

29. *Monetary Policy and the Management of the Public Debt,* Report of the Subcommittee on General Credit Control and Debt Management of the Joint Committee on the Economic Report, 82 Cong. 2 sess. (1952), p. 57.

30. *Ibid.,* pp. 69–77. See also the Hearings of the subcommittee, which include extensive discussion of virtually all the interrelationships between monetary and fiscal policy. *Monetary Policy and the Management of the Public Debt,* Hearings before the Subcommittee on General Credit Control and Debt Management of the Joint Committee on the Economic Report, 82 Cong. 2 sess. (1952).

bility has been unimpressive to date, probably more because it has not been used aggressively than because it is an inadequate tool. Monetary policy should have been used more aggressively after 1946.

4. Fiscal policy is a more powerful tool than monetary policy.

5. The present powers of the Federal Reserve are adequate to halt and reverse inflation; but aggressive use of available powers risks deflation and mass unemployment and probably means declining government bond prices.

6. It is important that the Federal Reserve be free to use monetary restraint against inflation. Yet this restraint must be used cooperatively with the Treasury and with due concern for the latter's task of managing the public debt. Thus, both Federal Reserve independence and its cooperation are needed.[31]

7. The present degree of Federal Reserve independence from the executive branch is about right. However, Federal Reserve participation in federal macroeconomic policymaking might be improved, without the loss of desirable independence, if a consultative national monetary-fiscal policy council were established to advise the President.

8. The Federal Reserve's independence from day-to-day pressures from Congress is also about right, though it might be desirable to bring the Federal Reserve's budget under congressional review and its expenditures under formal government audit.

9. Substitution of a more formal gold standard for existing reliance on responsible monetary and fiscal management in combating inflation and depression found little or no support.[32]

31. Chairman Martin, Allan Sproul (president of the New York Reserve Bank), and Secretary Snyder all agreed on the need for close cooperative relationships between the Federal Reserve and the Treasury.

32. For a more complete analysis, see G. L. Bach, "The Economics and Politics of Money," *Harvard Business Review*, Vol. 31 (March–April 1953), pp. 84–96.

5

THE EISENHOWER YEARS

THE EISENHOWER ADMINISTRATION, Stein writes, confirmed the revolution in fiscal policy of the preceding two decades.[1] The great depression and the Second World War had seen the emergence of Keynesian fiscal policy as a dominant theme and the relegation of money and monetary policy to minor roles. Easy money was widely thought to have failed the test of the great depression; monetary policy was at best permissive in the financing of the Second World War. The gold standard, once a widely accepted guide to the proper amount of money in each nation, was cast aside everywhere throughout the Western world. "Managed economies"—through fiscal and monetary measures—were its successor, and to a degree the new administration accepted the change. But there was little experience on which to draw in managing national economies.

1. Herbert Stein, *The Fiscal Revolution in America* (University of Chicago Press, 1969), Chap. 11. Many economists believe that the "revolution" was far less advanced by the 1950s than does Stein. Detailed reports on macroeconomic policies during the 1950s are provided by Edward S. Flash, Jr., *Economic Advice and Presidential Leadership* (Columbia University Press, 1965), Chaps. 4–5; Wilfred Lewis, Jr., *Federal Fiscal Policy in the Postwar Recessions* (Brookings Institution, 1962), Chaps. 5–6; Stein, *The Fiscal Revolution*, Chaps. 11–13; A. Jerome Clifford, *The Independence of the Federal Reserve System* (University of Pennsylvania Press, 1965), Chaps. 9–10; and Asher Achinstein, *Federal Reserve Policy and Economic Stability, 1951–1957*, U.S. Library of Congress, Legislative Reference Service, for the Senate Committee on Banking and Currency, 85 Cong. 2 sess. (1958).

As the great depression drew the spotlight from monetary to fiscal policy, so the years following the Second World War turned it back to money and monetary management. The vast monetary expansion during the Second World War, combined with bond pegging in the postwar years, highlighted the role of monetary expansion in producing inflation. Too much money and too few goods to buy with it turned out to be the major postwar economic problem—not the stagnant economy forecast by many Keynesians. Whether the large wartime increase in the money stock caused the ensuing inflation or merely permitted it to happen is debatable; that it played an important role in the postwar inflation is hardly subject to disagreement. The Federal Reserve–Treasury accord of 1951 restored flexible monetary policy to a potentially important role. But it did so in a world where scholars were still generally convinced that fiscal policy was the powerful stabilization tool, and that shortages of aggregate demand and economic slack were greater threats than was inflation.

The Republicans also inherited the Employment Act of 1946 and with it (though somewhat precariously) a Council of Economic Advisers, which brought professional economists nearer the center of economic policymaking than before.

Into this setting the Eisenhower administration brought a tentative, nondoctrinaire economic philosophy. In accepting federal government responsibility for helping to keep the economy healthy and growing, the new government sought to avoid the extremes of both depression and inflation. It saw the federal budget as having a significant impact on the level of economic activity, but it rejected the prevalent Keynesian view that the level of economic activity could be managed effectively through deficits and surpluses in the federal budget alone. Certainly it denied that only fiscal policy was important.

Arthur F. Burns, chairman of the new Council of Economic Advisers, and George M. Humphrey, secretary of the treasury, in many ways typified the new administration. Burns came to Washington from the National Bureau of Economic Research and a distinguished career as an empirical investigator in the field of business cycles. His approach to economic analysis was careful, thorough, pragmatic. He suspected that business cycles such as the United States had known in the past would return in the 1950s, and that the government's principal economic problem would be to avoid cyclical excesses. Widely respected in academic circles, Burns became the economics schoolmaster for President Eisenhower and his administration.

Secretary Humphrey represented the conservative businessman's point of view. He had little time for Keynesian ideas, or indeed for other theoretical-intellectual approaches to the problem of economic stability. He stood firmly for a balanced budget and fiscal responsibility. He was quick, abrupt, a man of decisive action, and a pragmatist, more at home with other businessmen and men of affairs than with economists. To a considerable extent, the flavor and history of the Eisenhower years are exemplified by these two men, their contrasting approaches, and the interactions between them.

1953-54: The Business Cycle Again?

The first years of the Eisenhower administration saw the development of its style in formulating and carrying out macroeconomic policy. In January 1953 the new administration found a prosperous economy. Private investment and industrial production were at new highs. Unemployment had been below 3 percent. The Korean war was ending. The sharp burst of price inflation brought on by the Korean war had ended.

In this setting, Burns at the Council of Economic Advisers, Humphrey at the Treasury, and William McChesney Martin, Jr., the new chairman of the Federal Reserve Board, all feared a further surge of inflation. Some academic economists warned of a possible downturn, but they received little attention. The government's main concern was to temper the upswing and avoid inflation.

President Eisenhower moved early to establish a new high-level Advisory Board on Economic Growth and Stabilization (ABEGS) under Burns's chairmanship. The committee included representatives of the heads of the Treasury, Agriculture, Commerce, and Labor Departments, the Budget Bureau, and the Federal Reserve, as well as Gabriel Hauge of the White House staff. As an advisory body, ABEGS was to keep the President "closely informed about the state of the national economy and the various measures necessary to aid in maintaining a stable prosperity."[2] Thus, easy and regular contact among Burns, Humphrey, and Martin was assured, and they consulted actively.

At the Federal Reserve, the Federal Open Market Committee (FOMC) saw the economy as expanding rapidly and the demand for credit strong. In January 1953 the discount rate was raised from 1.75 to 1.88 percent, and shortly thereafter to 2 percent, and reserves were tightened through open market operations to damp the boom. On the fiscal front, the Korean war excess profits tax was scheduled to expire on June 30, 1953; and, although Burns, Humphrey, and Eisenhower all wanted the tax removed eventually because it discriminated against investment, they strongly urged Congress to continue it for at least another six months. Congress reluctantly agreed. On the spending side, Eisenhower cut President Truman's proposed fiscal 1954 budget appropriation from $73 billion to $64 billion, most of the reduction being in defense, foreign aid, and related areas. The President and Budget Director Joseph M. Dodge urged further reductions in government departments and agencies as part of a general restrictive budget policy aimed at restoring fiscal responsibility after the spending surge of the Truman administration.

Early 1953 brought the first test of Federal Reserve–Treasury relations under the new administration. With bank reserves under growing pressure from the Federal Reserve, the commercial banks sold government bonds heavily to obtain funds to meet loan demands. In April a large Treasury bond offering was weakly received, and concern developed at the Treasury and in the financial community over the tightening money market. After extensive consultations with the Treasury, the Federal Reserve in May "began operating to ease pressure on bank reserves, not primarily because it foresaw at that time a recession in the making but because of the sudden appearance of more tension in the financial market than it considered appropriate."[3] Nevertheless, in early June the government securities market was virtually demoralized; there

2. *Economic Report of the President, January 1954*, p. 121.

3. *January 1954 Economic Report of the President*, Hearings before the Joint Committee on the Economic Report Pursuant to Sec. 5(a) of Public Law 304, 83 Cong. 2 sess. (1954), p. 668.

were practically no bids for U.S. Treasury securities. Hurriedly the FOMC fed more reserves into the market and in July reduced reserve requirements. The net effect of these actions was to increase the reserve funds available to member banks by more than $2 billion and to change the tone of the money markets from restraint to ease—even though inflation, not unemployment, was the dominant concern.

In retrospect, it is clear that the economy turned down sometime between March and July 1953. Business inventories were accumulating rapidly, and the cutback in government expenditures was proceeding apace. By early autumn, CEA economists and the Federal Reserve were both convinced that inventories were seriously out of line. In September, Burns reported to the President and the cabinet that a "readjustment" might be on the way. Interagency task forces were established under ABEGS to conduct "an intensive study of measures to promote the stability and growth of our economy and specific economic programs and policies to be pursued in the event of a general slowing down of economic activity."[4]

By late autumn, the administration welcomed an expiration date of January 1, 1954, for the excess profits tax, as well as for Korean war excises and personal income taxes. The total tax reduction on that date was estimated at roughly $5 billion, but credit for this can hardly be given to flexible fiscal policy. The expiration date had been set long before by Congress, quite apart from countercyclical considerations.

In retrospect, antirecession monetary policy got off to a good start, albeit somewhat accidentally because of the weaknesses in the money market noted above; and the Federal Reserve's strong moves toward monetary ease helped significantly to check the downswing. But fiscal policy deserved poor marks. The 1953–54 recession was due in considerable measure to the rapid cutback in defense expenditures at the end of the Korean war, while the associated postwar tax cuts were delayed by the administration until the recession was well under way. Even then, they fell short of offsetting cuts in expenditures. Not until early 1954 was most of the administration convinced of the need for counter-recessionary measures.

4. *Economic Report of the President, January 1954,* p. 123.

Throughout this period the council and the Federal Reserve worked closely together. Martin and Burns lunched together frequently and got along well. They respected one another, and their economic views were consonant. Apparently Burns from time to time prodded the Board toward easier money after the recession was a clear reality, but in general Martin and Burns held compatible views.

Burns and Humphrey were also in frequent communication, both informally and through participation in weekly cabinet meetings. The two men were friendly, but not personally close. Their policy views differed sharply as the recession developed. Humphrey opposed increases in federal spending and in the federal deficit. Burns pushed hard for easier mortgage terms to stimulate housing, but made only limited headway against the opposition of Humphrey and the housing agencies. The CEA suggested speeding up expenditures in the spring of 1954, and Burns obtained cabinet agreement that federal public works spending should be increased by $1 billion above planned levels. Throughout, Burns and other administration officials placed great emphasis on restoring and maintaining business confidence.

Over all, Burns's efforts to prod the administration into reasonably flexible counter-recessionary measures can be described as modestly successful. His support of moderate intervention to keep the economy stable was consistent with, though not based on, the Keynesian fiscal policies of the preceding administration's economists. However, there is little evidence that the rest of the Eisenhower administration accepted even Burns's fiscal ideas with any enthusiasm.

Still, Burns and his council emerged from the episode with substantially increased prestige. The recession was in fact brief and mild. Both the President and other observers were inclined to give substantial credit to the economists, especially Burns, who had helped lead the way through the dangers of recession. Burns somehow managed to be simultaneously a symbol of recovery, modern economics, fiscal responsibility, and conservatism. Interestingly, the Federal Reserve, which engaged in the most aggressive counter-recessionary measures, received far less public acclaim.

Early in his administration, Eisenhower developed a strong liking and respect for Burns and invited him to brief the cabinet on economic affairs at nearly every cabinet meeting. Sometimes Burns would talk as long as half an hour, and Sherman Adams reports that the President "listened to him with fascination."[5] Moreover, Burns and the secretary of defense were the only administration officials who had regular private weekly meetings with the President.[6]

During this entire period, Martin and Humphrey also maintained close communication through regular Monday lunches, other meetings, and frequent telephone calls. The Federal Reserve nonetheless remained somewhat aloof from the inner circles of government policymaking. It had only recently regained its independence and did not want to risk losing it again so soon.

Interestingly, Sherman Adams suggests that George Humphrey lost standing with the President on economic issues, and Martin gained, when Humphrey in 1953 "slowed down normal growth" by bringing out "an attractive issue of . . . bonds that mopped up enough money that would otherwise have gone into corporate stocks and mortgages to cause a mild panic." Adams continues: "Coming to the rescue, William McC. Martin, Chairman of the Federal Reserve Board, took prompt steps to ease the situation, lower interest rates and loosen up the money supply. The crisis

5. Sherman Adams, *Firsthand Report: The Story of the Eisenhower Administration* (Harper, 1961), p. 156.

6. Burns has described his role as CEA chairman in some detail in "Heller's 'New Dimensions of Political Economy,'" *National Banking Rview*, Vol. 4 (June 1967), p. 374: "During 1953–1956, for example, the Chairman of the Council had weekly scheduled meetings with the President—a privilege that only one other member of the government, the Secretary of Defense, enjoyed. He had full access to the President at other times and he used it when necessary. He represented the Council at weekly Cabinet meetings, made frequent reports on current and emerging policy requirements, and participated actively in Cabinet debates on economic matters. He served as Chairman of various Cabinet committees and used the opportunity to advance the Council's program. He worked closely with the Secretary of the Treasury and the Chairman of the Federal Reserve Board. He and his Council colleagues spent a good part of practically every day striving for a consensus on policy issues with representatives of the various departments and agencies. The Council thus fought tirelessly within the Executive establishment for the policies that it deemed needed and proper. The Council did not, however, take to the stump and fight in the public arena for the President's program. It refrained from this essential political activity because it felt, by and large, that professional economists should stick to their knitting, that economic counseling and political advocacy could get in one another's way, and that economists should not devote their precious time to do what politicians—who at least then were not in short supply—can do better."

passed, but it left its mark as an error in Humphrey's fiscal calculation and raised some questions about the stability of the administration's money policies."[7]

From the outset, however, Eisenhower took the position that the Federal Reserve was indeed a substantially independent agency, and he carefully kept hands off. He writes that, although the Federal Reserve was independent, "Another whose counsel I valued highly was the Chairman of the Federal Reserve Board, William McChesney Martin. Though not a member of the Executive branch, he worked tirelessly to further fiscal responsibility and sustain the value of our currency."[8]

Reasonably close working relations among the senior staffs of major agencies contributed substantially to the generally effective policy discussions. David Lusher, a senior economist at the CEA, established the widely known "Lusher Tuesday group" (or "Lusher's lunches") for senior economic analysts from the three or four agencies primarily responsible for macroeconomic policy. The top CEA staff on monetary-financial matters was on loan from the Federal Reserve; and Under Secretary of the Treasury for Monetary Affairs W. Randolph Burgess had been for many years with the New York Federal Reserve Bank. However, there is little doubt that the principals were strong-minded men who throughout made the basic policy decisions.

1955–58

Macroeconomic policy formation in the 1954–58 cycle was similar to that in 1953–54. Communication among the chief policymakers and their senior staffs was generally good, and there is little evidence that any of them acted without reasonable consultation with the others. The policy differences that did occur primarily reflected differing analyses of the economic situation, rather than quarrels over the appropriate monetary-fiscal policy mix.

In summary, the economy, with the help of stimulative fiscal and monetary policies, rose rapidly in late 1954 and 1955. Substantial inflation in commodity prices reappeared, and wage rates rose rapidly through union negotiations and in free markets. Reflect-

7. Adams, *Firsthand Report*, p. 161.
8. Dwight D. Eisenhower, *Waging Peace, 1956–61* (Doubleday, 1965), p. 460.

ing its concern about inflation, the administration moved to hold down budget expenditures and restrain rising prices. The Federal Reserve, on the other hand, maintained relatively easy money until mid-1955, although Burns had urged restraint earlier.

From late 1955 through early 1957 the economy presented a perplexing mixture of characteristics. On some fronts (industrial production and employment) the boom leveled off near the end of 1955, and the trend of economic activity was horizontal until 1957. On the other hand, private investment continued strong; and prices, wage rates, and wage costs continued to rise, reflecting "sectoral" or "cost-push" inflation in the eyes of many observers. In late 1955 the Federal Reserve moved to tighten credit substantially, then eased slightly to facilitate Treasury financing, and then tightened further during 1956 and early 1957.

In retrospect, by mid-1957 the economy had clearly slipped into the recession of 1957–58. By this time Burns's successor, Raymond J. Saulnier, and the council were urging immediate steps to offset the developing recession. But the Federal Reserve authorities held credit tight and in August 1957 even raised discount rates, in spite of concern (reported throughout 1957 in the FOMC minutes) that inflation might be giving way to recession as the central problem.

The contraction that began in 1957 was sharp. By early 1958, both Federal Reserve and administration officials were agreed on the need to fight recession, and strong steps were taken in that direction.

Several episodes during the 1954–58 period deserve special attention.

First, although central banks are usually thought to be more conservative than governments, the Federal Reserve moved to monetary restraint in 1955 more slowly than the White House and the council wished. Burns, Humphrey, and Eisenhower were agreed in early 1955 that inflation was re-emerging as the major problem and that the economy's growth rate could not be sustained. But not until 1956 did the FOMC fully agree with this analysis and take positive steps to halt rising prices, even though by mid-1956 industrial production and total output were moving more sideways than upward.

Second, two episodes in 1955 and 1956 indicate the nature of working relations between the Federal Reserve and the Treasury. In November 1955 the Treasury needed to finance over $12 billion of certificates and notes. As was customary, the refunding was undertaken after Treasury–Federal Reserve agreement on terms for the new issues. However, the refunding was not well received, and Treasury officials became alarmed that disorder would develop in the government securities market. Accordingly, even though many officials (including the CEA) stressed the need to restrain inflation, the Treasury appealed to the FOMC to support security prices actively in the open market. In a hurried action, the committee voted nine to three to absorb up to $400 million of the new certificates.

This special supportive action by the Federal Reserve did not escape the notice of Congress or the press; the accord of 1951 was still fresh in mind. It was widely suggested that the Federal Reserve, instead of acting independently, was in effect still under the thumb of the Treasury. In its 1955 Annual Report the Federal Reserve explained its action by pointing out that the committee could not ignore the secretary of the treasury's request, nor could it fail to take into account the possible psychological deterioration of the entire securities market if the issue were a failure. Moreover, the seasonal need for credit was rising rapidly, which also argued for additional bank reserves.

Many congressmen were not convinced. Senator Paul H. Douglas observed:

This is the type of . . . coercion of the Federal Reserve System by the Executive which I regard as improper. The Treasury should determine the terms of its issues, and if they misjudge the market they should be punished accordingly. . . . They should not call on the Reserve to bail them out and inflate the money supply in order to cover up a mistake in the terms of yield.[9]

In reply, Chairman Martin objected strongly to the use of the word coercion. He maintained that the episode showed the need for practical cooperation:

I think you have to recognize that the Treasury and the Federal Reserve are partners, each with a 50-percent interest, if you want to put it that way. Neither one of us is subservient, one to the other. It is our endeavor to see that the Treasury is successfully financed and

9. *Nomination of William McChesney Martin, Jr.*, Hearings before the Senate Committee on Banking and Currency, 84 Cong. 2 sess. (1956), p. 21.

neither the Treasury nor the Federal Reserve should ignore the dictates of the market; and neither the Treasury nor the Federal Reserve benefit by having the Treasury fail at any time.[10]

Senator J. W. Fulbright, chairman of the Senate Committee on Banking and Currency, told Martin that it was ridiculous to talk about the independence of the Federal Reserve System:

[We should avoid] kidding ourselves and kidding the public that we do actually have an independent agency independent of the influence of the Treasury. I do not quite think we have, and I do not quite think we are ever going to have. After all, the President does appoint the members and nominates them, and the Executive is going to have that very basic influence. . . .

I do not believe there is any real independence . . . except in the sense that you can quit. You do not have the power to continue your own way in the face of the pressure the White House is able to exert through the Treasury. . . .[11]

Martin, however, reminded the committee that Congress had given certain responsibilities to the System and that it was free to change them at any time. He argued that this was a desirable arrangement on practical grounds:

. . . the reason for having [such an arrangement] was that the Federal Reserve System, which stands at the bar of public opinion just the same as anyone else, ought to have in this field a reasonable opportunity to make its decisions, insulated from direct policy pressures or private pressures.[12]

He continued by saying that this "reasonable opportunity" did not mean isolation from the Treasury any more than it meant compulsion or coercion by the Treasury or by the President, regardless of the wishes of the Federal Reserve. On the other hand, the Federal Reserve had to take into account its responsibilities, including the successful financing of the government. If the Board were to sit incommunicado in an ivory tower, it would not be doing its job.

April 1956 brought another test of the Federal Reserve's willingness to oppose the Treasury on its financing plans. The Federal Reserve by now considered inflation to be a major problem and was moving to tighten bank credit. In April, despite the open opposition of the secretary of the treasury, the secretary of commerce,

10. *Ibid.*, p. 22.
11. *Ibid.*, pp. 66–67.
12. *Ibid.*, p. 24.

and the chairman of the Council of Economic Advisers, the Federal Reserve Board approved an increase in the discount rate. Again, congressional watchdog committees were in action, and Chairman Martin explained the circumstances as follows:

Pursuing our method of cooperation, I began discussions with Secretary Humphrey. In February of that year, Governor Balderston and I had a meeting with Secretary Humphrey and there was a disagreement as to the nature that the economy was developing. We were so convinced; we discussed it with various people, and in a series of meetings from about the middle of February until the last week in March. By the last week in March the position of the Federal Reserve ... was that it would be wise for us to go up in the discount rate.... We finally reached a point where there was no meeting of the minds that could be had, and there was nothing for the Federal Reserve to do except to go and act. And we acted.[13]

Martin referred to this episode as an illustration of the Federal Reserve's being "independent within the government." This independence does not allow the System to pursue a course contrary to basic national economic policies, but it does provide freedom for the Federal Reserve to exercise considerable independent judgment in the complicated field of monetary and credit policy. He stated:

We feel ourselves bound by the Employment Act and by the Federal Reserve Act. And in the field of money and credit ... we consult with them [the administration] but we feel that we have the authority, if we think that in our field, money and credit policies, that we should act differently than they, we feel perfectly at liberty to do so.[14]

Throughout, Congress was jealous of its prerogative to control the Federal Reserve, though except for a few individuals like Representative Wright Patman, congressmen were generally reluctant to intervene. Sometimes they were not sure that Chairman Martin and the Federal Reserve paid much attention to their views. In 1956, when Martin had made the point that the Federal Reserve was responsible not to the President but to Congress, Douglas questioned him as follows:

SENATOR DOUGLAS: Do you regard the Federal Reserve Board as an agent of the Executive or the agent of Congress?

13. *Investigation of the Financial Condition of the United States,* Hearings before the Senate Committee on Finance, 85 Cong. 1 sess. (1957), Pt. 3, p. 1362.
14. *Ibid.,* p. 1361.

MR. MARTIN: I regard it as an independent agency of the government.

SENATOR DOUGLAS: To whom is it responsible? To the Executive or the Congress?

MR. MARTIN: It is responsible to Congress. . . .

SENATOR DOUGLAS: Mr. Martin, I have had typed out this little sentence which is a quotation from you: The Federal Reserve Board is an agency of Congress. I will furnish you with scotch tape and ask you to place it on your mirror where you can see it as you shave each morning, so that it may remind you.[15]

Third, the press and public opinion in 1956 did indeed play the role Martin ascribed to them. They followed administration–Federal Reserve differences avidly and were quick to criticize. And the Federal Reserve did indeed stand before the bar of public opinion. A detailed account of this process during part of 1956 is given in the Appendix as an example of the workings of the system.

Fourth, a "new inflation" in this period raised difficult problems of analysis and policy for both monetary and fiscal authorities. The recovery of 1954–57 brought substantial price inflation well before unemployment was reduced to acceptable levels. In spite of the boom, unemployment stayed above 4 percent, compared to under 3 percent in 1953. Wage rates and unit wage costs rose rapidly, and many observers attributed the inflation to a "cost-push" phenomenon. This was in contrast to the "demand-pull" that had characterized most inflations, where aggregate demand substantially exceeded aggregate supply potentialities. Partly because of rising labor costs, business investment in plant and equipment increased rapidly, and with it bank credit. Prices in some sectors of the economy were bid up sharply, but few offsetting decreases appeared elsewhere. Thus, the 1955–57 inflation was also called a "sectoral" inflation, because any shift in demand would lead to higher average prices if some prices rose and none fell.

In retrospect, it is not clear that either the cost-push or sectoral analysis fully explains the inflation of this time, but they contributed to the perplexity of both monetary and fiscal policymakers. Previously it had been presumed under the simple Keynesian analytics that expansionary monetary-fiscal policy was called for as long as there was substantial underemployment of labor and plant and equipment. Now the authorities faced the apparent dilemma of

15. *Nomination of William McChesney Martin, Jr.,* Hearings, 1956, pp. 23–25.

choosing full employment *or* stable prices. Federal Reserve and top administration officials both stressed the need to break the spiral of inflationary expectations that increasingly characterized the postwar economy. Policy actions were generally consistent with this rationalization, and inflationary expectations surely were undercut, laying the basis for the long period of stable prices from 1958 to 1965. But unemployment remained stubbornly high, and U.S. growth lagged behind that of most Western nations. Optimal policy under such circumstances was far from clear.[16]

1958–60

The downswing from mid-1957 to early 1958 was one of the sharpest on record and one of the shortest. The upswing that followed was also short, but weak. The macroeconomic policy followed during the cycle can be described briefly. Both fiscal and monetary policymakers were tardy in recognizing the downswing, but once they did, in 1958, an appropriately expansionary stance contributed substantially to a quick recovery. However, almost as soon as the trough was passed and recovery was under way, both fiscal and monetary policy rapidly became more restrictive. This not only tended to prevent the economy from recovering fully, but also contributed to another recession almost immediately—in 1960. What were the main new lessons of 1958–59 for the policy process?

First, both fiscal and monetary authorities recognized the sharp contraction promptly in 1958. The "inside lag" (between a cycle turning point and counteraction by the authorities) was short—only a few months. But the 1957–58 downturn was so sharp it could hardly be missed.

Second, the policy coordination process worked well. The CEA, the Treasury, the Federal Reserve, and the White House were in effective communication throughout, and apparently all recognized the rapidly changing signals at about the same time. Moreover, both monetary and fiscal restrictions were then eased rapidly. On the fiscal side, this involved mainly a speedup of federal expen-

16. For a detailed analysis of this period, see *Staff Report on Employment, Growth, and Price Levels,* Prepared for Consideration by the Joint Economic Committee, 86 Cong. 1 sess. (1959), often called the "Eckstein Report."

ditures, with cooperation between the executive and Congress. On the monetary side, reductions in reserve requirements, reductions in the discount rate, and open market purchases were used to stimulate recovery.

Third, Stein describes fiscal policymaking in this downswing as "the near miss of 1958"—looking toward the outright adoption of deficit-period tax cutting in 1964. But this interpretation seems optimistic. Burns, by then back at his posts at Columbia University and the National Bureau of Economic Research, favored a tax cut to fight the recession, even if the consequences were a budget deficit. Some senior staff economists in the government swung to this view. But at top policymaking levels, both Robert B. Anderson, Eisenhower's new secretary of the treasury, and Chairman Martin of the Federal Reserve continued to consider inflation the number one danger, once the recession was clearly stopped in early 1958. Raymond Saulnier at CEA shared this view, and in 1959–60 this triumvirate persuaded Eisenhower of its validity against conflicting arguments. Modern fiscal policy had not yet arrived.

The President's deep commitment to avoiding inflation while maintaining a growing economy was reemphasized in the letter transmitting his Economic Report in January 1959, when the recession of 1957–58 had barely been reversed. Although unemployment was still above 5 percent, Eisenhower devoted nearly half of his letter to arguing for a program for "economic growth with stable prices." He wrote:

Our objective must be to establish a firm foundation for extending economic growth with stable prices into the months and years ahead. This will not come about automatically. . . . Finally, an indispensable condition for achieving vigorous and continuing economic growth is firm confidence that the value of the dollar will be reasonably stable in the years ahead.[17]

The concluding chapter of the report was entitled "A Program for Economic Growth With Price Stability"; it argued for a balanced budget and careful controls over expenditures to avoid inflation and provide the basis for firm economic growth, with primary reliance on the private sector.

By January 1960, with continued slack in the U.S. economy, with slower growth in the United States than in other countries, and with the end of his administration in sight, Eisenhower in-

17. *Economic Report of the President, January 1959,* p. v.

creasingly emphasized the classical economic notion that government deficit spending, financed by borrowing, in a recession would *compete* for private savings and thereby reduce the level of private investment. Government deficits might thus *slow* economic growth, even with slack in the economy. Burns, from his post at Columbia, warned that another recession was on the way and urged a shift in emphasis; but Eisenhower, Anderson, and Saulnier refused to go along.[18]

Secretary Anderson appears to have been very influential in this period; his thoughtful analysis impressed Eisenhower more than had Humphrey's blunt, simplistic judgments, even though Humphrey was closer personally to the President. Saulnier and his CEA appear to have had much less influence on policy than had Burns, with his strong personal position at the White House and around Washington. ABEGS was dormant, and Anderson took the lead in establishing regular meetings with the chairman of the CEA, the director of the budget, and the chairman of the Federal Reserve Board—the informal group later called the "quadriad" in the Kennedy administration. Anderson's previous service as vice-chairman of the board of the Federal Reserve Bank of Dallas facilitated understanding between the treasury and the Federal Reserve.

If "timely flexibility" is important for fiscal policy, as the Eisenhower administration emphasized many times, the experience of 1957–58 suggests that such flexibility is more feasible on the expenditure side than on the tax side. Some expenditures can be accelerated without the approval of Congress; and in any case, Congress is apt to move quickly on expenditure increases to fight unemployment. By contrast, at least a decade ago, tax cuts to fight recession were unpalatable to most congressmen and to the public. While one may blame Eisenhower for not proposing a tax cut in 1958, it is unlikely that Congress would have approved such a proposal.[19]

18. In 1959 the President appointed a Cabinet Committee on Price Stability for Economic Growth under the chairmanship of Vice President Nixon, with Dean W. Allen Wallis of Chicago as executive director. This committee carefully examined the problem of inflation and issued a balanced report on its causes and effects. However, the committee became increasingly a special enterprise of the Vice President; it did not have the close working support of the White House and received little attention.

19. Academic economists raised another doubt about the case for a temporary tax cut to fight recession. Milton Friedman, in his influential *A Theory of the*

Fourth, in the late 1950s serious concern began to arise about the balance of payments. The January 1960 *Economic Report of the President* stressed for the first time the large deficit in the U.S. balance of payments and indicated concern over a "continuing adjustment problem" in international trade that would avoid unsustainable balance-of-payments deficits.[20] The Federal Reserve in its *Annual Report* for 1960 also showed for the first time cautious concern over the continuing large payments deficit and gold drain.[21] Although public statements were restrained, the minutes of the FOMC show growing anxiety over the balance-of-payments problem and possible loss of confidence in the dollar abroad. It is clear that this factor strengthened the determination of both the Federal Reserve and the administration to avoid a resurgence of inflation that would weaken the U.S. trading position abroad and confidence in the dollar, thereby generating further capital outflows.

In retrospect, the Eisenhower fiscal policy of 1958–60 was one of the major fiscal policy mistakes of the postwar period. The push was for a big surplus instead of the "timely flexibility" against economic slack that administration officials emphasized so frequently in their public pronouncements. With a recession in 1960, the administrative budget surplus was $1 billion, while the full-employment budget surplus soared to nearly $15 billion, as restrictive tax policy created a "fiscal drag" on economic growth. The monetary authorities at the Federal Reserve by and large shared the White House view. Money was tight in 1960, though the Federal Reserve acted to ease it somewhat after early 1960. Lack of communication and coordination cannot be blamed for the failures of monetary and fiscal policy during this period.[22]

Consumption Function (Princeton University Press for National Bureau of Economic Research, 1957), argued that consumer spending depends largely on "permanent" income, so a temporary tax cut might be of limited value in stimulating consumption.

20. Pp. 111–23.

21. *Forty-seventh Annual Report of the Board of Governors of the Federal Reserve System for 1960,* pp. 12–18.

22. In the late 1950s, a special Commission on Money and Credit was established under the auspices of the Committee for Economic Development. This commission produced a substantial report and some twenty books, covering the entire range of monetary arrangements and policy. For an official retroview of policy and policymaking during the 1950s, as seen by the top officials of these two agencies, see the volume prepared for the commission by the Board of Governors of the Federal

The Policy Process: Evaluation

How effective was the macroeconomic policy process during the Eisenhower years? How well were its major elements coordinated?

THE EVIDENCE

Figure 1 shows the economy's performance during the 1950s, focusing on the principal goals identified in Chapter 2—real output compared to potential, unemployment, price level changes, and the balance of payments. If the test of a policy is its outcome, Figure 1 should provide central answers as to the effectiveness of macro policy during the Eisenhower years.[23]

Judged by these standards, the Eisenhower administration and the Federal Reserve might be given an over-all grade of "good" in the early years and no better than "fair" in the later ones. War imbalances were worked out of the economy without major disruptions. The major shortfall was in economic growth and employment in the years 1957–60, although on the credit side inflation was substantially eliminated during this period.

How far these observed results reflected goals sought by the various authorities, how far varying use of the policy instruments available, and how far inadequacies of the instruments for achieving the desired goals, is hard to discern. Although the economy's performance was mixed, it might have been worse (or conceivably better) without the policies that were followed. Moreover, monetary and fiscal authorities do not directly control real output, employment, and prices, but only intermediate variables, which in turn influence the ultimate goal variables.

Figure 2 offers alternative intermediate measures of the impact of fiscal and monetary policies on the economy. They provide evidence of the specific actions taken by the fiscal and monetary authorities and may be compared with the results shown in Figure 1.

Reserve System and the United States Treasury Department, *The Federal Reserve and the Treasury: Answers to Questions from the Commission on Money and Credit* (Prentice-Hall, 1963).

23. Figure 1 does not explicitly include "even keeling" the market for Treasury financing or maintenance of stability in financial markets, both of which are also clearly important Federal Reserve operating objectives. However, money market conditions (Figure 2) provide a related indicator.

FIGURE 1

The Goals of National Economic Policy, 1952–60

Growth of Gross National Product

Billions of 1958 dollars (ratio scale)

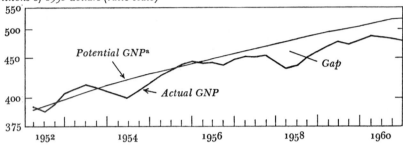

Unemployment and Prices

Percent

Balance of Payments[c]

Millions of dollars

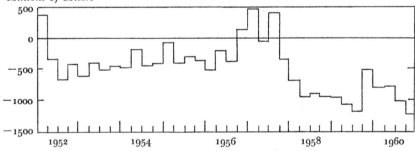

Sources: Gross national product and price deflator, U.S. Office of Business Economics, *The National Income and Product Accounts of the United States, 1929–1965, Statistical Tables* (1966), pp. 8–9, 158–59; potential GNP, Council of Economic Advisers; unemployment rates, U.S. Bureau of the Census, *Business Conditions Digest* (February 1970), p. 108; balance of payments, 1952–59, U.S. Department of Commerce; 1960, *Business Conditions Digest* (July 1969), p. 106. The data used in the figures are seasonally adjusted quarterly totals at annual rates.

a. Trend line of 3½ percent through middle of 1955 to 1960 IV.

b. Percentage change in GNP price deflator at annual rates.

c. 1952–53, net receipts and payments; 1954–59, net change in monetary assets and liquid liabilities; 1960, liquidity balance.

FIGURE 2

The Instruments of National Economic Policy, 1952–60

Fiscal Policy: The High-Employment Budget

Billions of dollars

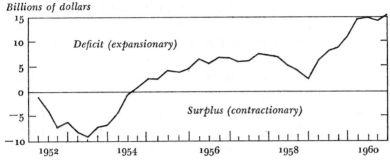

Monetary Policy: Interest Rates and Free Reserves

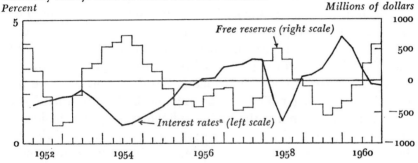

Monetary Policy: Money Supply and Monetary Base

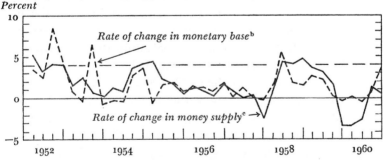

Sources: High-employment budget, Federal Reserve Bank of St. Louis, *Review*, Vol. 49 (June 1967), pp. 10–11; money supply, *Federal Reserve Bulletin*, Vol. 55 (October 1969), pp. 790–92; monetary base, Federal Reserve Bank of St. Louis; yield on 3-month Treasury bills, *Federal Reserve Bulletin*, various issues; free reserves, U.S. Bureau of the Census, *Business Cycle Developments* (January 1968), p. 76. The data used in the figure are seasonally adjusted quarterly totals at annual rates.
a. Yield on 3-month Treasury bills.
b. Currency plus demand deposits.
c. Member bank reserves plus currency outstanding.

Parallel movements of these intermediate indicators, as was pointed out in Chapter 3, is not necessarily evidence of effective coordination between monetary and fiscal policies, since optimal policy may require changes in the mixture of fiscal and monetary measures. Policy coordination, as defined in Chapter 3, is measurable primarily by the records of communication and decisions agreed upon among policymakers, as reported above. Nonetheless, the historical record of the intermediate policy variables themselves, when judged in the light of changing economic conditions, can throw some light on the coordination issue.

As for *fiscal policy,* there is now widespread agreement that the high-employment budget provides perhaps the best single measure of the impact of government fiscal policy on the economy. This measure (in the top panel of Figure 2) shows what the federal budget surplus (positive or negative) would have been if the economy had been operating at roughly full, or high, employment (say, with 4 percent unemployment). Fiscal authorities were not consciously aiming policy at affecting the high-employment surplus in the 1950s, nor is the high-employment surplus a basic goal in itself. Nevertheless, the figure is a useful indicator of the net impact of fiscal decisions on the economy. If the full-employment surplus or deficit changes from one period to the next, this indicates the changing impact of the federal budget on the economy.[24]

There is less agreement as to what data best indicate the net effect of monetary policy on the economy. Policymakers generally had their eyes on the broad economic goals indicated in Chapter 1. But the relation between their actions and these ultimate goals is complex and sometimes unclear. On a day-to-day basis they watched primarily intermediate variables (for example, free reserves and short-term interest rates), which in turn influence the ultimate performance of the real economy. These intermediate variables were thus both targets for policymakers and also indicators of what policymakers were doing and of their impact on the economy.

24. For a simple description, see *Economic Report of the President, January 1962,* pp. 78–84. A more complete analysis is presented by Michael E. Levy, "The Full Employment Budget Surplus," in *Fiscal Policy, Cycles and Growth* (National Industrial Conference Board, 1963).

Four separate intermediate targets, or indicators, for monetary policy are shown in the two lower panels of Figure 2.

1. "Free reserves" are one measure of the looseness or tightness of monetary policy. These are the excess reserves of the commercial banks minus any borrowings from the Federal Reserve. If free reserves are negative, banks usually feel pressed to restrict their lending. The Federal Reserve can add to or subtract from bank reserves and strongly influence the level of free reserves. But free reserves have shortcomings as a target indicator of Federal Reserve policy, because they reflect not only the Federal Reserve's actions but also the collective decision of the commercial banks as to how much free reserves to hold; individual banks can control their own free reserves to a considerable extent by borrowing, lending, and investment decisions. Nonetheless, Federal Reserve officials clearly considered the volume of free reserves as their primary intermediate target during the 1950s.[25]

2. Short-term interest rates (shown on the same panel) are considered by some to be the best measure of the looseness or tightness of monetary policy. In fact, however, they are a seriously imperfect indicator and target because they reflect the action of the Federal Reserve in limiting or expanding the stock of credit, private supplies of credit, and also the demand side of the market, which is controlled by private business and individual borrowing decisions. They are only partially controllable by Federal Reserve action.

3. The rate of growth of the money stock is now widely used as a measure of monetary policy, though it received little attention during the 1950s. Over many years, total real output has increased perhaps 3 or 4 percent a year, and many observers argue that when the money supply grows at about that rate, it is roughly in balance, or "neutral." Thus, in the bottom panel of Figure 2, a 4 percent line is added to show the extent to which the money supply grew

25. See, for example, "An Explanation of Federal Reserve Actions, 1933–68," Federal Reserve Bank of St. Louis, *Review,* Vol. 51 (July 1969); and Karl Brunner and Allan H. Meltzer, *An Alternative Approach to the Monetary Mechanism,* Prepared for the Subcommittee on Domestic Finance of the House Committee on Banking and Currency, 88 Cong. 2 sess. (1964). Most economists now criticize the use of free reserves as a target for, and indicator of, monetary policy. See especially A. James Meigs, *Free Reserves and the Money Supply* (University of Chicago Press, 1962), Chap. 2.

by more or less than that rate. But this measure too suffers from the fact that it reflects both Federal Reserve policies and the decisions of private banks and borrowers as to the form in which they hold their liquid assets. In any case, the Federal Reserve clearly paid little attention to the money stock per se during the 1950s. The word "money" hardly appears in the FOMC minutes for that period.

4. The growth in the "monetary base" (member bank reserves plus currency outstanding) provides a measure of the underlying base for growth in the money stock and in bank lending and investing.[26] It is substantially controllable by the Federal Reserve. As the economy grows, presumably this base should also grow at roughly the same rate if its effect is to be neutral. Thus, here again the 4 percent line indicates the extent to which the monetary base grew faster or more slowly than that rate.

Monetary experts disagree as to which of these four series provides the best indicator of monetary policy. But there is little doubt that, during the Eisenhower years, although the Federal Reserve accepted the goals of the Employment Act of 1946, the immediate target of monetary policy was free reserves and stability in the money markets. The tri-weekly directives from the FOMC to the manager of the System account generally mentioned broad economic conditions, but in such general terms that it is impossible to judge how much weight was being given to different goals; the specific directive was usually in terms of free reserves and money market conditions.

SOME PRELIMINARY OBSERVATIONS

Over-all evaluation of the macro policy process is the task of Chapter 7; but brief preliminary observations on the Eisenhower years may be appropriate here.

1. Neither fiscal nor monetary policymakers specified their goal structures, except in very general terms. Thus, evaluation of the policy process is difficult. Insofar as the results seem unacceptable, it is hard to distinguish clearly how much of the shortfall was due

26. This concept was little emphasized during the 1950s. Different economists define the monetary base differently. The base used here can also be defined as the sum of holdings of government securities by the Federal Reserve, member bank borrowings, Federal Reserve float, gold plus foreign currencies held, Treasury currency outstanding, and certain other minor items.

to differences among the policymakers' preferred goal structures, and how much to unsatisfactory use of monetary and fiscal policy instruments.[27]

2. Both monetary and fiscal authorities were reasonably quick in responding to the recessions of 1953–54 and 1957–58, but in retrospect their general thrust during the decade appears to have been over-restrictive. This was true especially in 1959–60, when both policies were strongly restrictive despite increasing slack in the economy.

3. Monetary decisions were made somewhat more flexibly than fiscal decisions. Although Federal Reserve authorities were rather slow to adopt restrictive measures in 1955, they moved more flexibly than fiscal policymakers in the recession of 1957–58, in 1958–59, and when restrictions were relaxed in 1960.

4. Flexibility on the fiscal side came mainly through "built-in" (or automatic) flexibility in tax receipts, which fluctuate more sharply than national income as the economy fluctuates, and through expenditure decisions—not through stabilizing changes in tax rates by administration-congressional action. Especially during the latter part of the decade, the fiscal authorities clearly underestimated the "fiscal drag" build-up in tax receipts and the consequent full-employment surplus as the economy grew.

5. There is little evidence that either monetary or fiscal authorities recognized adequately the problem of lags in the economic effects of their actions. In fact, lags are a mixture of short- and long-run effects of both monetary and fiscal policy. Thus the data shown in Figure 2 are of limited value in assessing the impact of fiscal and monetary measures on real output, employment, and prices.

6. Judged by the amount of discussion and informal agreement on policy mixes, coordination of monetary and fiscal policies was generally good, though with lapses and some disagreements. Monetary policies were generally adapted to what Federal Reserve officials thought fiscal policy would be, more often than the reverse.

7. Supplementary macroeconomic tools, such as housing credit,

27. Several econometric attempts to infer from observed data what Federal Reserve officials' (possibly subconscious) goal structure must have been are reported in Chap. 8. In general, they give most weight to high employment and short-term money market stability, much less to inflation control except toward the end of the decade, and virtually none to balance-of-payments considerations.

farm credit, Veterans Administration loans, and the like, were seldom used flexibly to counter cyclical swings in the 1950s. By and large, Congress and the responsible agencies viewed these programs in terms of their special purposes, such as that of assuring adequate education and housing to returning veterans.[28]

28. However, housing credit policy, somewhat by accident, was generally countercyclical during the 1950s. Federal housing credit through both the Federal Housing Administration and the Veterans Administration was available only at or below a federally approved ceiling rate. Hence, federal housing credit tended to flow out freely during recessions, when private lending rates were below the ceiling, but to be cut off in boom periods when market rates rose above this ceiling rate. For a more complete discussion, see Jack M. Guttentag, "The Short Cycle in Residential Construction, 1946–59," *American Economic Review*, Vol. 51 (June 1961).

6

THE KENNEDY-JOHNSON YEARS

THE 1960S HAVE BEEN CALLED by some observers "the soaring sixties." Others use less rosy terms. As case studies in macroeconomic policymaking, the Kennedy-Johnson years offer a variety of experiences, ranging from the 1962–64 push for a new fiscal policy to speed the economy upward, to the multifaceted program to restrain inflation without causing unemployment in an overheated Vietnam war economy.

Monetary-Fiscal Policy in the 1960s

A sample of five episodes during the Kennedy-Johnson years is examined in this chapter to illustrate the macroeconomic policy process.[1] As in Chapters 4 and 5, there is no attempt to provide a complete analysis of economic and monetary-fiscal events during

1. Detailed accounts of macroeconomic policymaking in the Kennedy-Johnson years are provided by Herbert Stein, *The Fiscal Revolution in America* (University of Chicago Press, 1969), Chaps. 15–18; and Edward S. Flash, Jr., *Economic Advice and Presidential Leadership* (Columbia University Press, 1965), Chaps. 6–7. A concise summary of federal fiscal policy during the 1960s is provided in "Federal Fiscal Policy in the 1960's," *Federal Reserve Bulletin*, Vol. 54 (September 1968), pp. 701–18. Walter W. Heller's *New Dimensions of Political Economy* (Harvard University Press, 1966), Arthur M. Okun's *The Political Economy of Prosperity* (Brookings Institution, 1970), and Theodore C. Sorensen's *Kennedy* (Harper & Row, 1965), especially Chaps. 16–17, provide an authoritative, inside look at policymaking on particular economic issues in the Kennedy administration.

the decade; the episodes are chosen because of the light they may shed on the policymaking process.

DAWN OF THE NEW ECONOMICS

The Kennedy administration inherited a recession when it took office in January 1961. It had at hand a task force report, written largely by economist Paul Samuelson, warning of the danger of continuing slack and recommending active fiscal policy to avoid it. The new Kennedy team of economists included Walter Heller, Kermit Gordon, and James Tobin at the Council of Economic Advisers, David Bell, director of the budget, Carl Kaysen in the White House, and a steady flow of outside academic consultants. All these men were committed, in varying degrees, to the active use of fiscal policy to help stabilize the economy and to assure stable growth without inflation.

At the Treasury, Secretary Douglas Dillon, a respected financial authority and former high official in the Eisenhower administration, had doubts; and these doubts were shared by Chairman William McChesney Martin, Jr., at the Federal Reserve. They knew the arguments for an active fiscal policy, but nonetheless remained concerned about the dangers of inflation, of a large unbalanced budget, and of a weakening U.S. balance-of-payments position. Dillon was soon joined by Robert V. Roosa from the Federal Reserve Bank of New York as under secretary of the treasury; Roosa played a leading role in both international monetary arrangements and debt management. His views were similar to those of Dillon, and the generally conservative trio of Dillon, Roosa, and Martin constituted a powerful force in the new administration.

The President's Economic Report of January 1962 presented the case for the "New Economics" strongly and lucidly. The new Council of Economic Advisers wrote:

Faster economic growth in the United States requires, above all, an expansion of demand, to take up existing slack and to match future increases in capacity. Unless demand is adequate to buy potential output, accelerating the growth of potential is neither an urgent problem nor a promising possibility.[2]

To analyze the impact of government fiscal policy on the economy, the council emphasized a new concept, the "full-employment surplus." This was an estimate of what the federal budget surplus or

2. *Economic Report of the President, January 1962*, p. 108.

deficit (on the national income and product accounts basis) would be if the economy were operating at substantially full employment (generally assumed to be 4 percent unemployment in the official statistics). The council said:

As the economy returns to the full employment track, the full employment surplus will need to be kept from growing indefinitely, and perhaps to be reduced. The choice—or rather the division, for it is unlikely to be an "either-or" matter—is between reductions in tax receipts and increases in government expenditures. . . . A pragmatic decision will almost certainly involve both. It is unlikely that the most urgent unmet needs of the population will lie all in the area of private consumption or all in the areas traditionally allotted to public consumption and investment.[3]

When the full-employment budget was in surplus, it exercised net restraint on over-all economic activity.[4] And the full-employment budget would move steadily toward surplus, by perhaps $5 billion to $7 billion annually if tax rates and government expenditures remained constant as national income grew. This was because tax receipts would rise more than proportionately with rising incomes. Thus the federal budget would exert a steadily increasing "fiscal drag," which would make it more and more difficult to maintain a healthy, fully employed economy without either tax reductions or increased government spending.

In January 1962 President Kennedy reported to Congress that "the economy has regained its momentum; [it has responded] to the Federal Government's efforts, under the [Employment] Act [of 1946], 'to promote maximum employment, production, and purchasing power.' "[5] Federal fiscal policy—through wider unemployment insurance benefits, increased federal aid to the states for unemployment benefits, liberalized social security benefits, funds for home building, and federal aid under the Area Redevelopment Act—contributed significantly to the recovery.[6] Monetary policy helped, too. After the restraint of early 1960, the money stock rose rapidly, reflecting the addition of new reserves and

3. *Ibid.,* pp. 142–43.
4. By stressing the full-employment surplus, the CEA hoped to divert attention from the actual budget surpluses, which led many noneconomists to support increases in taxes or reductions in spending.
5. *Economic Report of the President, January 1962,* p. 3.
6. When the Berlin blockade in 1961 stimulated military spending, the new CEA won its first victory for the New Economics by successfully opposing proposals within the administration to *raise* taxes.

large-scale bank lending, while interest rates remained approximately stable.

But by mid-1962 the upward thrust of the economy faltered again. Unemployment seemed stuck at around 5 percent. The rate of growth of real gross national product declined. Profits turned down. The Kennedy administration, like the Eisenhower administration before it, apparently failed to take into account the large increase in tax revenues that was generated automatically as recovery proceeded; it abandoned its expansionary antirecession fiscal policies almost as soon as the recovery was under way.[7] In 1960 the full-employment budget surplus had shot up to nearly $15 billion, and it stayed above $10 billion through 1961 and 1962. It rose sharply again to nearly $15 billion in 1963, although the administrative budget of the government continued in heavy deficit. While the leveling off in 1962 was only a "mini-recession," it served to focus attention again on the failure of the economy to recover strongly from the recessions of 1958 and 1960, and there was increasing support for a large tax cut to stimulate the economy.

As early as April 1961, in order to stimulate investment and economic growth, the President had recommended a special "investment tax credit" of 7 percent for business firms investing in depreciable equipment. But Congress did not respond. With the slowdown of 1962, the council and Budget Director Bell strongly urged passage of this legislation. For their part, Chairman Wilbur Mills of the House Ways and Means Committee and Secretary Dillon supported these changes but continued to doubt the case for general tax reduction to stimulate over-all demand. Congress moved slowly.

President Kennedy spoke at a Yale University commencement on June 11, 1962, asking the nation to set aside its "myths" about big government, fiscal policy, and the federal debt. This reflected his growing concern over the state of the economy and over the clichés that the CEA and White House economists convinced him were basic blocks to economic progress. The U.S. growth rate lagged behind those of almost all the Western industrialized nations. At the urging of both the council and the Treasury, Kennedy had

7. Against the advice of several of its top economists (it should be added), who urged a tax cut in mid-1962.

sent to Congress on May 8 a bill to give the President standby authority to reduce taxes temporarily to combat recession. He was impressed by Heller's and Tobin's accounts of strong European economies and the apparent willingness of European governments to use deficit financing.

On June 7 the President announced at a press conference:

A comprehensive tax reform bill which in no way overlaps the pending tax credit and loophole-closing bill offered a year ago will be offered for action by the next Congress, making effective as of January 1 of next year an across-the-board reduction in personal and corporate income tax rates which will not be wholly offset by other reforms—in other words, a net tax reduction.[8]

The big push for a tax cut, based on the New Economics, was under way.

But the President's announcement left much to be determined later, and within the administration there were widely diverse views. The Treasury, Council of Economic Advisers, Budget Bureau, and White House staffs, together with a score of part-time consultants, such as Joseph Pechman, Harvey Brazer, Richard Musgrave, Otto Eckstein, and E. Cary Brown, under Stanley Surrey, director of the office of tax legislation in the Treasury, worked hard and long to draft an acceptable tax bill. The secretaries of labor and commerce in general supported this effort. But Secretary Dillon continued to have reservations, as did Martin at the Federal Reserve.

The Kennedy administration's investment tax credit, passed in late 1962 after long debate, was the first step down the road toward an active fiscal policy to combat lagging economic growth. It is noteworthy that the tax relief was to corporations, not consumers; its objective was direct stimulation of business investment to promote faster growth. No less striking is the fact that the bill was pushed through Congress against widespread opposition from many of the businessmen it was intended to benefit. Revision of depreciation schedules by the Treasury in 1962 to permit more tax flexibility was a parallel step. These tax stimuli helped, but not enough to move the economy up sharply.

On December 14, 1962, President Kennedy spoke to the Eco-

8. *Public Papers of the Presidents of the United States: John F. Kennedy, 1962* (1963), p. 457.

nomic Club of New York on his tax program. He viewed it as a crucial effort, declaring that:

. . . an economy hampered by restrictive tax rates will never produce enough revenue to balance our budget just as it will never produce enough jobs or enough profits.

In short, it is a paradoxical truth that tax rates are too high today and tax revenues are too low and the soundest way to raise the revenues in the long run is to cut the rates now. . . .

I repeat: our practical choice is not between a tax-cut deficit and a budgetary surplus. It is between two kinds of deficits: a chronic deficit of inertia, as the unwanted result of inadequate revenues and a restricted economy; or a temporary deficit of transition, resulting from a tax cut designed to boost the economy, increase tax revenues, and achieve . . . a budget surplus.[9]

It was an effective speech; the President was pleased with the warm response of his business audience.

In January 1963 President Kennedy at last sent the administration's new tax bill to Congress. It marked the boldest fiscal move in a generation. Although much opposition remained, Heller, the council, and the new economists had won their first battle. Nevertheless, the President clearly felt uneasy and inhibited by congressional and voter opposition. His public statements revealed concern over an unduly large federal deficit. " 'Wilbur Mills,' he said one day, 'knows that he was Chairman of the Ways and Means before I got here, and that he'll still be Chairman after I have gone —and he knows I know it. I don't have any hold on him.' "[10] Former President Eisenhower entered the fray with a letter to Congressman Charles Halleck, calling the combination of "a massive deficit . . . lavish new spending and huge tax cut . . . fiscal recklessness";[11] he urged a cut in the spending side of the Kennedy budget.

Throughout 1963 the economy continued to grow slowly; unemployment stubbornly refused to drop. Heller and the council persistently argued the advantages of a massive tax cut to provide more spendable income. Conservative congressmen and businessmen remained unconvinced, pointing to the already sizable deficit. The controversy was confused by the emphasis placed by many

9. *Ibid.*, pp. 879–80.
10. Sorensen, *Kennedy*, p. 426.
11. *Ibid.*, p. 431.

participants (notably Kennedy, Dillon,[12] and Mills) on reforming the tax system simultaneously with the tax cut. Senators Hubert Humphrey, Clifford Case, Jacob Javits, and Kenneth Keating favored an immediate tax cut, but it was opposed by Senators Harry Byrd, Robert Kerr, and Willis Robertson, and even by Senator Paul Douglas, a leading liberal Democrat and economist. Congressman Mills remained unenthusiastic about a cut.[13]

The U.S. balance of payments provided an important backdrop for the tax debate. From 1960 onward, alarm was expressed both here and abroad about the steadily worsening state of the U.S. international payments position, and about the persistent drain on the U.S. gold stock, as foreigners converted rising dollar balances into gold. Talk of "fiscal irresponsibility," "lack of discipline," and U.S. "inability to deal with the unions and inflation" was heard widely in banking and business circles, even though the U.S. inflation rate remained well below that of most European countries.

In 1962, at Heller's suggestion, President Kennedy had established a cabinet-level committee—the Cabinet Committee on Economic Growth—composed of the secretaries of the treasury, labor, and commerce, and the director of the budget, and headed by the chairman of the CEA. Martin, though not a member, was usually invited to attend meetings. A smaller "troika" was also formed, composed of the heads of Treasury, the Budget Bureau, and the CEA. The troika rapidly developed into a powerful forum for discussing over-all government economic policy. Martin was invited from the Federal Reserve, making a "quadriad," when the issues being discussed involved monetary policy. The President himself usually attended meetings; he was intrigued by issues of economic policy and read avidly the memos sent to him by Heller and Dillon. At the staff level, senior economists in the Treasury, Budget Bureau, and the CEA were in almost constant communication. At the top and lower levels, a mutual liking and respect contributed substantially to effective policy coordination. At the CEA, the Treasury, the Budget Bureau, and the White House, top Kennedy

12. Strongly backed by Assistant Secretary Surrey who had headed President-elect Kennedy's pre-inauguration task force on tax policy.

13. See James L. Sundquist, *Politics and Policy: The Eisenhower, Kennedy, and Johnson Years* (Brookings Institution, 1968), Chap. 2.

appointees were men of worldly style and intellectual distinction. It also helped that Heller, Tobin, Gordon, and Bell (and Paul Samuelson and others on the outside) knew and liked each other before coming to Washington.[14]

But Kennedy was not to see the New Economics implemented in the form of a tax cut. The tax bill was one of the first measures pushed by President Johnson in 1964, and a $14 billion tax reduction bill was passed by Congress in February, which reduced the full-employment surplus from nearly $15 billion at an annual rate to little more than zero by mid-1965. In the final version, nearly all the tax reform provisions were deleted. After the Kennedy tax message of January 1963, it had taken a full year to convince doubters within the administration, among the public, and most important, in Congress, before the tax cut could become a reality.

In perspective, the tax cut of 1964 reflected growing support for the active use of fiscal policy. A consensus was achieved by continuing debate within and outside the administration over a period of at least three years. Without Chairman Heller and the strong Kennedy council it is doubtful that the New Economics could have been sold to the President, the Washington doubters, and the public. Without a strong and sympathetic White House staff (especially Carl Kaysen) and support from the director of the budget, it is doubtful that the President could have been won over from his generally conservative inclinations on fiscal policy. Without a thoughtful, intellectually inclined secretary of the treasury, the revolution in fiscal policy might well have been blocked much longer.

The CEA deserves full credit for pushing through the new ideas, but its role should not be overemphasized. The tax proposals in the President's tax message of January 1963 reflected in broad spirit the new economics, but with all their force, the ideas of Heller and his colleagues could not have prevailed if a politically adept secretary of the treasury had opposed them strongly and had been supported by the chairman of the Federal Reserve Board.

14. Both the council and the Treasury used academic consultants extensively during the Kennedy and the Johnson years. Council use was on an ad hoc basis; at Treasury, Seymour Harris of Harvard served as chairman of a large group of academic consultants (twenty or so), who met with the secretary two or three times a year. In addition, more intensive work was done by individual academicians on particular problems.

The campaign for modern fiscal policy was won by persuading Dillon, Martin, and congressional leaders—not by overrunning their opposition. Throughout, the close, informal working relations among all the parties concerned—in the administration and in the Federal Reserve—were of crucial importance.

Through the Kennedy years the Federal Reserve Board, Chairman Martin, and monetary policy generally remained in the background. Some enthusiastic advocates of tax cutting and the new economics publicly doubted that money mattered, one way or the other. More moderate economists (including Tobin, who was the council's expert on monetary policy) believed that a permissive policy, whereby the money stock would grow with rising income and interest rates would be held down, was essential to the success of fiscal policy, albeit not the prime mover. Only a few economists, mainly in academic life, argued that growth of the money stock was the key to growing aggregate demand and economic health.[15]

Throughout, monetary policy was permissive if not aggressively expansionary. The monetary base and the money stock were expanded steadily, at an average rate of 3 or 4 percent annually—substantially higher than during the late 1950s. Interest rates crept up as the demand for credit rose steadily, but credit at market rates was freely available except for a brief period of tightness in 1963, and total bank credit expanded rapidly.[16]

With the revival of interest in money later in the 1960s, many economists argued that it was indeed the expansionary monetary policy that deserved credit for the apparent success of the tax cut of 1964. In view of the events of 1964 and the following years, credit should go either to the tax cut or to expansive monetary policy, or to both. Assigning credit to one or the other calls for sophis-

15. In an attempt to open more effective channels of communication with academic economists, the Federal Reserve Board in 1963 invited a small group of leading monetary economists, chaired by the author, to meet with it several times annually to discuss policy problems. The exact composition of the group varies with the policy issues under discussion.

16. It is not clear whether during this period the Federal Reserve authorities had a long-run strategy of open market operations. Most attention was focused on adjusting to current business conditions and on "defensive" open market operations aimed at offsetting the short-run destabilizing effects of Treasury financing, currency drains, shifting float, and gold flows on free reserves and interest rates. See Jack M. Guttentag, "Defensive and Dynamic Open Market Operations, Discounting, and the Federal Reserve System's Crisis-Prevention Responsibilities," *Journal of Finance*, Vol. 24 (May 1969).

ticated economic analysis, a problem that is discussed further in Chapter 7.[17]

THE BEGINNINGS OF INFLATION—1965

In 1965 the New Economics faced its first serious test on how to deal with inflation. Whether or not policy and performance were cause and effect, the gross national product (GNP) moved rapidly upward, almost precisely as advocates of the new economics had predicted. A year after the tax cut, GNP had risen more than $40 billion, the increase predicted by the CEA using Keynesian multiplier analysis—and also predicted by money stock analysis, as a few monetarists pointed out. Unemployment fell steadily from nearly 6 percent to just over 4 percent at the end of 1965. Federal Reserve authorities increased the monetary base at a rate of about 4.5 percent annually; the money supply, though fluctuating sharply, grew by about 5 percent over the year.

But in mid-1965, for the first time since 1958, wholesale prices began to rise appreciably. Conservative observers argued increasingly that unemployment was down nearly to the desired 4 percent level, that the economy was showing signs of overheating, and that the rise in wholesale prices was an ominous omen, threatening the return of inflation.

On June 1, 1965, in a speech at Columbia University, Chairman Martin noted "disquieting similarities" between the then-current prosperity and the situation in the late 1920s, although the main theme of his speech was the need for further improvement in the U.S. balance of payments. Newspapers headlined the implicit crash warning, and the stock market dropped sharply. President Johnson and other top administration officials rushed to reassure the nation; Johnson emphasized that there was "no reason for gloom or doom." By the middle of the month Congress had passed an administration-sponsored bill calling for a reduction in excise taxes.

Employment continued to rise, and the stock market steadied. The rift, if there was one, between the Federal Reserve and

17. The "wage-price guideposts" proposed by the council in the 1962 Economic Report played a significant role in the macroeconomic policies of the Kennedy and Johnson administrations. They are not considered here because this chapter presents only a sample of macroeconomic policy problems and actions.

the administration seemed to have been patched over. Chairman Martin told the press on June 11 that "there is nothing in the [Columbia] speech that I want to change," but a few days later in a speech at Rutgers University he stressed only the international aspects of the problem with no reference to domestic dangers. Representative Wright Patman, continuing his familiar criticism of the Federal Reserve and tight money, suggested that Chairman Martin ". . . has outlived his usefulness as a public servant in charge of America's central banking system."[18] Business indicators were somewhat mixed during the summer months, and Secretary of the Treasury Henry Fowler was quoted by the *New York Times* of June 30, 1965, as saying it is "quite likely that we could have a leveling-off or a period of recession" before resuming a fast rate of growth.

But the President's announcement in late July that the United States would commit an additional fifty thousand men to the war in Vietnam ended the fears of recession. Instead, fear of inflation spread through the business and banking communities. President Johnson and Gardner Ackley, the new chairman of the CEA, exerted strong pressure on unions and business leaders to hold wages and prices within the "guideposts" laid down by the administration in 1962. On September 27 the *New York Times* headlined: "Threat of New Inflation Dominates Economic and Business Discussions," and business and academic economists predicted further price rises. The President cautioned the nation to "stop, look, and listen" before it took actions that would undermine the "balanced expansion." The wholesale price index rose by 3 percent over the year.

President Johnson, unlike his predecessor, had little interest in detailed discussions of economic issues. The quadriad, which had thrived under President Kennedy, gradually atrophied, not by design but because it did not well serve the Johnson administration's style. While there were no serious rifts, contacts between the Treasury and the CEA, on the one hand, and the Federal Reserve, on the other, became less frequent. As had been the practice for more than a decade, the secretary of the treasury and the chairman of the Federal Reserve Board lunched together nearly every Mon-

18. *Wall Street Journal,* June 11, 1965, p. 3.

day, and sometimes they or their senior staffs had a followup luncheon on Wednesdays, to discuss especially debt management issues. The troika continued to operate effectively, and an administration position was generally worked out by these three agencies with the White House staff. But minor irritations further undermined informal communications between the Federal Reserve and the Treasury-CEA. Related staff contacts dwindled.

On several occasions during the summer and autumn of 1965, Chairman Martin, in the inner councils of the administration, stressed the danger of overheating the economy. He reported a growing feeling among his Federal Reserve colleagues that the time might be coming for a rise in the discount rate to slow the inflationary expansion. Publicly he supported a general tax increase. Alfred Hayes, president of the New York Federal Reserve Bank, openly advocated tighter credit. Aluminum price increases, announced early in November, were denounced as inflationary by an angry President Johnson and by Ackley. They threatened to sell Defense Department stockpiles if necessary to hold down the price of aluminum. But the official administration policy was watchful waiting until the fiscal year 1967 outlook in the military budget was clarified.

On December 1, 1965, the Bureau of Labor Statistics consumer price index reached another record high, and the President announced plans for immediate talks with members of the quadriad on the economic outlook. A press statement, however, said that the President was "not unduly concerned," and "didn't consider inflation a major threat at this time." Secretaries Willard Wirtz (of Labor) and John Connor (of Commerce) emphasized the strength of the economy and noted that full employment still had not been reached, even though there were shortages of labor in skilled occupations.

The President was in Texas recovering from a minor operation, and the announced quadriad meeting did not take place. On December 3 Martin told Secretary Fowler that he expected to go ahead soon with a rise in the discount rate if his Federal Reserve colleagues agreed. Apparently Fowler did not realize the imminence of Federal Reserve action. The Board had been divided on discount action for some time, and Martin's vote on December 4 broke the tie. On December 6 the Board announced an increase in the discount rate from 4 to 4½ percent. *Business Week* headlined: "Bankers Applaud. Businessmen Accept."

President Johnson definitely did not applaud. He immediately called Martin and Ackley to Texas for consultation. Commenting on the Federal Reserve action, he noted the lack of "full facts" and termed the move "premature," but Martin indicated no intent to revoke the Federal Reserve action. The news media headlined the "Administration–Federal Reserve Showdown" and reported that both Johnson and Secretary Fowler strongly resented what they considered Martin's breach of faith in raising the rate then, rather than waiting until after the new budget was complete and an overall anti-inflation program could be developed. Neither the Federal Reserve, the CEA, nor the Treasury had been able to get Defense Department estimates on defense spending for 1966, though it was widely speculated that there would be a large increase.

Democrats in Congress were even more critical. Representative Wright Patman called for immediate curbs on the powers of the Federal Reserve; Senator Russell Long called the action "Dickens's Christmas Carol in reverse"; Senator Douglas termed it "brutal." Yale's James Tobin wrote a sharp criticism for publication in the *New York Times*. But most bankers, many businessmen, and many academic economists appeared to support the Board's action against incipient inflation.

Chairman Patman announced immediate hearings by the Joint Economic Committee (JEC) to investigate the apparent breach between the Federal Reserve and the administration. Before the JEC, Martin argued his position persistently through severe questioning, as well as in his prepared statement:

. . . the actions simply extend the policy that the Federal Reserve has been following of permitting money and credit to expand enough to satisfy the needs of our growing economy but not so much as to threaten inflationary disturbances. . . .

I can assure you that the administration has been kept continuously informed of the position of the Federal Reserve System and that there has been a continuing frank exchange of views between the Federal Reserve and administration officials, both before and after the Board's actions. The administration and the Federal Reserve are equally dedicated to doing everything possible to assure the most rapid growth of our economy compatible with reasonable stability of prices and reasonable equilibrium in our international payments.[19]

Martin contended that because of planned Treasury financing over the weeks ahead, it would have been technically almost impossible to raise the rate before late January or February 1966 if the early December action had been rejected. His testimony[20] throws light on policy relations at the time:

SENATOR JAVITS: You sought the concurrence of the administration [on the rate increase]?

MR. MARTIN: I did, indeed.

SENATOR JAVITS: In other words, you testified at the very end of your statement that you informed the administration, and conferred with them, consulted with them, but you did not testify that you sought its concurrence. You now say that you did?

MR. MARTIN: I did, indeed.

SENATOR JAVITS: Now whose concurrence did you seek?

MR. MARTIN: I would like to have had the concurrence of the President, the Secretary of the Treasury, the Chairman of the Council of Economic Advisers. I did not consult beyond that.

SENATOR JAVITS: But you asked for their concurrence?

MR. MARTIN: I urged them. I presented the situation as I saw it, and I indicated to them what the problems were, as I saw it. They did not agree with me. It was a very friendly and very useful discussion, and I also reported to my colleagues that I had done this.

SENATOR JAVITS: Now did you, nonetheless, go ahead, and after their refusal to concur?

MR. MARTIN: I did.

SENATOR JAVITS: Now may I ask you whether you think any change in law or practice is required or desirable for the better coordination of your own activities and those of the administration in power, whatever it may be, in respect to their fiscal and economic policy as contrasted with your monetary policy?

MR. MARTIN: There has been a lot of discussion, as you know, Senator, about this, and it may be that there could be some improvements in the informal procedures which have been developed through the years, where I usually have lunch with the Secretary

19. *Recent Federal Reserve Action and Economic Policy Coordination*, Hearings before the Joint Economic Committee, 89 Cong. 1 sess. (1966), Pts. 1 and 2. These two volumes present a detailed account of the discount episode, including statements by all Federal Reserve officials and numerous other witnesses. The Martin statements noted are on pp. 14–15 of Pt. 1.

20. *Ibid.*, pp. 67–68.

of the Treasury on Monday. Treasury representatives come over to the Board frequently on Wednesday, almost as a routine matter. We have occasional meetings with the Council of Economic Advisers, and since Secretary Anderson's time, we have had small groups—recently the group has been called the Quadriad—that have met with the President periodically. The Quadriad has met about once a month. . . .

In the event, as in the current case, where the Federal Reserve . . . have done their best to discuss this matter and have a different conclusion from the other members of the Quadriad, should they be bound by law to go along? If they were, it seems to me that there is no real need for a Federal Reserve Board. It would probably be better to replace the Board with a Cabinet official. . . .

I told Secretary Fowler on the morning of December 3 that I intended to act, if the Board would back me. I did not—I couldn't commit the Board. . . . I didn't know whether the Board would support me or not.

That tempers rose over the discount action is understandable. Within the administration, private discussions among the senior troika members and their staffs had indicated growing concern that inflation would develop before full employment was achieved. But President Johnson, reflecting his strong populist leanings, had long opposed high interest rates and apparently believed that the Federal Reserve authorities and private bankers could indeed hold interest rates down if only they wanted to. Thus, according to one White House aide, the President saw the increase in interest rates as almost a personal vindictive act on the part of Chairman Martin.

In retrospect, the December discount action appears to have been a minor episode. But President Johnson's and Secretary Fowler's resentment produced a new coolness in administration–Federal Reserve relations. Clearly, Federal Reserve action reflected both honest differences of judgment on the economic situation and misunderstanding as to the degree of Federal Reserve commitment.[21] Inadequate information from the Department of Defense on its spending plans underlay the entire situation.

In the weeks following, the Federal Reserve System moved strongly to assure adequate bank credit at the new higher rate—

21. One Federal Reserve official unofficially explained the event: "It was a real misunderstanding. The real fact is that Joe Fowler just didn't believe Martin would do it, no matter what he said."

possibly because of the administration's criticism. The monetary base increased at an annual rate of more than 7 percent between the last quarter of 1965 and the first quarter of 1966, although interest rates continued to climb. Six months later, as economic expansion continued unchecked, there was growing agreement (even among economists in the administration) that, in fact, the Federal Reserve had been right.

THE "CREDIT CRUNCH" OF 1966

Coincident with the discount rate increase of December 1965, the Federal Reserve took another, little-noticed step. Under its Regulation Q, the Board raised from 4 to 5½ percent the ceiling interest rate that member banks could pay on time deposits. This was designed to improve the ability of commercial banks to compete for the funds of savers against both savings and loan associations (which had traditionally paid higher rates than commercial banks) and open market instruments, such as Treasury bills and corporate securities. By late 1965 both savings and loan rates and short-term market interest rates were well above those paid by commercial banks; as a result, the commercial banks were steadily losing market position, especially on the West Coast, where S&Ls offered peak rates for funds to re-lend in the rapidly expanding housing market.

This change in Regulation Q quickly shifted the balance of market power. Large commercial banks wasted little time in offering sharply increased rates on time "certificates of deposit" (CDs), which for large borrowers were substantially equivalent to demand deposits or highly liquid securities, since they could be sold to other lenders. These developments were to play a major role in the coming "credit crunch" of mid-1966.

Later in the year, the economy moved up sharply. Soaring expenditures on the Vietnam war and on domestic programs produced a highly stimulative budget deficit. Vietnam expenditures were consistently underestimated by the administration, and before mid-year unemployment was below the "interim" target level of 4 percent. Prices began to rise over a broad front. Wage settlements rose rapidly, breaching the administration guideposts for noninflationary wages and prices. Chairman Ackley of the CEA reputedly favored a tax increase by early 1966, but did not speak out against the position of the President. The U.S. balance of payments continued in deficit and generated increasingly urgent pleas for restraint at home and overseas. The U.S. gold stock continued to decline steadily. Newspapers at home and abroad reported speculation about the soundness of the dollar.

Although the Federal Reserve provided bank reserves freely in early 1966, in April it moved to slow economic expansion and rising prices, since there appeared to be little likelihood of a tax increase. From 6½ percent, the annual growth rate of the money stock fell to zero by mid-summer. Net borrowed reserves exceeded $300 million. Interest rates edged toward historic highs.

Unlike expansionary fiscal policy, which largely reflected soaring outlays for the Vietnam war, tightening monetary policy represented a conscious effort by the Federal Reserve to check the inflationary forces, which it saw as endangering continued stable growth. Whether the Federal Reserve authorities intended as drastic a pattern of restraint as emerged is unclear from the minutes of the Board and the Federal Open Market Committee (FOMC) meetings. Federal Reserve officials emphasized their reluctance to have monetary policy bear the entire brunt of checking the overheating economy and recognized the sharp impact of tighter credit on the construction industry. But they made clear that they would act to help stabilize the economy and maintain the value of the dollar as it became necessary.

Rapidly tightening money, inflationary expectations, and booming demand created severe strains in the money markets during the late spring and summer. At the same time that the Federal Reserve Board restricted the flow of new reserves, private demands for funds soared, both to finance current outlays and in anticipation of expected increases in interest rates and tighter money.

The impact on savings and loan associations and the housing market was dramatic. S&Ls were already hard pressed for funds. Interest rate competition forced their costs up rapidly, while income from outstanding mortgages—issued earlier at lower rates— could not be increased. There was at the same time a general weakening in the housing market from overbuilding, particularly in the California area. Federal Housing Administration funds for mortgages were unavailable at prevailing high interest rates. S&Ls faced the July 1 interest payment date with apprehension, and rightly so. They had a net loss of $3 billion in customer savings during the first half of the year.

For its part, the Federal Home Loan Bank Board (FHLBB, the federal supervisory authority for federally chartered and insured savings and loan associations) on the one hand tried to discourage the S&Ls from over-extending themselves through rate competition for funds and, on the other hand, provided liquidity for assets of seriously endangered S&Ls. Resources of the FHLBB were, however, limited to its own reserves, plus its power to borrow directly from the market and (to a limited extent) from the Treasury. Only the Federal Reserve had basic power to create new money, and its power to extend credit directly to the FHLBB or to savings and loan associations was uncertain.

The state-municipal bond market also bore the brunt of the financial squeeze. States and municipalities have borrowed heavily since the Second World War, and the commercial banks have bought a large share of these tax-exempt bonds. When the reserve positions of banks were squeezed, the net acquisitions of tax-exempts by commercial banks dropped toward zero as new issues continued to pour onto the market. Prices fell sharply, and yields rose correspondingly.

These pressures came to a climax in late August and early September. Mortgage money was scarce, even at the new high interest rates. For a few days, there was virtually no market for municipal bonds; the imminent failure of two leading bond houses, which were caught with large inventories of unsold municipals, was rumored on Wall Street. The news media were filled with talk of financial panic.

Not surprisingly, as fears of the unavailability of credit spread, business and other borrowers rushed to get new loans or to draw down their existing lines of credit. The extraordinary bulge in credit demand was described by a high Federal Reserve official:[22]

In addition to the heavy current demands for credit, the major immediate cause of the highly unsettled conditions in late August was a growing apprehension over the ability of the markets to accommodate the pressures that seemed to be building up for September. In particular, it was expected that large fall loan demands would at

---

22. Alan R. Holmes, "Review of Open Market Operations in Domestic Securities," in *Fifty-Third Annual Report, Board of Governors of the Federal Reserve System Covering Operations for the Year 1966*, p. 232.

that time be converging on a banking system that faced the possibility of a large-scale runoff of maturing negotiable CD's. To this was added a growing concern over the capacity of the market to digest a sizable offering of Treasury tax-anticipation bills . . . and an expected sale of FNMA participation certificates and other Federal agency offerings in September.

Simultaneously, bankers, who were increasingly concerned over their ability to meet loan commitments, moved to build up free reserves and to reduce or eliminate their indebtedness to the Federal Reserve, so as to enhance their positions for more borrowing if a "crunch" should come.[23]

By September it was clear that a possible crisis loomed. On September 1, 1966, the Federal Reserve sent letters to all member banks assuring them that if they made only essential loans, it stood ready to provide such credit as was needed by individual banks to service their legitimate loan demands. The discount window would be open to all member banks that followed a policy of restricting new loans to bona fide, noninflationary business loans.

The Federal Reserve also moved rapidly, through open market operations, to provide the reserves needed to stabilize the nation's money markets. Within a few weeks the markets, though shaky, were back on a more or less even keel. On September 26, under its new statutory powers, the Board lowered to 5 percent the ceiling rate on bank time deposits of less than $100,000 in order to ease further the drain on savings and loan associations. Beginning in October, the Federal Reserve eased credit further. Both the monetary base and the money stock resumed their earlier rapid rise of over 6 percent a year. Interest rates declined moderately, and credit was again readily available.

Throughout this period, there was continuous communication among the CEA, Treasury, and Federal Reserve, and frequent communication with the FHLBB and the Federal Deposit Insurance Corporation (FDIC). The differences over the increase in the discount rate in December 1965 had left a distinct coolness between the President and Secretary Fowler on the one hand, and Chairman Martin and the Federal Reserve on the other. But all

23. Lively, detailed reports on the "crunch" are presented in Hyman P. Minsky, "Private Sector Asset Management and the Effectiveness of Monetary Policy: Theory and Practice," *Journal of Finance,* Vol. 24 (May 1969), pp. 223 ff., and Guttentag, "Defensive and Dynamic Open Market Operations," pp. 257 ff.

were determined that there should not be another breakdown of communication. Regular meetings of the quadriad were reestablished, and both the Treasury and the Federal Reserve took special pains to assure an adequate exchange of information. John Horne, chairman of the FHLBB, and his senior staff became involved as the housing credit crunch developed. Ackley and James Duesenberry of the CEA worked closely with the financial authorities on credit market developments. While Secretary Fowler apparently favored steps by the Federal Reserve and the FHLBB to raise interest rate ceilings further in order to reduce pressures on Treasury securities held by banks and savings and loan associations, apparently neither he nor Ackley objected strongly to the Federal Reserve's tightening of credit restraint during the summer.[24]

The House and Senate attacked the problem by approving, on September 13, the Financial Institutions Supervisory Act of 1966. The new law provided flexible authority for all federal financial supervisory agencies to set maximum rates of interest payable on time deposits of various kinds and sizes; expanded the permissible range of reserve requirements on time deposits in member banks; and authorized the Federal Reserve to buy and sell obligations of all federal agencies, thereby enabling it indirectly to provide liquidity for mortgages and other financial institution assets outside the commercial banks. While Federal Reserve authorities had developed emergency plans in midsummer to provide funds to the housing market if they were needed, the new law made clear the Federal Reserve's ability to provide liquidity for the entire financial system, not merely for the commercial banks. It also gave clear parallel powers to the FHLBB and the banking authorities to establish ceiling rates on time accounts at banks and at savings and loan associations. Finally, the bill required the several federal supervisory agencies to consult before acting under their new powers.

Hearings on the financial institutions bill probed the coordination between the Federal Reserve and the FHLBB.[25] Chairman

24. Chairman Martin has been widely credited with, or blamed for, the tight money policy of mid-1966. But Martin was away from the Board recuperating from an operation through this entire period. Vice Chairman J. L. Robertson was in charge, and he reports that the Board did not bother Martin with information or requests for advice until he was ready to return in the autumn.

25. *Financial Institutions Supervisory Act of 1966*, Hearings before a Subcommittee of the Senate Committee on Banking and Currency, 89 Cong. 2 sess. (1966).

Horne of the FHLBB testified that he had no advance notice of the December 1965 Federal Reserve action raising Regulation Q ceilings for commercial banks. Chairman Patman of the House Banking and Currency Committee questioned Horne as follows:[26]

THE CHAIRMAN: . . . under the law, the Employment Act of 1946, it is the duty of the Federal Reserve to coordinate these actions with the other agencies effectively. Were you consulted prior to that announcement of the increase in rates on December 6, 1965?

MR. HORNE: No, sir. I was not. . . .

THE CHAIRMAN: Do you not think the action of the Federal Reserve really jeopardizes the security of the savings and loans and other thrift institutions of this country, Mr. Horne?

MR. HORNE: Mr. Chairman, there is no question but what if the present development continues and grows in intensity, that there is definitely going to be a danger here that I think no one wants.

James J. Saxon, comptroller of the currency, testified similarly:[27]

. . . it [the Federal Reserve] did not consult our office, either, as a matter of fact. I received the first word of the announcement of the change in regulation Q from the Monday morning newspapers, to be frank with you.

Chairman Martin acknowledged that there had not been adequate consultation with the other supervisory agencies before the December action. In response to repeated questions, he testified:[28]

. . . there was a deficiency on my part that they [the other agencies] were not brought in. This was a very difficult period and I make no bones about it. I wish they had been consulted. It would not have changed the decision, but it would have given them prior notice.

REPRESENTATIVE REUSS: Do you think that perhaps . . . it might have been a good thing, in terms of public policy, to have a statutory board that looks at overall monetary policy instead of allowing one board to make a unilateral decision . . . ?

MR. MARTIN: No, I don't think it would be desirable to have such a statutory board, but I agree that we ought to be better coordinated. . . .

---

and *To Eliminate Unsound Competition for Savings and Time Deposits,* Hearings before the House Committee on Banking and Currency on H.R. 14026, 89 Cong. 2 sess. (1966).

26. *To Eliminate Unsound Competition,* Hearings, pp. 74–75.

27. *Ibid.,* pp. 280–81.

28. *Ibid.,* p. 556.

In fact, these hearings were attacking a problem largely past. Immediately after the December furor over the increase in the discount rate, President Johnson directed Secretary Fowler to establish more effective coordination among the financial supervisory agencies. This led to the establishment of an informal committee, which includes representatives of the Federal Reserve, the FHLBB, the FDIC, and the comptroller of the currency. Vice Chairman J. L. Robertson represents the Federal Reserve Board. The other agencies are represented by their chief officials. Chairmanship of the group rotates among the members. Active, almost continuous communication among them and their senior staffs continued during the tense weeks of the summer of 1966, as well as with Ackley and Duesenberry at the CEA. Thus, it was possible for all to testify that there had been close working coordination since December 1965, whatever the situation had been before then.

But increased communication failed to produce an integrated, consistent set of macroeconomic policies during 1966. On the contrary, stop-and-go action by the Federal Reserve carried almost the entire burden of stabilization, while fiscal policy was strongly expansionary throughout and the other financial supervisory agencies provided little help.

THE 1968 BALANCE-OF-PAYMENTS PROGRAM

The balance of payments was an important constraint on U.S. macroeconomic policymaking during the Kennedy-Johnson years. The United States was in deficit through most of the 1950s, but it was not until 1958 that the U.S. gold stock began to decline rapidly as foreigners converted a substantial part of their new dollars. During the period 1958–60, the U.S. payments deficit (liquidity basis) rose sharply to nearly $4 billion, and the soundness of the American dollar began to be challenged by conservative financiers here and abroad.

Early in 1961 President Kennedy established the Cabinet Committee on Balance of Payments, headed by Secretary Dillon and including the secretaries of state, commerce, defense, and agriculture, as well as the chairman of the CEA. Martin of the Federal Reserve was invited to all the meetings. This committee met frequently under Dillon's strong leadership to discuss the critical balance-of-payments situation. Moreover, the balance of payments was often an important topic in the deliberations of the troika and the quadriad. According to their contemporaries, both Dillon and Under Secretary Robert Roosa were men of style, with unusual understanding of the intricacies of international finance. Heller and the council, as well as Carl Kaysen, who was Kennedy's top White House assistant on international economic affairs, argued that the nation was paying too much attention to cries of alarm from abroad and to the balance-of-payments deficit. They believed that restoring prosperity at home was the primary problem.

In fact, Sorensen reports that Kennedy's associates in the administration believed almost unanimously that he was too concerned about the balance of payments. But Kennedy sided with Dillon and Roosa:

"I know everyone else thinks I worry about this too much," he [Kennedy] said as we pored over what seemed like the millionth report on the subject [the balance-of-payments problem]. "But if there's ever a run on the bank, and I have to devalue the dollar or bring home our troops, as the British did, I'm the one who will take the heat. Besides it's a club that De Gaulle and all the others hang over my head. Any time there's a crisis or a quarrel, they can cash in all their dollars and where are we?"[29]

He was painfully aware that the gloomy rumors that triggered the gold drains in 1960 emanated from Wall Street, as well as from bankers overseas.

But doubts about the soundness of the dollar grew instead of receding. Balance-of-payments issues were under constant consideration by the heads of the ten major Western central banks at their regular meetings in Basel, by the Group of Ten (representing the major governments), and by other ad hoc and continuing groups, such as Working Party III of the Organisation for Economic Co-operation and Development (on balance-of-payments and international financial problems). Martin and others from the Federal Reserve, as well as Heller, Tobin, Gordon, and Robert Solow were all heavily involved. While most day-to-day operations of the United States in the exchange markets and on currency swaps, sales of "Roosa bonds,"[30] and the like were handled by the New

29. Sorensen, *Kennedy,* p. 408.

30. In 1961 the United States, at the suggestion of Under Secretary of the Treasury Robert Roosa, offered to sell to foreign governments bonds denominated in their own national currencies. This guaranteed only a fixed amount in their own

York Federal Reserve Bank, ultimate authority clearly lay with Dillon and Roosa at the Treasury, and, through them, with the President. All agreed that there had to be a single U.S. position on international monetary questions.[31]

In the Johnson administration, Secretary Fowler and Under Secretary Frederick Deming, who replaced the Dillon-Roosa team, maintained the Treasury's leadership, but with important changes. President Johnson himself was little interested in the technical aspects of balance-of-payments issues, whereas President Kennedy had spent many hours on them. Moreover, Dillon's expertise in international economic affairs and his close personal relations with Kennedy gave him considerable power, which he wielded shrewdly. Secretary Fowler's relations with President Johnson were cordial, but less close. In the Johnson administration, the cabinet-level Balance-of-Payments Committee met less and less frequently; members often sent their delegates to meetings. But an informal undersecretary-level committee, chaired by Deming and including members from the Council of Economic Advisers, the Federal Reserve, and the State and Commerce Departments, played an increasingly important role in analyzing and formulating U.S. international payments policy.

Academic economists argued increasingly for a rise in the dollar price of gold or a dramatic changeover to freely floating exchange rates. The administration, however, spoke with a united voice. The price of gold would remain at $35 an ounce, stable exchange rates would be maintained, and the United States would continue its slow but steady progress toward payments equilibrium. International policy differences among the council, the Federal Reserve, Treasury, State, and Commerce were small during 1966–67. All

---

currencies for countries that kept their exchange rates pegged to the dollar; but for those that chose not to devalue their currencies in case the United States did, it offered the equivalent of a gold guarantee. See Herbert G. Grubel, *The International Monetary System* (Penguin Books, 1970), pp. 147–48.

31. Oddly enough, however, the directives to Charles Coombs (who managed day-to-day affairs on the foreign desk) and the New York Federal Reserve Bank on currency swaps were issued by the Federal Open Market Committee, as were directives to Alan Holmes on the domestic desk for open market operations. Apparently this dual responsibility of the New York Bank to the Treasury and the FOMC led to no serious problems, though Washington officials report that at times both the Treasury and the Federal Reserve Board had to remind the bank that it was their agent, not an independent authority.

were concerned about the uneasy international monetary situation; all agreed that action was needed to slow the gold drain and improve the U.S. payments position; and all agreed that this needed to be done without dramatic repressive action on U.S. foreign trade and capital exports, or on the domestic economy.

Although concern was expressed repeatedly in committee investigations of the U.S. international economic position, Congress showed little inclination to accept a major tax increase as a way of curbing the domestic inflation and the payments deficit. The administration turned mainly to voluntary and mandatory direct controls of various sorts. Foreign aid was tied to purchasing in the United States. "Buy American" preferences were prescribed for U.S. military needs abroad and at home. The interest-equalization tax on foreign borrowing in the United States was continued. Voluntary "quota" programs were established for U.S. businesses and banks in order to check the capital outflow. With tightening reserves and rising interest rates at home, the commercial banks actually developed a return flow of capital from Europe and failed to use even their allowed quotas of capital exports.

Neither the administration nor the Federal Reserve cared much for the hodge-podge of controls. There was little support for mandatory limitations on capital exports. Meanwhile the U.S. surplus on goods and services dwindled as inflation in the United States accelerated; by late 1967 the surplus was nearly gone. By December it became obvious within the administration that the fourth quarter figures would be deplorable, as the capital outflow resumed after the British devaluation. The fourth quarter payments deficit (annual rate–liquidity basis) was $7 billion.

At the same time, it had become apparent that the existing international monetary system, relying on gold and dollars as its primary reserves, would sooner or later have to be altered substantially. In 1966–67 there was virtually no increase in total international monetary reserves (which consisted mainly of gold and dollars), although world trade continued to grow by 6–8 percent a year.

Facing these problems, Fowler and Deming at the Treasury, Martin and Dewey Daane at the Federal Reserve Board, and Hayes and Coombs at the New York Federal Reserve Bank worked to achieve agreements among the leading nations to improve the basic system and protect against crises of confidence in major currencies. International negotiations proceeded at various levels, with Fowler and Martin in close contact with their counterparts in foreign treasuries and central banks. Deming, Daane, Arthur Okun, and Duesenberry of CEA, Francis Bator and Edward Fried of the White House staff, the New York Federal Reserve Bank, and others at the under secretary level carried on international negotiations on details. And working parties of the OECD and of the Group of Ten were in almost continual contact.

At Rio de Janeiro in September 1967, agreement in principle was achieved at last on the establishment of special drawing rights (SDRs) as a new form of international reserve, to be issued through the International Monetary Fund. But tension in the international monetary system continued. The free market gold price crept upward, and an uneasy peace overhung world monetary markets, disturbed intermittently by continuing doubts about the ability of the United States to meet its commitments in gold. Mainly to reassure the rest of the world of our willingness to maintain the price of gold at $35 an ounce, the administration asked Congress to eliminate the 25 percent gold cover against Federal Reserve notes, thereby freeing several billions of dollars in gold for use in meeting international commitments.

With a huge payments deficit in late 1967, the administration decided on a major policy statement to be made by President Johnson on January 1, 1968. The new program was developed in hurried, secret sessions. Fowler and Deming at the Treasury, Ackley, Duesenberry, and Okun at the CEA, Martin, Robertson, Daane, and Hayes at the Federal Reserve, Fried in the White House, and George Ball and Anthony Solomon at State devised an over-all balance-of-payments program in late December. Secretary of State Dean Rusk had little interest in international economic issues and participated only infrequently in making policy in this area.

At the working level, the voluntary capital export controls program had been developed and managed since 1964 by a sub-cabinet-level committee headed by Robertson, vice chairman of the Federal Reserve Board. This committee developed the details of the 1968 capital controls program. Robertson reports that, as in 1964, most of the committee's recommendations were accepted by the cabinet-level committee and the White House.

Most important, the administration and the Federal Reserve agreed that stronger monetary and fiscal measures must be taken to check inflation in the United States. The President therefore vigorously renewed his 1967 request for an income surtax, which had been delayed in Congress for an entire year.[32]

But the January 1 program was not enough. Confidence in the entire international monetary system faltered. On March 16, to check a massive drain, British authorities closed the London "gold pool," through which the dollar-gold parity was maintained with the cooperation of the other major Western nations. Over the weekend, the treasury secretaries and central bank heads of seven major nations met secretly in Washington and agreed on a revolutionary shift to a new "two-tier" international gold system. Major central banks agreed to buy and sell gold only to each other and other central banks that chose to abide by the agreement; the price of nonmonetary gold was set free to move with market forces.[33] This ended the episode.

The important role of senior staff work throughout these developments should be emphasized. Close working relations between the Federal Reserve and the Council of Economic Advisers (on both international and domestic issues) reflected the growing number of economists appointed to the Board itself, as well as the skillful maneuvering of Daniel Brill and Robert Solomon—directors of domestic and international research, respectively, at the Federal Reserve—in working with their counterparts at the CEA and in other agencies. Throughout, it is clear that the competence of the technical staff of the Federal Reserve was vital in explaining the Board's important role. By contrast, the CEA relied heavily on the staff work of other agencies, and the senior economic staffs at Treasury and State were also limited. Indeed, the Federal Reserve provided several key persons to other agencies—Deming had been president of the Minneapolis Federal Reserve Bank; Roosa had been vice president of the New York Bank; and Solomon, Frank

32. The original request of Jan. 1, 1967, was for a 6 percent surtax to become effective at mid-year; this was increased to 10 percent in August.

33. For a brief, official summary, see *55th Annual Report of the Board of Governors of the Federal Reserve System, 1968*, pp. 331–32. In late 1969 the plan was modified to provide a $35 an ounce floor under the free-market price for newly mined gold through International Monetary Fund purchases at that level, if this seemed appropriate to the signatories.

Schiff, and Albert Koch from Federal Reserve research staffs served, on loan, as senior staff members at CEA, continuing a tradition of two decades.

Finally, a prestigious "outside" balance-of-payments advisory committee, established in 1966 at the request of President Johnson and chaired by former Secretary Dillon, had an important role in developing U.S. positions. Charles Kindleberger of the Massachusetts Institute of Technology, a leading international economist, served as secretary to the committee, but academic consultants generally played less significant roles than during the Kennedy years.

CONGRESSIONAL INTERVENTION IN MONETARY POLICY

For the first time since the 1920s, serious pressures developed in Congress during the mid-1960s for more direct congressional control over Federal Reserve policy. For more than fifty years, congressional committees (especially the Senate and House Banking and Currency Committees and the Joint Economic Committee) have intermittently called Federal Reserve officials before them to explain their actions and answer criticisms. Since the 1930s, Representative Wright Patman of Texas has been a vigorous critic of the Federal Reserve as banker-dominated, tight-money-oriented, and insufficiently responsive to the people; after he became chairman of the House Banking and Currency Committee in the 1960s, he was increasingly able to call the Federal Reserve to account.

But for the most part, Congress was content to let its committees maintain surveillance of the Federal Reserve. Only in crises, such as that preceding the accord of 1951, did most congressmen become intimately concerned with Federal Reserve policymaking and its impact on the economy.

Nationwide debate on the effectiveness of monetary and fiscal policies increased steadily as the Federal Reserve first tightened credit drastically in 1966 and then resumed expanding credit at a very rapid rate in 1967–68. The Joint Economic Committee, chaired by Senator William Proxmire, pressed the Federal Reserve increasingly for an explanation of its "stop-go" policies and its (allegedly) inflationary policy in 1967–68. Proxmire argued that rapid growth in the money stock was inflationary and rejected Federal Reserve arguments that high interest rates and free reserves indicated that money was very tight. Proxmire, Representative

Henry Reuss of Wisconsin, and Patman joined in criticizing Federal Reserve policy, though for somewhat different reasons, with some support from other congressmen.

In its report on the President's Economic Report of 1967, the Joint Economic Committee said:

The committee urges that the monetary authorities adopt the policy of moderate and relatively steady increases in the money supply, avoiding the disruptive effects of wide swings in the rate of increase or decrease.

The committee is impressed with the increasing weight that many economists give to the importance of a steady rise in the money supply. Such rate of increase should be more or less consistent with the projected rate of growth—generally within a range of 3–5 percent per year. Sudden changes in the money supply give rise to instabilities in the economy.[34]

A year later, the Joint Economic Committee reiterated this emphasis, urging that the Federal Reserve keep the annual growth rate of the money stock between 2 and 6 percent and that, whenever the rate varied from this range, the Federal Reserve System should be obliged to report to Congress the reasons therefor.[35]

The committee further urged the Federal Reserve authorities to set forth publicly at the beginning of each year, as specifically as possible, their judgment as to the monetary policy that would be appropriate during the year, given the expected state of the economy. In demanding such reports, the committee emphasized that:

Just as Congress has the authority to fix Government expenditures and taxes, and thus largely to determine the budget surplus or deficit, the Congress has the responsibility of reckoning with the monetary consequences of its action. While the monetary authority granted to the Congress by the Constitution has been delegated to the Federal Reserve System, it behooves the Congress to provide some guidance to the Federal Reserve on how the System should see to the support of the Government's credit and, in particular, to what extent Congress regards the expansion of Federal Reserve credit as an appropriate way to finance any part of the deficit.[36]

In the committee's *1968 Joint Economic Report*, Representative Henry Reuss urged even more strongly the case for a rule prescrib-

34. *1967 Joint Economic Report,* Report of the Joint Economic Committee on the January 1967 Economic Report of the President, 90 Cong. 1 sess (1967), p. 14.

35. *Standards for Guiding Monetary Action,* Report of the Joint Economic Committee, 90 Cong. 2 sess. (1968), pp. 16–19.

36. *Ibid.,* p. 19.

ing a reasonably stable rate of growth in the money stock. He wrote:

> In recent years, dialog between the Joint Economic Committee, in its annual reports, and the Federal Reserve System, in the minutes of the Open Market Committee, might as well have been conducted in Urdu on the one side and Swahili on the other. The Joint Economic Committee, in its 1967 Report, urged upon the Fed "the policy of moderate and relatively stable increases in the money supply, avoiding the disrupting effects of wide swings . . . generally within a range of 3 to 5 percent per year." Our "advice" is obviously not being followed.

Noting a typical directive from the FOMC to the manager of the open market account, Reuss emphasized the complex explanations the Federal Reserve gave for its vagueness. He continued:

> Was the Fed continuing to create money at the rate of 9 percent— in the face of the Joint Economic Committee's 3 to 5 percent "advice" —because of Treasury borrowing, the level of production, expectations about future tax increases, worries about residential construction, or what? What weight was assigned to these factors? We are not told. Obviously, the Joint Economic Committee and the Fed are not talking the same language.[37]

In an attempt to specify more clearly just how such a rule could be used, Reuss urged a growth rate of 3–5 percent for the money stock, but added seven qualifications as special cases in which the Federal Reserve might reasonably depart from this range.[38]

These debates led to special hearings before the Joint Economic Committee in May 1968. Academic economists were split on the issue. Governor George Mitchell testified for the Federal Reserve Board, urging the need to consider many factors other than just the money stock, a position consistently taken by the Federal Reserve over many years. Senator William Proxmire urged Mitchell

37. *1968 Joint Economic Report,* Report of the Joint Economic Committee on the January 1968 Economic Report of the President, 90 Cong. 2 sess. (1968), pp. 44, 45.

38. Reuss's exceptions included adjustment for shifts of deposits from time to demand, or vice versa; larger increases in the money stock in case of cost-push inflation; special funds to help Treasury financing for short periods; deviations justified by balance-of-payments problems; and deviations when monetary policy threatens to disrupt the home building industry. It is interesting to note that in responding to the Reuss proposal, the Federal Reserve urged that the Reuss exceptions were so broad that they might well turn the System into an engine of inflation, especially through the cost-push inflation exception.

to give more precise and detailed explanations of Federal Reserve policy.

CHAIRMAN PROXMIRE: Supposing you were required . . . to come before the Congress after each quarter in which you had either not increased the money supply at the rate of 2 percent, or had increased the money supply at a rate of more than 6 percent, to explain the reason for it, come before this committee, for example; this would not strain you?

MR. MITCHELL: No.

CHAIRMAN PROXMIRE: You would just come up and tell us why you did it? Would there be any objection to that?

MR. MITCHELL: No, I do not think so. Mr. Brill (Federal Reserve director of research) just reminded me we do it twice a year in the Federal Reserve Bulletin now in effect.

CHAIRMAN PROXMIRE: You do it in the Bulletin, but we would prefer to have you come up and question you in detail and in public— a vigorous cross-examination.[39]

But when Proxmire pushed Mitchell for an advance statement on planned policy changes, quarter by quarter or year by year, Mitchell was not prepared to acquiesce.

Soon thereafter, Representative Patman obtained, through the House Committee on Banking and Currency, the reactions of some seventy experts, inside and outside the government, on both the monetary rule and the extent to which the Federal Reserve was responsive to the public interest.[40] In his reply Chairman Martin reiterated the well established Federal Reserve position against the rule, and the Board's willingness to provide Congress with detailed information on Federal Reserve policy after the fact. He specifically offered to send to Congress the confidential reports prepared by the staff for each meeting of the FOMC, so that Congress could see precisely what information was being used in arriving at policy decisions.

Secretary Fowler and the Council of Economic Advisers supported the Federal Reserve's argument against the monetary rule, as did a number of banks and academic economists. However, a

---

39. *Standards for Guiding Monetary Actions,* Hearings before the Joint Economic Committee, 90 Cong. 2 sess. (1968), p. 133.

40. *Compendium on Monetary Policy Guidelines and Federal Reserve Structure,* Subcommittee on Domestic Finance of the House Committee on Banking and Currency, 90 Cong. 2 sess. (1968).

majority of the academic economists polled (perhaps a biased sample) indicated a preference for the kind of money stock rule proposed by the Joint Economic Committee; there were differing views on the Reuss exceptions. Patman also found considerable academic support for closer congressional control over Federal Reserve operations, and for a closer tie between Federal Reserve policies and government fiscal policies as prescribed by the President. However, the JEC is not a legislative committee, and there was little evidence that the majority of the legislative Banking and Currency Committees favored any major increase in congressional control over Federal Reserve operations.

The Policy Process: Evaluation

Figures 3 and 4 (on pages 146 and 147) summarize the course of monetary and fiscal policies during the Kennedy-Johnson years, carrying forward the series used in Figures 1 and 2. Again, Figure 3 shows the performance of the economy—real output compared with potential output, unemployment, price-level changes, and the U.S. balance of payments (liquidity basis). Figure 4 presents the full-employment budget as a measure of fiscal policy and four alternative measures of monetary policy—free reserves, short-term interest rates, and the growth rates of the money stock and of the monetary base.[41]

Given both multiple intermediate targets and multiple ultimate goals, what can be said about the effectiveness of macroeconomic policymaking during the Kennedy-Johnson years? The following generalizations appear warranted.

1. In light of performance, macroeconomic policy was reasonably successful in the 1961–68 period. The eight years were a time

41. The warning in Chap. 5 bears repeating. Neither the Federal Reserve authorities nor independent monetary experts agree as to which of the four measures of monetary policy was, or should have been, the primary target of Federal Reserve action. Early in the decade, Federal Reserve authorities stressed the amount of free reserves and money market conditions, as they had during the 1950s. In later years, the Federal Reserve began to watch carefully variations in the money stock. In 1966 it began to compute daily a "bank credit proxy," which provided a rough surrogate for the money stock (including time deposits), and FOMC policy directives to the manager of the System's open market account now usually include a desired level of bank credit along with free reserves and money market conditions.

of unprecedented, continuing, prosperous growth, by far the longest on record. Moreover, especially during the last half of the period, the growth rate of real output was high, averaging nearly 5 percent a year, well above the 3–3½ percent average for the preceding century. Prices began to rise appreciably beginning in 1965, but even the 4 percent increases of the 1966–68 period, while objectionable to many observers, were modest in comparison with those in earlier inflations; only toward the end of the decade did inflation and inflationary expectations come to the fore as major problems. Finally, despite repeated international crises of confidence, U.S. trade and capital exports, and those of the world as a whole, increased steadily to unprecedented levels during the 1960s. Direct capital controls somewhat impeded capital flows, but repeated warnings of impending international financial collapse and world-wide recession, by conservatives and by the financial press, again and again proved unwarranted.

This performance of the economy was not, of course, necessarily attributable to macroeconomic policy. Post hoc, propter hoc reasoning is hazardous. Perhaps the economy would have performed as well or better with a different set of macroeconomic policies, or with no conscious stabilization policies at all. But the evidence on the basis of performance is generally favorable, with reservations.

2. In the 1960s, the rationale of economic policy shifted away from ad hoc measures to combat business fluctuations toward a focus on continued stable economic growth as such. To proponents of the new economics, this was a significant change, since it emphasized measures to keep the economy growing smoothly rather than waiting until corrective measures were needed against booms or recessions. "Stop-go" measures were generally to be avoided.

But this change must not be overemphasized. The policy implications of the two approaches are similar in many instances, and many observers doubt that the business cycle is extinct. Some advocates of the New Economics spoke of "fine-tuning" the economy with frequent policy changes to keep it growing evenly along the line of full employment without inflation; but many skeptics doubted then, and still doubt, that such precision is possible with our limited knowledge of the "outside" lags in monetary and fiscal policy, even if the inside lag could be eliminated.[42]

42. It is important to note that the Council of Economic Advisers, the official advocate of the New Economics, carefully avoided talk about "fine-tuning" in its

3. During the 1960s, modern fiscal policy came into its own as a major, consciously used force for stable economic growth—and fell short of expectations. The big tax cut of 1964 receives high marks from most observers, but it passed Congress only after a long delay. The Johnson income surtax of mid-1968 was again the right action, but it came at least two years late. In 1967–68, and probably in 1963–64, both the administration and Congress lagged behind the country, certainly behind the monetary-fiscal experts, in supporting stabilizing tax policy. The record on smaller tax changes (excises, payment dates, social security taxes, and so on) to encourage stable economic growth was somewhat better, though mixed.

On the spending side, the fiscal policy record was hardly better; in the years 1965–68 it was highly destabilizing. The level of federal spending was set primarily by program objectives, with little serious attention to stabilization needs. Federal expenditures on Vietnam, and to a lesser extent on domestic programs, were consistently underestimated by the Department of Defense, the Budget Bureau, and administration staff economists. There were from time to time minor slowdowns and speedups in spending by the administration, but the massive overstimulation of the economy in the 1965–68 period dominates the picture.

4. Viewed alone, monetary policy displayed overreaction to economic changes—a stop-go policy of the sort widely criticized in other nations. The mini-crisis of mid-1966, when the Federal Reserve tightened credit dramatically, is the outstanding example, but having slowed the upsurge, the authorities returned almost immediately to a highly expansionary policy of growth in the monetary base and in money in 1967 and 1968.

own official statements. CEA members, especially in later years of the Kennedy-Johnson administrations, became increasingly convinced of the complexity of the problem and aimed at getting only roughly stable growth in aggregate demand along a full-employment-without-inflation path. Federal Reserve authorities were even more wary about claiming ability to fine-tune the economy. Heller's *New Dimensions in Political Economy* and Okun's *The Political Economy of Prosperity* provide authoritative statements by former CEA chairmen. Unfortunately, fine-tuning has seldom been defined precisely by those who use it. At one extreme, any discretionary attempt to stabilize the economy might be called fine-tuning. At the other, fine-tuning might mean only day-to-day or week-to-week intervention, for example, in the short-term money market. Obviously, in the latter sense, tax policy cannot be used for fine-tuning, but monetary policy might.

In terms of traditional "timely flexibility," the Federal Reserve's performance was reasonably good. The inside lag before it took action was fairly short—a few months at the most. But given the growing evidence of long and uncertain outside lags in the effect of monetary policy on the real economy, just how much stabilizing force these changes exerted is not clear.[43]

Federal Reserve performance was generally better when judged by the interest rate and free reserve targets than by changes in the monetary base or stock of money. This is not surprising, since during much of the decade the Federal Reserve clearly focused its actions more strongly on free reserves and on short-term interest rates than on the money stock or the monetary base per se.

The preceding criticisms of the Federal Reserve need to be substantially softened, however, because the major policy shifts reflected primarily attempts to offset erroneous fiscal policies, or uncertainty about them, in 1966 and in 1967–68. It is possible to conclude that monetary policy failings came about largely through attempts to compensate for poor fiscal policy. The Vietnam war made the last half of the decade particularly difficult for both fiscal and monetary policymaking. One may hope that some of these difficulties would not occur in more normal periods.

5. If coordination is defined as active discussion among policymakers, macroeconomic policymaking deserves high marks

43. Most outside observers agree that by usual countercyclical standards, the Federal Reserve's recognition and reaction pattern was generally satisfactory. Rendigs Fels and C. Elton Hinshaw (in *Forecasting and Recognizing Business Cycle Turning Points* [Columbia University Press for National Bureau of Economic Research, 1968]) conclude that the FOMC pattern of recognition of National Bureau of Economic Research turning points during the postwar period varied from one to nine months before the cyclical turn. That is, there is substantial evidence that the FOMC was becoming concerned about a turning point that far in advance. The FOMC confirmation pattern was generally firm within three to six months after the NBER turning point date—that is, the Federal Reserve took action on the basis of its conclusion that the turning point occurred within that period. The FOMC thus did about as well as other leading forecasters. Its advantage (if it had any) was that it was somewhat quicker in firming up the decision on the turn once it had occurred.

Karl Brunner and Allan H. Meltzer (in *An Alternative Approach to the Monetary Mechanism* [Prepared for the Subcommittee on Domestic Finance of the House Committee on Banking and Currency, 88 Cong. 2 sess., 1964]), though highly critical of the Federal Reserve, emphasize that the FOMC recognition and action pattern was generally good. Their criticism is focused on the use of free reserves and money market conditions as the major intermediate targets of Federal Reserve policy.

FIGURE 3

The Goals of National Economic Policy, 1961–68

Growth of Gross National Product
Billions of 1958 dollars (ratio scale)

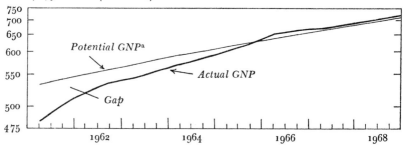

Unemployment and Prices
Percent

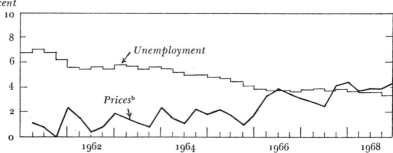

Balance of Payments[c]
Millions of dollars

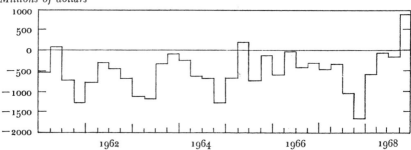

Sources: Gross national product and price deflator, U.S. Office of Business Economics, *The National Income and Product Accounts of the United States, 1929–1965, Statistical Tables* (1966), pp. 9, 159, and *Survey of Current Business*, Vol. 48 (July 1968), pp. 19, 50, and Vol. 49 (July 1969), pp. 17, 48; potential GNP, Council of Economic Advisers; unemployment rates, U.S. Bureau of the Census, *Business Conditions Digest* (February 1970), p. 108; liquidity balances, *Business Conditions Digest* (July 1969), pp. 82, 106. The data used in the figure are seasonally adjusted quarterly totals at annual rates.

a. Trend line of 3½ percent through middle of 1955 to 1962 IV, 3¾ percent from 1962 IV to 1965 IV, and 4 percent from 1965 IV to 1968 IV.

b. Percentage change in GNP price deflator at annual rates.

c. Liquidity balance.

FIGURE 4

The Instruments of National Economic Policy, 1961–68

Fiscal Policy: The High-Employment Budget
Billions of dollars

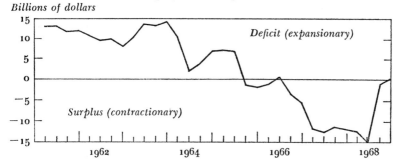

Monetary Policy: Interest Rates and Free Reserves

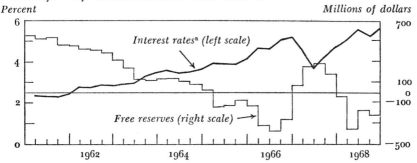

Monetary Policy: Money Supply and Monetary Base
Percent

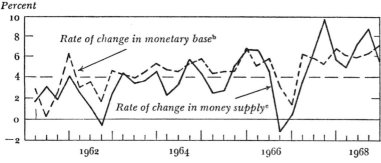

Sources: High-employment budget, Federal Reserve Bank of St. Louis, *Review*, Vol. 49 (June 1967), pp. 10–11, and "Federal Budget Trends" (Feb. 20, 1970, processed), p. 3; money supply, *Federal Reserve Bulletin*, Vol. 55 (October 1969), pp. 792–93; monetary base, Federal Reserve Bank of St. Louis; yield on 3-month Treasury bills, *Federal Reserve Bulletin*, various issues; free reserves, U.S. Bureau of the Census, *Business Cycle Developments* (January 1968), p. 76, and *Business Conditions Digest* (October 1969), p. 77. The data used in the figure are quarterly totals seasonally adjusted at annual rates.

    a. Yield on 3-month Treasury bills.

    b. Member bank reserves plus currency outstanding.

    c. Currency plus demand deposits.

147

through the 1960s. Only once, in the Federal Reserve's December 1965 discount and Regulation Q rate changes, was there a significant breakdown in communication. And this instance represented more a disagreement over timing than a lack of communication. At top levels, the troika and quadriad served well, and there was a nearly continuous exchange of views among the principals—though there was some coolness immediately following the 1965 differences. Equally important, close working relationships developed at the under secretary and senior staff levels.

The main failures in coordination were between Congress and the administration on fiscal policy. They were attributable not to a lack of coordinating machinery but to serious differences of judgment among the authorities concerned (Congress, the administration, and the Federal Reserve) as to what policies were best.

6. The record of the stabilization authorities on forecasting was uneven in the 1960s, as in the 1950s. The forecasts of different economists inside and outside the government differed widely at times, for example, in the 1966 slowdown and when the surtax was enacted in mid-1968. Forecasts following the tax cut of 1964 were more in agreement and were generally accurate. The performance of government economists was about as good as that of sophisticated outsiders, perhaps somewhat better.

Although the advocates of policy "rules" argue that their approach would obviate the need for forecasts as a basis for policy, as a practical matter it is hard to see how the monetary and fiscal policymakers can escape the forecasting problem, in view of the fact that both monetary and fiscal measures have lagged effects. Since the length of these lags is uncertain, as was emphasized above, policymaking combined only moderately reliable forecasts with uncertain outside lags in policy effects. Given this combination, it is difficult to attribute the generally good performance of the economy during the decade to wise macroeconomic policy, except when major policy changes occurred—for example, the tax cut of 1964 and monetary restraint in 1966.

7. As in the preceding decade, the failure of the monetary authorities to define unambiguously their ultimate and intermediate policy targets makes it hard to evaluate the effectiveness of monetary policy alone and in combination with fiscal policy. Clearly, Federal Reserve action could and did have a quick impact on

money market conditions. But equally clearly, there was a substantial delay before it affected the ultimate targets of employment, output, and prices.

8. Increased use of legal interest rate ceilings on time deposits at banks and savings and loan associations raised new problems of coordination in the mid-1960s, and in retrospect, they are open to serious criticism as a major policy instrument. After 1965, with credit generally tight, ceiling interest rates became the cutting edge of monetary policy and a major determinant of which sectors of the economy would bear the brunt of a tight money policy. While there was active communication among the Federal Reserve, other banking agencies, and the FHLBB after December 1965, there was little coordination before that time—perhaps understandably, since there had previously been little need for coordinating ceiling interest rate policies. The Financial Institutions Supervisory Act of 1966 provided parallel powers to the FHLBB and the bank supervisory agencies to set ceiling rates on time deposits, authorized the Federal Reserve to provide liquidity for savings and loan association assets in time of crisis, and directed them to consult in determining policies on interest ceilings. This mechanism may be adequate, but the different policy goals of the agencies involved suggest that conflicts may recur in the future.

9. It is difficult to tell whether the Joint Economic Committee's strong push for a monetary "rule" established by Congress to guide Federal Reserve policy reflects more than a passing surge of congressional concern. In any event, it reemphasizes the close supervision Congress can exercise over Federal Reserve policies whenever it wants to, and probably reflects a lasting move toward more complete Federal Reserve disclosure and reporting of reasons for its policy actions. But Congress did not change the basic legislation governing the Federal Reserve System, nor does it show any great inclination to do so. The 1965–68 episode thus shows that there is a strong congressional (and public) sentiment for keeping the Federal Reserve free from the pressures of "politics," in either Congress or the White House.

10. The answer to the question whether the balance between U.S. international and domestic policies was satisfactory during the 1960s depends largely on the criteria applied. U.S. international economic policymaking was well coordinated under the

general leadership of the secretary of the treasury, working closely with Chairman Martin at the Federal Reserve, with the Council of Economic Advisers, with special assistants in the White House, and to a lesser extent with high officials at the State and Commerce Departments and other agencies. While one may disagree with the policies that evolved, there is no obvious way in which other administrative or policymaking arrangements could have produced a better or more unified U.S. policy.

PART THREE

TOWARD MORE EFFECTIVE
POLICYMAKING

7

LESSONS OF EXPERIENCE

What are the lessons of experience for more effective macroeconomic policymaking?

The coordination of macroeconomic policies can be usefully assessed only if the criteria for judgment are specified. Over the half century surveyed in Chapters 4–6, the goals of macroeconomic policymakers shifted substantially. But since the Second World War, high-level employment, rapid, stable economic growth, and reasonably stable prices have been generally accepted as dominant goals—all consistent with substantial freedom of initiative and economic choice for the individual and for business. During the past decade, equilibrium in the international balance of payments must be added as an important constraint on domestic policymakers, or as a fourth goal; and throughout the period certain agencies have emphasized particular goals—for example, the Federal Reserve has been concerned throughout with stability in the financial markets.

Monetary and fiscal policies do not act directly on employment, growth, and prices. Rather, fiscal policy affects disposable income, profits, business expectations, and the like. Monetary policy affects interest rates, bank reserves, and financial expectations. Each policy focuses directly on intermediate variables, which in turn affect the ultimate goals of employment, growth, and price stability.

Figures 1 through 4 (on pages 104, 105, 146, and 147) review the performance of the economy since 1950, and monetary and fiscal policies as measured by the high-employment budget surplus and four different monetary indicators.[1] The major objective of this chapter is to evaluate macroeconomic policymaking, but since different policymaking processes may be biased toward particular results, it is necessary also to consider briefly the quality of the results produced by alternative policy procedures.

Performance of the Economy

Compared with earlier decades, the stability and growth rate of the American economy over the past twenty years have been generally good. There has been no major depression, and throughout the decade of the 1960s there was not even a recession. Although there have been periods of slack and underemployment, real growth has been faster than in previous periods. Inflation, though persistent, has been moderate by historical standards, except during war periods. On balance, the economy deserves a grade of "very good" on its performance over the past two decades.

But how much of this good performance was due to conscious economic policy is a debatable question. Good fiscal and monetary policy would presumably move toward restraint when the economy is excessively inflationary and toward stimulus when the economy sags below desired growth and employment levels. On some occasions monetary and fiscal policy (as judged by their intermediate indicators) were right; on others they were not. Indeed, sometimes they have been destabilizing though both have avoided the wild fluctuations found in earlier periods of war and depression.[2]

But the impact of monetary and fiscal policy cannot be precisely assessed because the economy's performance reflects a variety of both policy and nonpolicy forces, and because both fiscal and monetary policy affect employment, growth, and prices only after substantial, and uncertain, time lags. Even if policy, as judged by the

1. The usefulness and shortcomings of these indicators are discussed on pp. 53–54 and 106–08.

2. In retrospect, the fiscal and monetary policies proposed by leading government economists have generally been superior to the policies actually adopted by the policymakers. This is true especially since the 1930s.

intermediate indicators, appears correct in relation to the current state of the economy, it may in fact be destabilizing, since its effects are spread over months or even years. Thus, the correlation between policy indicators and ultimate goals provides an imperfect guide to the quality of policymaking. How the economy has performed in the past only partly measures the effectiveness of macroeconomic policies.

Fiscal Policymaking

The decades from the 1930s through the 1960s saw a revolution in American fiscal policy and policymaking. In 1929 almost no one thought of the federal budget as a positive instrument for mitigating booms and depressions. The conventional wisdom called for annual budget balance and for resolute action to achieve that balance, even in the face of massive unemployment and depression. Three decades later, the Kennedy-Johnson tax cut of 1964 marked the culmination of a long campaign to sell expansionary fiscal policy, even in the face of an already large federal deficit. By 1967–68, the argument over the proposed Johnson federal surtax to slow expansion and halt inflation rested largely on the need, or lack of need, for federal fiscal restraint. Along the way, in the late 1950s and early 1960s, smaller fiscal changes (for example, the investment tax credit of 1962) were increasingly considered in terms of their impact on economic growth and stability.

But the revolution was a halting one. As late as 1969, Representative Wilbur Mills, perhaps the most powerful member of Congress on tax issues, still spoke of a balanced budget as a desirable norm in its own right; and many congressmen, as well as many businessmen and other influential citizens, still questioned whether federal deficits and surpluses were proper weapons against recession and inflation. The tax cut of 1964 had been under consideration for two years before President Kennedy and then Congress were convinced of its need. The Johnson surtax of 1968 was passed by Congress only after a year of uncertainty on the part of the President followed by almost a year and a half of bitter controversy between the administration and Congress. Only an optimist or a wishful thinker could say that by 1969 the case for flexible stabilizing fiscal policy was widely accepted and operationally feasible.[3]

In perspective, six propositions summarize the lessons of fiscal policymaking since 1930.

1. Acceptance of federal fiscal policy as a flexible economic stabilization instrument has broadened dramatically, but it is still uneasy and uncertain—among congressmen, high government officials, leading businessmen and bankers, and the man in the street.

2. The inside lag for fiscal policy (the delay between actual developments in the economy and policy action) is long and uncertain. On taxes and government spending, the President proposes, Congress disposes. While presidential proposals can influence the over-all direction of fiscal policy, the ultimate power lies on Capitol Hill. The administration has very limited power to change expenditures and none to change tax rates without specific congressional authorization.

Congressional consideration of tax changes proposed by the administration is usually long and searching. Appropriations must go through Congress annually, and appropriations subcommittees have powerful chairmen who exert great power over particular programs. There is no general procedure whereby Congress systematically considers the over-all fiscal (stabilization) impact of the expenditures and taxes it votes. Serious and persistent underestimates of military spending by the Department of Defense have repeatedly upset administration fiscal planning and Federal Reserve monetary planning. Though there have been some successes in achieving timely fiscal action, political theory and organizational reality offer little hope for flexible stabilizing fiscal action under present policymaking arrangements. Indeed, the White House, the Treasury, and the Bureau of the Budget on the one hand and Congress on the other have frequently become involved in bitter controversy; the 1967–68 conflict over the need for a tax increase and/or expenditure control is a classic example.

3. In the 1960s, looking back over the 1950s, Wilfred Lewis, Jr., wrote (in *Federal Fiscal Policy in the Postwar Recessions* [Brookings Institution, 1962], p. 275): "Progress can be discerned over the postwar period, from one recession to the next, in the public and political acceptance of unbalanced budgets as an appropriate means of combating recession. It remains true, however, that balanced budgets and 'fiscal responsibility' are powerful ideas. Only for brief periods near the cyclical troughs has opposition been relaxed to deliberate additions to the massive budget deficits that inevitably accompany recession."

3. The *outside* lag of fiscal policy (the delay between fiscal action and its effect on employment and prices) is also substantial. While some effects of fiscal changes come quickly, the direct effects on real gross national product and prices are certainly spread over several quarters, and the combined direct-indirect effects apparently may extend as long as two years or more.

4. Much of the short-term stabilizing impact of American fiscal policy has come through built-in (automatic) mechanisms. With a progressive tax structure, upward movements in the economy, and indeed the general growth process, generate an increasing federal surplus, which, other things being equal, acts to damp upward expansion. Conversely, the same factors tend to reduce the force of a downswing, since the decline in income reduces tax liabilities more than proportionally. Given the dominance of growth in the American economy, the primary effect of this automatic mechanism is to produce a fiscal drag on economic expansion.[4]

5. Destabilizing fiscal policies (errors) have been an important cause of both inflations and recessions over the past half century, especially but not exclusively in war periods. Merely to eliminate destabilizing policies would mark a major advance in fiscal policy-making.

6. Even when differences arose, communications between the administration and Congress seldom broke down more than briefly. Neither can operate effectively without the other. Treasury, Budget, and White House officials report long hours negotiating with and "educating" key congressional officials on the entire fiscal picture. Fiscal policy deadlocks between the administration and Congress more often reflected differences over policy goals and over control of the federal budget than a breakdown of communication per se.

Why was the performance of fiscal policy so mixed? It was partly because neither the administration, nor Congress, nor their economists were notably successful in forecasting changing needs for fiscal expansion or restraint. But even after economic forecasts were generally accepted, neither the administration nor Congress moved rapidly to adjust fiscal policy accordingly. On occasion, no-

4. A convenient summary of the effects of built-in fiscal stabilizers is provided in *Policies to Combat Depression,* a Conference of the Universities-National Bureau Committee for Economic Research (Princeton University Press for National Bureau of Economic Research, 1956).

tably in 1965–66, the failure of the Department of Defense to provide accurate spending forecasts represented a serious breakdown of fiscal policymaking within the administration.

These failures did not occur through ignorance; economic arguments for stabilizing fiscal policy were well presented by economists inside and outside the government to policymakers, both in the White House and on the Hill. Delays were more generally attributable to the political and fiscal processes. Neither the administration nor Congress showed any enthusiasm for prompt increases in taxes or reduced spending when fiscal restraint was required. Given an outside lag of months or even years, the delays were even more serious. Improved fiscal policymaking offers perhaps the greatest possibilities, and the least hope, for a major improvement in our macroeconomic policymaking. Merely avoiding destabilizing effects would be a significant improvement. Hopes for "fine tuning" the economy through fiscal policy, over months or even quarters, find little support in the record. New policymaking procedures are needed if fiscal policy is to become a more useful stabilization tool.

Monetary Policymaking and Monetary-Fiscal Coordination

Responsibility and authority for fiscal policymaking are shared, somewhat uneasily, by Congress and the administration in office. Monetary policy is largely the responsibility of the Federal Reserve, a quasi-independent agency. As a practical matter, however, the Treasury too has substantial monetary powers, and the Federal Reserve has invariably taken into account probable fiscal policy and Treasury debt-management problems in determining monetary policy. The fiscal-monetary relationship is thus asymmetrical; fiscal policy is customarily made under the assumption that monetary policy will be adjusted appropriately, while monetary policymakers must usually take actual and probable fiscal actions as given. Therefore, monetary policymaking can be evaluated only in the context of Treasury and administration policies, on the one hand, and congressional actions on the other.

The lessons of modern monetary history highlight both the potentialities and the weaknesses of monetary policy:

1. Monetary policy has made its greatest contribution (a) when it has produced a roughly stable increase in the monetary base and the money stock along the economy's growth path while keeping interest rates roughly stable (1960–64); and (b) when it has moved flexibly to offset developing recessions or expansions (in 1954, 1958, 1960).

2. In general, the Federal Reserve has a good record in promptly recognizing changing economic conditions and in responding to them reasonably quickly. Perhaps its policy reactions were wrong, and it certainly missed on some turns in the economy (for example, in mid-1968); but given the state of knowledge on economic processes and forecasting, it would probably be unreasonable to expect the Federal Reserve to have done much better in its analysis of economic change.

3. Federal Reserve officials showed little awareness of the importance of long and variable outside lags in the impact of monetary action on real output, employment, and prices. Thus, their generally good record in recognizing cyclical turns in the economy does not necessarily mean that the resulting policy actions were stabilizing. By and large, policy was geared to reacting quickly to changes in the economic climate. Federal Reserve policy action influences money market conditions almost instantaneously, but its impact on consumer spending, business investment, output, and prices is spread out over a year or two, or even longer. Thus, quick Federal Reserve response to changing economic conditions is not enough. The Federal Open Market Committee's concentration on money market indicators and its concern for "even keeling" the market for Treasury securities contributed to its inadequate concern for lags in effects on the real economy and commodity and labor prices.[5]

4. The disastrous liquidity collapse in the early 1930s was the Federal Reserve's greatest failure. The other major monetary pol-

5. For a discussion of lags in monetary and fiscal policy, and the extensive literature on the subject, see "The Channels of Monetary Policy: A Further Report on the Federal Reserve-MIT Econometric Model," by Frank de Leeuw and Edward M. Gramlich, *Federal Reserve Bulletin*, Vol. 55 (June 1969), especially pp. 485–91; Thomas Mayer, "The Lag in the Effect of Monetary Policy: Some Criticisms," *Western Economic Journal*, Vol. 5 (September 1967), pp. 324–42; and Albert Ando and others, "Lags in Fiscal and Monetary Policy," in E. Cary Brown and others, *Stabilization Policies*, prepared for the Commission on Money and Credit (Prentice-Hall, 1963), pp. 1–163.

icy shortcomings have been associated with support for, or inadequate attempts to counteract, inflationary Treasury-administration finance during wars. War financing over three wars and bond-pegging after the Second World War exemplify the former; the actions taken in 1966 and 1969, the latter. Thus, the major failures in stabilizing monetary policy do not reflect a lack of discussion among policymakers but the choice of dubious policies in spite of, or as a result of, such discussion. The Federal Reserve's recent stop-and-go policies are explainable largely as efforts to adjust to government fiscal policies. These relationships are considered in greater detail in (6), below.

5. As a result partly of the Treasury's interest in stable money markets and low interest rates, partly of dubious monetary analysis, Federal Reserve authorities have frequently placed too much weight on free reserves and short-term interest rates and too little on the monetary base and money stock as intermediate policy targets. Pre-1965 policy directives and discussions were couched almost entirely in money market and interest rate terms, with intermittent emphasis on even keeling the market for Treasury financing. More recently, Federal Reserve authorities have placed increased weight on the monetary aggregates. In many circumstances, similar policies are called for by both targets, but especially in periods of inflationary expectations, interest rates may be seriously misleading indicators. For example, in 1967–68 what was apparently intended as a policy of moderate restraint (since the Reserve authorities responded primarily to interest rate and free reserve indicators) seems instead to have been one of monetary stimulus; reserves and the money stock grew rapidly to maintain acceptable interest rates and money market conditions in the face of soaring demands for credit. In mid-1968, the Federal Reserve, expecting strong fiscal restraint, mistakenly eased further. By 1968–69 experts generally agreed that spiraling interest rates reflected an expectation of continued inflation and monetary expansion rather than tight money; and in 1969 the Federal Reserve moved to a more restrictive stance despite unprecedentedly high interest rates and a crescendo of complaints from the money markets.

More research will throw a clearer light on the monetary and fiscal mechanisms. Given present information, it seems that before

1968–69 the Federal Reserve was excessively concerned with maintaining short-run money market stability and even keeling during Treasury financing periods; "defensive" open market policy aimed at avoiding short-run instability often dominated the thinking of the Federal Open Market Committee in Washington and "the desk" in New York. The Federal Reserve could stabilize short-term interest rates by varying the money supply, or it could maintain stable growth in the monetary base, permitting interest rates to fluctuate with shifts in the demand for credit. But it could not do both, and for the most part it chose the former.

Recently most Federal Reserve officials have come to include changes in the monetary base and money stock as important intermediate policy indicators, along with free reserves and interest rates. But experts still differ on whether money, the monetary base, bank reserves, or unborrowed reserves is the best policy target among the monetary aggregates, if some such target is appropriate. Uncertainty concerning the appropriate weights for these different intermediate targets under different circumstances makes any evaluation of Federal Reserve policymaking during much of the postwar period necessarily tentative. But giving monetary authorities the benefit of the doubt, in view of existing uncertainty about the monetary mechanism and optimal goal structures, does not remove the serious question about the effectiveness of monetary policy for promoting stable growth without inflation. At the least, it points toward policy principles that take into account inflationary expectations, forecasting problems, and the lagged effects of policy actions.

6. As measured by discussion and common consideration of important policy issues, coordination between the Federal Reserve and the Treasury-CEA-administration has been generally good. Such discussions have not always produced policy agreements (for example, they did not in 1956 and late 1965), but serious differences have been rarer than is often thought. Counterdirectional movements of fiscal and monetary policy often (for example, in 1966 and mid-1968) reflected agreement, not disagreement, among policymakers in the administration and the Federal Reserve.

Individual styles in the White House, the Council of Economic Advisers, the Treasury, and the Federal Reserve have varied, and with them the amount of interagency exchange of information and discussion. The Federal Reserve was more intimately involved in over-all macro policy discussions under Presidents Roosevelt, Kennedy, and Johnson than under President Truman. At the highest level this reflected primarily the relations of the Federal Reserve chairman with the White House and other top administration officials. Marriner Eccles was directly involved through the 1930s in both fiscal and monetary policymaking, although his relations with Secretary of the Treasury Morgenthau were often less than cordial. Eccles's influence waned with President Truman and Treasury Secretary John Snyder.

Throughout his regime, Chairman William McChesney Martin, Jr., was on reasonably close working terms with the Treasury, the Council of Economic Advisers, and the White House, although the warmth of these relationships varied. Working relations between the Federal Reserve and the Treasury on debt management were maintained even in periods of sharp disagreement between the two agencies—for example, following the Second World War and after the break in December 1965.

President Eisenhower intermittently used a quadriad, and its active use was resumed by President Kennedy. Communication among the quadriad agencies varied over the years, reflecting personalities and particular circumstances, with only a few real breakdowns. Especially in the early Kennedy years, Martin, Douglas Dillon, and Robert Roosa often sided together on monetary-fiscal policy matters against Walter Heller, Kermit Gordon, James Tobin, David Bell, and Carl Kaysen at the council and the White House. President Johnson had less interest in the details of monetary and fiscal policy, and formal use of the quadriad faded in his administration. But communication on major issues was reasonably close, even preceding the much-publicized quarrel over the Federal Reserve's increase in the discount rate in December 1965.

The Federal Reserve throughout maintained a degree of independence, reserving its right to make final decisions itself. But it never, with the possible exception of the pre-accord break of 1951, made major policy changes without prior discussion of the situation with representatives of the administration. Three widely publicized instances of inadequate "coordination" (the period preceding the accord and the Federal Reserve–Treasury–White House differences in 1956 and 1965) were more newsworthy than disruptive economically, except for the open break in 1950–51.

Although preliminary fiscal discussions are often off the record within the administration, presidential recommendations and their consideration by Congress generate widespread public discussion. Thus, the Federal Reserve was generally well informed about the fiscal plans of the administration and Congress.[6] In contrast, the Federal Reserve seldom disclosed its plans for *specific* policy actions in intragovernmental discussions, but increasingly in recent years informal conversations and "leaks" among top officials and senior staff members have apparently provided an effective exchange of information, even on such issues. The growing number of trained economists on the Federal Reserve Board recently has helped to open communication channels, especially between the Board and the CEA. Close informal communication has developed among senior staff members under these principals—especially, for example, between Federal Reserve and Treasury staffs during the Dillon years, and between Federal Reserve and CEA staffs during the Ackley-Okun years.

It is not clear that closer communication between the Federal Reserve and the administration on monetary-fiscal policy issues would have made much difference in the policies actually adopted. Off the record, each has felt free to communicate its views on the policies of the other. Most differences reflected considered differences in policy judgments, not a failure to exchange information and views.

The degree of Federal Reserve independence from the Treasury and the White House, though legally unchanged since 1935, has varied substantially from time to time. Over the years, Federal Reserve–Treasury differences over details of financing and the like have been frequent. But especially in the last two decades, close Federal Reserve–Treasury consultation on debt management has prevailed, with reasonably continuous communication between the Federal Reserve and the White House–Treasury–CEA on monetary-fiscal policy interactions. This evaluation is not inconsistent with recurring tensions between Federal Reserve and White House–Treasury–CEA officials, reflecting the partial independence of the Federal Reserve from presidential control.

The power and influence of the Federal Reserve in over-all macroeconomic policymaking has usually been greatest when its

---

6. The breakdown of information on the soaring military budget in late 1965 and 1966 is a clear exception.

distance ("independence") from the administration has been least, and least when the distance has been greatest. Only on rare occasions (as in 1950–51) can the Federal Reserve risk a major confrontation with the President and his cabinet officials. For the most part, Federal Reserve influence on major policies must be exerted in the general shaping of government economic policy, or by marginal adjustments within the framework of general macroeconomic policy. Federal Reserve officials recognize clearly the need for a coordinated national economic policy, and they recognize that the President, within the determination of the Congress, must be fundamentally responsible for implementing this policy.

7. Federal Reserve officials have consistently affirmed that sustainable high-level employment and reasonably stable prices are their basic goals, the weight given each being dependent on the state of the economy. Improvement of the U.S. international payments position has been important since 1960. Cooperation with the Treasury in debt management and the maintenance of stable financial markets have been important, though secondary, goals throughout. On occasion, faster economic growth per se has been added to the list.

Nonetheless, the Federal Reserve has frequently been criticized as overly concerned with avoiding inflation and too little concerned with keeping unemployment low. Often, it has been argued, the Reserve authorities have been insufficiently responsive to the wishes of Congress and the public and too insulated from the political process.

Evaluation of the Federal Reserve's goal-setting and its success in achieving these objectives is difficult because the goals are stated only in general terms, without specification of the weights being given to each, and because there is substantial disagreement on what the goals should be. The Federal Open Market Committee minutes and other Federal Reserve publications make clear that the authorities have tried to follow a flexible policy, leaning toward expansion in recession periods and toward restriction during inflation, insofar as this was feasible, given war and peacetime fiscal policies. During the 1950s, "timely flexibility" was the keynote; from 1960 to 1964, gentle expansion; in 1966 and 1969, severe restriction; and in 1967–68, steady restraint (as the monetary officials watching interest rates saw it) or inflationary expansion (as it looked to money supply-oriented critics).

Over all, the Federal Reserve seems to have been more concerned with possible and actual inflation than has the administration or Congress. The tendency of governments to inflate the currency in search of prosperity extends back many centuries, even into biblical times. The growth of central banks, first private and then governmental, was intended to guard against the inflationary overissue of money. The supposed preference of central banks for stable money as against inflation—certainly in comparison to responsive democratic governments—is based on both history and political theory. The public complains more bitterly and votes the rascals out more readily if unemployment comes than if prices rise. There are clearly some levels of inflation that are so painful and destructive that they are no more acceptable to the public than is heavy unemployment; the hyperinflations following the First and Second World Wars are examples. But, the argument runs, a "little inflation" is generally less painful and disruptive to politicians and the public than is a "little unemployment."

The basic case for an "independent" central bank rests on precisely this presumption—that a central bank, at least partially insulated from day-to-day political pressures, will take a longer view and will value stable prices and sound money more highly than will, or can, a politically responsive President or Congress. In the Western industrialized countries, this presumption seems to be generally in accordance with the evidence over the last century or two.[7]

But it is easy to overemphasize this difference between central bankers and elected government officials. Federal Reserve officials have often argued the need for more restrictive monetary and fiscal policy (for example, in 1957–58 and 1965–68) when administration and congressional fiscal policy was expansionary. But in the postwar world, whenever unemployment has risen substantially (for example, to 5–7 percent), Federal Reserve officials have moved solidly toward monetary ease, even when they still warned of the danger of inflation. Numerous empirical analyses of Federal Reserve behavior since the Second World War confirm the sensitivity of Federal Reserve policy to substantial unemployment.

The Federal Reserve's fear of inflation has bulked larger when

7. See, for example, Etienne S. Kirschen and others, *Economic Policy in Our Time*, Vol. 1 (Rand McNally, 1964), especially Chap. 8, for a careful analysis of this historical evidence.

there has been pressure on the U.S. balance of payments—in the early 1930s and in the 1960s. Understandably, given a stable exchange-rate system, Federal Reserve officials feel responsible for the nation's international reserves. Even with elaborate international agreements among central banks for mutual aid and the two-tier gold system since 1968, the traditional feeling of central bank responsibility has remained.[8]

Thus, the conventional wisdom that central banks act as buffers against the political process in protecting the value of money is generally, but not completely, supported by Federal Reserve history. High employment and price stability appear to have been of more or less equal importance in Federal Reserve policymaking. Which goal dominated depended on varying circumstances; in general, most emphasis was placed on the goal where performance fell furthest short of aspirations.

8. From the outset, Congress has been impressed with the great importance of the monetary and banking powers delegated to the Federal Reserve System. It has kept a close eye on Federal Reserve behavior, through congressional committees and through periodic consideration of reform legislation. Hardly a year has gone by without committee or subcommittee hearings on some aspect of

8. On the relative importance of different goals, see, in addition to Federal Reserve officials' own statements, John E. Buehler and David I. Fand, "The Federal Reserve and Monetary Policy," *Michigan Academician*, Vol. 1 (Spring 1969), pp. 21–35; William G. DeWald and Harry G. Johnson, "An Objective Analysis of the Objectives of American Monetary Policy, 1952–61," in Deane Carson (ed.), *Banking and Monetary Studies* (Irwin, 1963); James W. Christian, "A Further Analysis of the Objectives of American Monetary Policy," *Journal of Finance*, Vol. 23 (June 1968), pp. 465–77; and Mark H. Willes, "Changing Goals of Monetary Policy: 1952–1966," *National Banking Review*, Vol. 4 (June 1967), pp. 503–07. Michael W. Keran and Christopher T. Babb (in "An Explanation of Federal Reserve Actions, 1933–68," Federal Reserve Bank of St. Louis, *Review*, Vol. 51 [July 1969], pp. 7–20) find generally dominant concern for financial market stability and even keeling, though this could be overridden by strong unemployment or inflation signals. Karl Brunner and Allan Meltzer argue in their studies that the Federal Reserve focused almost entirely on money market conditions, with no clear relationship between policy actions and the ultimate employment and price goals.

None of these studies, some using econometric techniques, finds a stable Federal Reserve trade-off function between price stabilization and employment in which price stability is dominant. Federal Reserve officials emphasized different goals at different times, and their policy actions were consistent with shifting goals. But all the studies agree that substantial and rising unemployment dominated when it appeared, albeit with a lag in some cases.

Federal Reserve policies or structure. For many years, the Federal Reserve Board chairman has been a prime witness in the annual Joint Economic Committee hearings on the President's Economic Report. These hearings are often thorough investigations of Federal Reserve monetary policies as well as of the economic outlook and the budget.

Thus the Federal Reserve has been far from free of congressional influence, on broad issues and on its day-to-day operations. Eccles writes of the great pains taken to keep Senator Carter Glass informed of, and agreeable to, the changes proposed in the Banking Act of 1935. Martin for years made a point of being in touch at least monthly with Representative Wright Patman, the System's leading critic in Congress. In recent years, the continuing efforts of Senator William Proxmire and Representative Henry Reuss have helped push the Federal Reserve to consider seriously changes in the money stock as a guide to monetary policy.

After the credit crunch of 1966, congressional criticism of the Federal Reserve mounted. Long-time critics like Patman, Proxmire, and Reuss pressed strongly in the Joint Economic Committee and the House Banking and Currency Committee for more frequent and detailed reports from the Federal Reserve on its policy actions, and for advance notification of major Federal Reserve changes. They urged that the Reserve keep the growth rate of the money stock between 2 and 6 percent annually, unless there were strong reasons to the contrary. They proposed that the Federal Reserve be given an annual directive by the President in his Economic Report.

Throughout these investigations and criticisms, Eccles, Martin, and other Federal Reserve officials consistently hewed to the same line. Congress established the System and directed it to act as a primary agency of monetary and credit control. The Federal Reserve accepts these responsibilities, which it exercises as an agent of Congress. Congress has turned over the operating responsibilities in this complex field to a specially composed government body, insulated from the day-to-day pressures of the administration and Congress. For Congress to specify detailed rules governing day-to-day Federal Reserve policy would be a serious mistake in the complex and changing world in which it must operate. But Reserve officials readily acknowledge their basic responsibility to Congress.

In the past few years, the Federal Reserve has partially drawn aside the veil of secrecy on its actions and the reasons for them. Detailed historical records have been made public through the mid-1960s. FOMC directives to the New York desk, with the reasons supporting them, are now released publicly about three months after each FOMC meeting. Since 1969, the Board has submitted to the Joint Economic Committee a detailed assessment of the coming quarter and the monetary policy implications of what it considers to be the most likely developments.

But in spite of these pressures and changes, it has been clear that the majority of Congress values highly the semi-independence of the Federal Reserve and has no intention of bringing the System's day-to-day operations under close congressional control. Attempts by Chairman Patman to bring this about have failed repeatedly, even in his own Banking and Currency Committee. Monetary affairs are complex and little understood by most congressmen. The fear of excessive "political" control of monetary policymaking is real and powerful in Congress and with the general public today, albeit less so than it was a half century ago.

Rules versus Authorities

One approach to solving the problems of macroeconomic policymaking would be for Congress to legislate "rules" to govern fiscal and monetary policy, instead of relying on discretionary "authorities" to act. To a limited extent the gold standard and annually balanced budget principles provided such standards, though they were frequently violated.

Since the Second World War, many economists (led by Milton Friedman), and recently some congressmen, have called for the Federal Reserve merely to increase the money stock at a stable rate (for example, 4 percent a year), eschewing attempts to offset short-run fluctuations in the economy. They argue that the Federal Reserve, however well-intentioned it may be, in fact intensifies fluctuations in the economy through sharp changes in the growth rate of the money stock, rather than damping these fluctuations. In part, they say, the Reserve authorities are misguided, watching interest rates and money market conditions rather than the money stock. The price level and unemployment rate are not satisfactory guides to policy because of the long lags between open market operations and their impact on prices and output. A rule prescribing stable growth in the money stock, they argue, would not prevent all fluctuations in the economy, but it would go a long way toward preventing wide swings. Big depressions or inflations could not occur without big decreases or increases in the money stock.[9]

A similar guide, or "rule," was suggested for fiscal policy, to replace the outmoded annually balanced budget rule. In 1947 the Committee for Economic Development suggested that the government, given its expenditure decisions, should always set taxes to produce a small budget surplus *at high employment.* As with the Friedman proposal, this rule would not completely stabilize the economy, but it would avoid large destabilizing swings in the federal budget. Supporters argue, somewhat as Friedman does, that however well-intentioned fiscal policy may be, politically it turns out to be slow, cumbersome, and often destabilizing. Therefore, Congress and the administration should put a constraint on themselves—that they will always match desired government expenditures with tax rates that will approximately balance the budget *at a high level of employment.*[10]

Figures 1 through 4 (pages 104, 105, 146, and 147) summarize the behavior of monetary and fiscal policy since 1950. Both have been erratic, fluctuating substantially over short periods and frequently out of phase with each other. Superficially, therefore, it would appear that the use of a stabilizing "rule" for monetary or fiscal policy, or both, might have helped to achieve stable economic growth without inflation. With such rules, coordination of monetary and fiscal policy would in fact be achieved.

The probable effects of a stable money growth rate have been analyzed intensively.[11] Leading studies, while subject to criticism

9. See, for example, Milton Friedman, *A Program for Monetary Stability* (Fordham University Press, 1960), Chap. 4; and Edward S. Shaw, "Money Supply and Stable Economic Growth," in Neil H. Jacoby (ed.), *United States Monetary Policy* (Praeger, for the American Assembly, 1964).

10. See, for example, Committee for Economic Development, *Taxes and the Budget: A Program for Prosperity in a Free Economy* (New York, 1947). Beardsley Ruml, aided by Herbert Stein, was largely responsible for this proposal.

11. See, for example, Franco Modigliani, "Some Empirical Tests of Monetary Management and of Rules Versus Discretion," *Journal of Political Economy*, Vol. 72 (June 1964), pp. 211–45; M. Bronfenbrenner, "Statistical Tests of Rival Monetary

on many points, conclude that a stable money growth rule would have produced more satisfactory results than did discretionary action in the big swings of the war periods and the great depression. They confirm the commonsense observation that anything approximating a stable money growth rule would have avoided the monetary-financial collapse of 1929–33 and the massive monetary expansion of the war periods. But the evidence for the nonwar years since the Second World War is less clear. Professor Modigliani concludes:

> In this one period [1952 through 1960] one finds that monetary management was rather effective. . . . It led to relatively small errors, except possibly through parts of the 1957–58 recession; and it outperformed, usually by healthy margins, all of the conventional rules. . . .
>
> At best, therefore, rules can provide only a rough guide for monetary management. But their function cannot, and should not, be to prevent the [monetary] authority from utilizing any other relevant information, or to relieve it from bearing the responsibility for the outcome.[12]

The evidence on a high-employment budget balance rule is similar. With such a rule, budget policy would have been far more expansive in the great depression, far more restrictive in the major wartime and postwar inflations. It is hard to see how a high-employment budget balance rule could have failed to improve our national fiscal performance. But no complex econometric simulation study of the combined private and public economy has yet been devised that can provide a fully convincing answer on how either monetary or fiscal policy rules would compare with discretionary policies in all likely situations. Nor has anyone explained how Congress and the President could be persuaded to yield to a "rule" their prized powers over taxes and expenditures. These objections

---

Rules," *Journal of Political Economy,* Vol. 69 (February 1961), pp. 1–14; and "Statistical Tests of Rival Monetary Rules: Quarterly Data Supplement," *Journal of Political Economy,* Vol. 69 (December 1961), pp. 621–25. There is a new, rapidly burgeoning literature on this issue, involving the use of computer-aided simulations to study the results of alternative monetary and fiscal policies. (See, for example, Edward Gramlich, "The Usefulness of Monetary and Fiscal Policy as Stabilization Tools," and Carl Christ, "Econometric Models of the Financial Sector," both in *Journal of Money, Credit, and Banking* [forthcoming].) These experiments suggest that results may differ substantially under differing circumstances, that both monetary and fiscal policy have substantial effects, and that the Modigliani conclusions cited here appear to be generally correct.

12. Modigliani, "Some Empirical Tests," pp. 243–44.

raise serious doubts that a mechanistic monetary or fiscal rule is a likely solution to macroeconomic policymaking problems. But the proposals both have very attractive aspects, and their implicit criticism of actual discretionary policies carries weight.

Debt Management

Debt management has been a small gun in the arsenal of macroeconomic policy, and it has received little attention in the preceding historical chapters. By law the Treasury has primary responsibility for borrowing funds when taxes fall short of the expenditures voted by Congress. Therefore the Treasury must decide continuously, in its new borrowing and refunding operations, what structure of debt to issue—long-, medium-, or short-term—and what interest rates to offer. What does the record indicate?

1. Debt policy is primarily the responsibility of the Treasury, but it has been made in cooperation with the Federal Reserve. While the Treasury could officially decide what securities it would issue at what rates, it has consistently counted on the help of Federal Reserve open market operations to keep the markets on "even keel" during large Treasury financings. In essence, the Federal Reserve has underwritten the success of Treasury issues by putting adequate funds into the market to assure generally stable interest rates at the agreed level. Thus, as a practical matter, Treasury and Federal Reserve authorities have worked together continuously in planning refundings and new-money issues.

This close coordination has periodically created the danger that the Treasury's desire for low interest rates would force the Federal Reserve into easier money policies than were optimal for over-all economic stabilization. The Treasury's interest in stable, low interest rates has underlain many of the most important monetary policy issues noted in the preceding section.

2. The Treasury and the Federal Reserve have had only limited powers to influence the economy through debt management. The Treasury can influence interest rates in the private economy by selling long- as against short-term maturities, or vice versa. Similarly, the Federal Reserve can temporarily influence the term structure of interest rates by buying or selling short- or long-term maturities. The total volume of debt outstanding in the economy

is massive, however, and these Treasury and Federal Reserve actions, often important in the short run, apparently have not had a large, lasting impact on the structure of total debt and on the term structure of interest rates. In recent years, the Treasury has had to refinance over $100 billion of debt annually. However, this total is still small in relation to the total volume of debt outstanding.[13]

3. Congress has set up a significant barrier to rational debt management by imposing a 4¼ percent ceiling on the rate the Treasury can offer on long-term bonds. The objective has been to hold down the interest cost of the national debt and to avoid the pain of high interest rates in periods of inflation. But in fact, as many economists have emphasized, the ceiling has simply forced the Treasury to borrow at short-term when long-term rates have risen above 4¼ percent. This has often increased, not decreased, total interest costs on the debt and has required short-term issues even when long-term ones would be more appropriate to economic stabilization. Nor does the legal ceiling hold down interest rates. They reflect the total demand for, and supply of, credit. When the Treasury has been unable to pay more than 4¼ percent on bonds, and the market rate is higher, it has not been able to sell bonds; the government demand for funds has shifted to the short-term market, thus increasing demand and effective interest rates there.

4. Congress has also traditionally imposed a ceiling on the total amount of government debt that can be issued. For years this "permanent" ceiling has been below the actual amount of debt outstanding, so Congress must establish higher "temporary" ceilings when it spends more than taxes bring in. Annual congressional re-

13. There is an extensive literature on debt management as a tool of economic stabilization. Few writers have been able to find significant effects of either Treasury debt management or Federal Reserve policy on the term structure of interest rates or on economic activity through them. See, for example, Franco Modigliani and Richard Sutch, "Innovations in Interest Rate Policy," in American Economic Association, *Papers and Proceedings of the Seventy-Eighth Annual Meeting, 1965* (*American Economic Review*, Vol. 56, May 1966), pp. 178–97; and replies of the Treasury, Federal Reserve, and Council of Economic Advisers to a question concerning debt management in *Compendium on Monetary Policy Guidelines and Federal Reserve Structure*, Subcommittee on Domestic Finance of the House Committee on Banking and Currency, 90 Cong. 2 sess. (1968). The Treasury wrote: ". . . it is unlikely that alterations in the maturity structure of the debt can ordinarily be brought about rapidly enough to have a major short-run influence on the liquidity of private investors, and, consequently, on their economic decisions" (p. 60).

view of the debt ceiling is partly a political ritual, partly a real constraint on the Treasury's freedom of action in handling the debt. Often the ceiling leads the government to shift expenditures outside the regular budget, using special "agency" bonds to raise funds for particular purposes. While this may technically avoid raising the national debt, it also usually involves higher interest costs and sometimes the use of uneconomically small special agency issues.[14]

Financial Supervisory Institutions and Interest Rate Ceilings

Fiscal and monetary policy are the main weapons in the government's macroeconomic arsenal. But from time to time specialized agencies concerned with housing, agriculture, veterans' affairs, and the like have been intimately involved in macroeconomic policy issues. Policy conflicts have often arisen in such instances, since the particular missions of these agencies transcend their concern for macroeconomic effects.

Disputes developed among the bank supervisory agencies in the 1930s. Establishment of the Federal Reserve System in 1913 as a voluntary, not a compulsory, association of commercial banks reflected a long tradition of state control over banks in the various states. There was strong "states' rights" opposition to requiring all banks to join any national organization. The result was a proliferation of bank supervisory agencies—the Federal Reserve, the Federal Deposit Insurance Corporation (FDIC), and the comptroller of the currency (in the Treasury Department), and also state authorities. Eccles argued that the Federal Reserve was unable to stimulate bank lending effectively when examiners from the other supervisory agencies were establishing more stringent requirements for acceptable bank loans. The FDIC, the comptroller of the currency, and many of the state banking agencies argued that the function of bank supervision was to protect the safety of deposits, not to participate in countercyclical monetary policy. Coolness

14. See Marshall A. Robinson, *The National Debt Ceiling: An Experiment in Fiscal Policy* (Brookings Institution, 1959). The disruptive effects of these and other congressionally imposed interest ceilings on federal loan guarantees are considered at greater length in the following sections and in Chap. 8.

among the agencies reached the point where they refused to share supervisory information with each other, even on banks that they jointly supervised. The situation was exacerbated by the fact that under the dual (federal-state) banking system, any member bank that disliked strict Federal Reserve regulation could simply withdraw from the System and become responsible only to the FDIC and a state supervisory agency.

In its annual report for 1938 the Federal Reserve Board attacked the complex and inefficient system of bank supervision, urging Congress to create a more unified supervisory system.[15] Eccles, in his memoirs, entitled the chapter dealing with this controversy, "Competition in Laxity," referring to the bickering and to the competitive efforts of the supervisory agencies to lure banks into their respective domains.[16] The same basic complexity of bank supervisory operations remains today.

In 1966 the credit crunch again focused attention on relationships among financial supervisory agencies. Generally tight money markets, high interest rates here and abroad, and an increasing tradition of competition among financial institutions have made the relative interest rates paid to savers by different financial institutions a matter of critical importance. Thus, if the Federal Reserve raised Regulation Q ceilings for commercial banks and the Federal Home Loan Bank Board (FHLBB) did not do likewise for savings and loan associations, a substantial flow of funds from the S&Ls to the banks could be expected. Similarly, if market interest rates on Treasury bills, commercial paper, and Eurodollar balances rose above the ceiling rates paid by banks and S&Ls, savers would shift funds into open market instruments or abroad. With such sensitivity to small differentials in interest rates, ceiling rate policy decisions by the supervisory agencies have become a cutting edge of monetary policy.

Governmental attempts to regulate the flow of credit among different institutions and markets reflect a growing unwillingness to accept allocation by market processes. Tight money falls especially heavily on home construction and to a lesser extent on state and local governments and new, small business firms. These are among

15. Pp. 1–18.
16. Marriner S. Eccles, *Beckoning Frontiers: Public and Personal Recollections* (Knopf, 1951), pp. 266–86.

the least attractive borrowers for most financial institutions when money becomes tight. Construction is particularly vulnerable because a large volume of housing credit flows through the savings and loan associations, which find it hard to attract savers' funds in tight money periods, when interest rates elsewhere rise higher than the S&Ls can afford to offer. Therefore, both the Federal Reserve and other financial regulatory agencies are under pressure to steer the flow of credit toward the S&Ls and thereby toward construction borrowers. The Federal Reserve and other bank supervisory agencies do so by trying to keep down competitive interest rates paid to savers by commercial banks. The FHLBB does it by providing direct subsidies and additional loanable funds to the S&Ls. Not surprisingly, when the government puts ceilings on some interest rates, savers seek other unregulated investments, and the government must extend regulation to other borrowers or see its credit-allocation goals undermined.

Moreover, Federal Reserve and FHLBB objectives are different. Congress created the FHLBB and the other housing credit agencies to aid home financing and stability in the credit markets that are closely related to housing. In general the FHLBB has tried to assure adequate credit in the housing sector in a way that will mesh with the general monetary policies of the Federal Reserve. But at times these objectives have conflicted. The Federal Reserve, as the nation's central bank, is responsible for both promoting stable economic growth and providing over-all liquidity for the nation's credit structure—but only indirectly for housing credit per se. It is not surprising that differences often arise between the Federal Reserve and the special-purpose credit agencies.[17]

17. For example, in 1968 John E. Horne, chairman of the FHLBB, repeatedly emphasized that the first objective of the Board was to maintain stability and assure adequate credit to housing markets, though he recognized also the pressure to cooperate with general monetary policy. He told an audience of mortgage bankers: "It is time we recognize that Federal credit programs, which are designed to deal with particular markets, are not always suitable for general stabilization. We must recognize that fluctuations in a given sector of the economy do not always coincide with fluctuations in the economy as a whole. Trying to make all Federal credit programs serve general stabilization policies at all times can lead to defeating the primary purposes of some, if not all, of these credit programs." ("Mortgage Markets—A New Look at Stability," address before the Twenty-Third Annual Conference for Senior Executives in Mortgage Banking, New York University, Jan. 12, 1968. See also *Report of the Federal Home Loan Bank Board for the Year Ending December 31, 1967*, pp. 48–52.)

These goal conflicts have not been limited to the FHLBB. The Federal Reserve has had comparable conflicts periodically with other federal financial agencies—for example, with the Department of Agriculture over farm credit programs, with the Veterans Administration over veterans' home loans, and with virtually all the federal lending and loan guarantee agencies.

Under President Kennedy, two major studies were made of the problem of coordinating federal credit programs and federal supervision of financial institutions. In 1962–63 the quadriad (Secretary of the Treasury Dillon, Budget Director Bell, CEA Chairman Heller, and Federal Reserve Board Chairman Martin) recommended a program of coordination through consultation by the heads and senior staffs of all federal credit agencies, whereby the interest rates and timing of all U.S. guaranteed issues would be subject to Treasury approval.[18] At about the same time, a special presidential committee of eleven top federal financial officials issued a detailed report on coordination of the policies of federal agencies that supervise private financial institutions. In general the recommendations were for coordination through consultation.[19] A similar review of the coordination of federal credit programs, required by the Participation and Sales Act of 1966, reached substantially similar conclusions.[20]

Consonant with these recommendations, an informal committee was established in 1966 by Secretary of the Treasury Fowler at the direction of the President to meet demands by Congress for better coordination of the supervision of financial institutions (see page 132). The committee meets regularly, and it considers the entire area of financial supervision, but not the broader policy issues, which are the sphere of the quadriad. The committee exercises no formal power over the participating agencies, but it has served well

18. *Report of the Committee on Federal Credit Programs to the President of the United States* (1963).

19. *Report of the Committee on Financial Institutions to the President of the United States* (1963).

20. *Federal Credit Programs,* Report by the Secretary of the Treasury to Congress, Senate Committee on Banking and Currency, 90 Cong. 1 sess. (1967). George F. Break, in *Federal Lending and Economic Stability* (Brookings Institution, 1965), provides detailed information on all major government direct-loan and guarantee programs since the Second World War. Break concludes that several of the programs could be used as flexible stabilizers and to some extent have been so used; but others have long lags and offer little promise for countercyclical use.

the goal of communication.[21] Informal discussions among the agency heads, and with the CEA and White House, have recently worked well. But given the overlapping responsibilities and different missions of the financial supervisory agencies, it will be surprising if minor frictions or more serious interagency differences do not recur.[22]

Federal Reserve Policymaking

In principle, it is said, the aerodynamics and wing-loading of the bumblebee would indicate that it cannot fly. Yet every day the bee defies the august authority of Isaac Newton and Orville Wright. In somewhat the same way, the Federal Reserve System appears on paper to be an extraordinarily complex and cumbersome piece of policymaking machinery. Yet in practice it has worked reasonably well over the past half century. The preceding pages have indicated the role of monetary policy and its interactions with fiscal policy in pursuing national economic goals. More specific attention to the Federal Reserve as a policymaking and operating body suggests the following conclusions:

GOALS AND RESPONSIVENESS TO PUBLIC OPINION

1. The Federal Reserve has consistently indicated that its goals are part of, and substantially the same as, the goals of general national economic policy.

2. In addition to their broad economic stabilization goals, the Reserve authorities have consistently sought to maintain stable, "even keel" conditions in national financial markets, mainly through "defensive" open market operations. As a bank supervisory authority, the Federal Reserve has shown consistent concern for the welfare of banks and related intermediaries in the financial

21. While James Saxon was comptroller of the currency, relations among the supervisory authorities were tense; communication was at best intermittent. Saxon openly defied other supervisory agencies and refused to share supervisory data with them. Since then, cooperation has improved.

22. It is clear that the separate operating goals of the credit agencies, as a practical matter, block their effective use as flexible monetary-fiscal stabilizers. Many economists would argue that *in principle* they should not be so used because of the danger that their special program missions might then be improperly subordinated to stabilization goals.

process. There is substantial basis for the criticism that short-term money market conditions and concern for the Treasury and bankers have received undue emphasis at the expense of the major economic goals indicated above.

3. Although individual congressmen and some economists have criticized the Federal Reserve as impervious to the general public welfare, Federal Reserve authorities have been sensitive to congressional pressures and to public opinion. They have consistently recognized their direct responsibility to Congress and, through it, to the public.

4. In its early years, the Federal Reserve was substantially influenced by private bankers and financiers. Since the 1930s, however, top Federal Reserve officials in Washington and at the twelve Federal Reserve banks have clearly considered themselves public officials, responsible to Congress and the public rather than to the banking industry.

FEDERAL RESERVE STRUCTURE AND POLICYMAKING

The present complex Federal Reserve organization reflects the regional banking needs of a half century ago, modified here and expanded there as the focus has shifted to national monetary policy and as new financial instruments have developed. How well the System has worked in practice is suggested by the preceding chapters. Like the bumblebee that flies, the System has done better than one would expect from its organizational structure.

1. *Public versus Private Control.* A half century ago, when the Federal Reserve was established, how far it should be controlled by private bankers and how far by the government was a hotly debated issue. Historically, central banks had grown out of private banks, and in 1914 most central banks abroad remained technically independent of their governments. But the Banking Acts of 1933 and 1935 radically shifted the balance of power toward Washington and toward a governmental status for the Federal Reserve.

Nonetheless, some observers still question the close relationships between Federal Reserve officials and commercial bankers. While they acknowledge that private bankers do not formally control the Federal Reserve, they argue that in practice the Reserve, like other regulatory agencies, has come, albeit subconsciously, to protect the interests of its industry. The proper weight to place on short-run financial market stability in the public interest is open to argument. One may question the wisdom of the Federal Reserve's emphasis on even keeling financial markets without concluding that the System is unduly influenced by either the banking industry or the Treasury.

2. *Regional versus Central Control.* In 1914 the Federal Reserve's major responsibilities were expected to be to provide regional rediscounting facilities, to centralize reserves to lessen the danger of banking crises, and to provide an elastic currency. The twelve Reserve Banks were expected to work closely with the commercial banks in their districts. Great emphasis was placed on the regional nature of the new Federal Reserve System.

Achievement of these goals has become routine. The central focus of the Federal Reserve is now national monetary policy—control over the aggregate money supply, its cost, and its availability. This is beyond doubt a national function. To have the various regional Reserve Banks operating at cross purposes would be unthinkable. Federal Reserve records show no consistent pattern of voting behavior by presidents as compared to Board members in Federal Open Market Committee decisions. Shifting coalitions, rather than stable voting blocs, have characterized FOMC voting during the past decade.

3. *Role of the Chairman.* The early history of the Federal Reserve is replete with bitter intramural battles over control of policymaking, especially control over newly developing open market operations in the 1920s. Under Marriner Eccles in the 1930s and 1940s, the FOMC spoke with a single voice. Eccles was the dominant figure in the System, with only Allan Sproul, president of the New York Bank, of a stature to challenge his dominance. The twelve-man open market committee, or even the seven-man Board of Governors, could not participate actively in high-level discussions of economic goals and policies, or in small groups charged with responsibility for carrying out these policies. Thus, both because of his personal strength and because of organizational realities, Eccles spoke for the Federal Reserve externally and dominated its operations internally.

Martin's operating style was different—calm, persuasive, low-key. Under him, all Reserve Bank presidents, not merely the Board members and those presidents who were formally members of the FOMC, participated regularly in FOMC meetings, which were usually held every three weeks. Although only the twelve FOMC members could vote, all present were free to express their opinions. Partly because of his skill in shaping a consensus that met his own views, Martin for many years was as successful as Eccles in achieving unanimous votes on the FOMC. But during the 1960s, new appointees to the Board by Presidents Kennedy and Johnson were not always Martin men (as they had been during the Eisenhower regime), and sharper differences began to develop among Board members. Split votes within the Board and on the FOMC became more common, though invariably with Martin on the majority side.

Externally, Martin's leadership position was as strong as Eccles's. Martin spoke for the System in negotiations with the President and other top government officials, in testifying before congressional committees, and in reporting to the public through speeches. Increasingly, other Board members and bank presidents spoke up as well, but there was no doubt that Martin was the leader of the System, and a dominant one.[23]

4. *FOMC Policymaking.* Federal Reserve policymaking, with a de facto nineteen-member open market committee at the core of the decision-making process, involves a lot of talk. The FOMC usually meets every three weeks for a thorough discussion of Federal Reserve policy. Critics have argued that the large size of this policymaking body has caused delay and compromise in policymaking. Under Chairman Martin, time was provided at the meetings for each official to say his piece, reflecting Martin's deep faith in decision by consensus. Inefficient though the procedure may have been, there is little evidence that it produced worse pol-

23. Studies of Federal Reserve voting procedures during the 1950s and 1960s indicate a clear leadership by Chairman Martin, but are not consistent with a "dictator" hypothesis or domination by any particular bloc on the FOMC. Chairman Martin's consistent role in voting with the majority is attributed especially to his skill in running the committee and summarizing consensus effectively, and to his further skill in smoothing over differences so as to obtain unanimous or nearly unanimous votes. Even when the chairman's influence over new appointments weakened in the 1960s, voting differences followed no consistent pattern that reflected differences among the Reserve Bank presidents and Board members, or among newly and previously appointed Board members. See William P. Yohe, "A Study of Federal Open Market Committee Voting, 1955–64," *Southern Economic Journal*, Vol. 32 (April 1966), pp. 396–405; and E. R. Canterbery, "A New Look at Federal Open Market Voting," *Western Economic Journal*, Vol. 6 (December 1967), pp. 25–38.

icy decisions than a smaller committee or a single official would have. But conversely, examination of the FOMC minutes provides little evidence that the quality of FOMC decisions has been improved substantially by having so many participants in the process; the main issues are usually well stated by early spokesmen, and the repetition is considerable.

The FOMC is the key body in domestic monetary policymaking. But the Board alone controls reserve requirements; and discount rates are set by the twelve Reserve Banks, subject to Board approval. This split authority makes no sense organizationally. In practice, it has led to few serious differences and delays. In the end the Board has prevailed when it stood united. But the elaborate division of authority no longer appears to serve any useful purpose, if it ever did.

5. *Board Members and Decision Processes.* The *modus operandi* of the Board itself and the role of individual Board members has varied widely over the past half century. During the long Eccles regime, the Board was frequently considered a rubber stamp for the chairman's strong opinions. By and large, the quality of Board members reflected this situation. Through much of the 1930s and 1940s, major monetary policy issues arose only infrequently (the rule was easy money throughout the late depression years and support for the Treasury security market during the Second World War). Much of the Board members' time was devoted to relatively minor matters—detailed supervision of Board and Reserve Bank operating procedures, and so on. There is little evidence that Federal Reserve policy would have been much different had Eccles been a single head of the System.

Under Martin, participation by individual Board members was substantially greater. Recent appointments to the Board have included a substantial number of trained economists, knowledgeable about central banking problems and policies. At the same time, pressure from the Board has led to the appointment of stronger Reserve Bank presidents, several of whom have been trained economists. These changes have been reflected in the tenor and quality of Board discussion of monetary issues, especially during the 1960s.[24]

24. Bank supervisory matters (mergers, bank holding companies, and the like) occupy a substantial amount of the time of some of the Board members.

6. *Role of the New York Bank.* During the 1920s, Governor Benjamin Strong, head of the New York Bank, was widely recognized as the leader of the Federal Reserve System. Under the Eccles regime, Allan Sproul, president of the New York Bank, was clearly the second spokesman for the System, often differing openly with Eccles. More recently, President Alfred Hayes of the New York Bank has been a respected senior spokesman for the Reserve Banks and for the System. The president of the New York Bank serves, ex officio, as vice chairman of the FOMC; and, perhaps more important, the New York Bank serves as agent for both the entire Federal Reserve System and the Treasury in conducting domestic open market operations and foreign monetary transactions.

The New York Bank officials responsible for these activities operate under directives from the FOMC and the Treasury.[25] But the New York Bank has a position of eminence unparalleled by any other Reserve Bank. As agent for the Treasury in international and domestic fiscal operations, it is in almost constant communication with top Treasury officials here and abroad on debt management and international monetary issues, and it participates for the Treasury in international negotiations. FOMC directives are, by tradition, broadly phrased, and they leave substantial discretion to the managers of the domestic and foreign desks on day-to-day transactions. For "defensive" open market operations, large powers rest in the hands of the domestic account manager. Even when the FOMC changes the directive substantially, the manner and rate of achieving these changes is left largely up to the manager.[26]

The position of the New York Bank is anomalous, further, in that it acts simultaneously as agent for both the FOMC and the U.S. Treasury, two independent entities, on overlapping domestic

25. The vice president of the New York Bank who serves as manager of the System's open market account has recently been made directly responsible to the FOMC.

26. John E. Buehler and David I. Fand, in "The Federal Reserve and Monetary Policy," report that in recent years the domestic account manager has tended to be somewhat more liberal in the execution of policy than was prescribed by the FOMC, but did not initiate major policy changes and implemented policy directives rapidly. Other writers, notably Karl Brunner and Allan Meltzer, feel that the New York Bank has had greater leeway, and they are more critical of its behavior and of the Reserve's heavy emphasis on free reserves and short-term money market conditions as major guides to policy.

and international matters. However, top officials of the Federal Reserve and the Treasury have generally agreed that the present arrangement not only is workable but also is the most practical. Someone has to carry on the highly technical day-to-day operations in the domestic and international money markets, and the New York Bank is the logical place to center these responsibilities.

Policy Dilemmas: Unemployment or Inflation

The 1950s and 1960s posed a major dilemma for macroeconomic policymakers. When unemployment was above 5 percent or so, prices were stable or rose only slightly. But when unemployment fell to 4 percent or less (in the years 1955–57 and 1965–69), the price level rose substantially. This was shown in Figures 1 and 3 (on pages 104 and 146). A similar problem had arisen earlier. Prices began to rise substantially in 1936–37 as aggregate spending grew rapidly in spite of massive unemployment.

To many observers this suggested a painful dilemma: how much inflation must be accepted in order to maintain a low rate of unemployment? Some saw the dilemma in the 1950s and 1960s as reflecting substantial changes in product and labor markets; increasing concentrations of business and union power in these markets permitted large sellers to demand and obtain higher prices and wages despite substantial unemployment. But others argued instead that a low level of unemployment need be accompanied by substantial inflation *only* when aggregate demand rises *rapidly*— for example, as it did in the 1965–68 Vietnam war boom. Predictably, according to this theory, rapid increases in aggregate demand would produce bottlenecks in labor and product markets and would drive up some wages and prices well before general high employment is reached. With a slower approach to high-level employment, markets can adjust more flexibly, and inflation need not be the price of prosperity.

An alternative explanation, which also stresses *changes* in the rate of inflation, not the level of prices per se, emphasizes expectations. If inflation is partly unanticipated, some prices (for example, wages) will rise more slowly than others (for example, the prices of final products). This decline in real wages leads to higher employment. But if expectations are adjusted so that everyone

184 Making Monetary and Fiscal Policy

anticipates inflation equally, the real wage-price ratio and employment return to their original levels. Thus, since rising inflation is usually partly unanticipated, it tends to reduce unemployment, but only temporarily.[27]

If either the rate-of-change or the anticipations theory is right (and there is considerable support for them), inflation helps significantly to reduce unemployment *only* when the rate of inflation is rising, or, more fundamentally, not fully anticipated. Once union members, businessmen, households, borrowers, and lenders come to expect 4 percent inflation, they adjust their wage and price demands and their spending-lending practices to this expected rate of inflation, so that it no longer has a stimulative effect on employment and output. The stimulus of inflation to employment comes mainly because real costs fall when money wages and interest costs rise more slowly than do selling prices.

By this reasoning, inflation is not necessarily the price of a low level of unemployment, except in a transitional or short-run sense. A continuing stable rate of inflation buys little in the way of higher employment.[28] If this analysis is correct, a policy of accepting "a little inflation to maintain full employment," whether by monetary or by fiscal authorities, may be shortsighted, though perhaps sometimes justified as a short-run expedient. Indeed, recent history suggests that more progress can be made in lessening this unemployment-inflation dilemma by improving the structural efficiency of labor markets than by monetary-fiscal policies.

The preceding paragraphs presume that both unemployment and inflation have costs that are real and substantial. The costs of unemployment are apparent—wasted potential output, idle work-

27. In principle, there is no reason why rising inflation should necessarily increase, rather than reduce, employment. If wages should rise faster than prices, unemployment would rise, not fall, temporarily. Historically, wage lag seems more common, but there are important exceptions (for example, in the 1954–57 period). Generally, insofar as inflation is caused by a labor-cost push, the result will be a decrease, not an increase, in employment, other things being equal.

28. In economists' terms, as was indicated in Chap. 3, it is by no means clear that there is a meaningful "Phillips curve" that indicates a stable relationship between the rate of inflation and the level of unemployment. This relationship may be a short-run or transient one, while in the longer run the level of unemployment is substantially independent of the rate of inflation. Barring continuing changes in the degree of monopoly power in labor or product markets, or other such market structure changes, professional economists increasingly support this long-run, short-run distinction.

ers, human misery, deprivation. Those of inflation are less obvious, since inflation may merely redistribute income and wealth. Measurement of these relative costs is a complex undertaking beyond the scope of this book. It is important to recognize here, however, that the relevant costs are those at the margin in most cases—the costs of a little more inflation against a little more unemployment. Clearly, both total output and employment *and* distributional effects must be measured. Unemployment due to inadequate aggregate demand does not strike workers at random; low-skilled, inefficient, young, often minority workers are usually laid off first and hired last. Similarly, inflation tends to shift income and wealth away from creditors to debtors, from those on relatively fixed incomes to those with flexible incomes. Moreover, the trade-off will be different depending on the initial conditions. The real costs of a little more inflation may be modest if the price level has been stable and rises only a little, but much greater if a rapid inflation is under way. The costs of a little more unemployment may be great in a recession, when older, skilled, immobile family heads are affected, but less in prosperous times, when beginners and young, mobile workers lose their jobs.

How one weights these various costs will influence policy choices when trade-offs are inescapable. Since different policymaking environments—for example, the relative independence given the Federal Reserve—may influence the kind of policy that results, it is important to bear in mind how the relative costs have been weighed.[29]

The growing frustration of policymakers and the public during the 1960s, as full employment without inflation proved an elusive goal, understandably led to growing support for direct government intervention to resolve the dilemma. President Kennedy's wage-price guideposts in 1962 were a first step in spelling out wage and price policies that would be consistent with high employment

---

29. I have spelled out my own analysis and preferences in *Inflation: A Study in Economics, Ethics, and Politics* (Brown University Press, 1958). Briefly, persistent moderate inflation has relatively little effect on total output and less effect on the distribution of income and wealth than has often been asserted. It redistributes real income and wealth to some extent from the aged, employees of nonprofit institutions, and, to a lesser extent, the poor to the rest of the population. Inflation is likely to be unstable upward, however, so there is substantial doubt that, as a practical matter, it can be sustained over long periods without accelerating.

and a stable price level. Various European "incomes policies" were aimed at the same goal during the 1950s. Some countries went as far as government-enforced wage and price behavior, including temporary wage-price freezes. Others stressed informal government-business-labor cooperation in arriving at wage-price behavior consistent with national noninflationary growth policies. In the United States, the guideposts were gradually transformed into direct government intervention in specific price and wage decisions that threatened the Kennedy and Johnson anti-inflation policies.

The evidence on the effectiveness of the wage-price guideposts is mixed. They apparently helped modestly to ease the unemployment-inflation dilemma during the 1962–65 period, but had little real effect when large excess demand pressures developed after 1965.[30]

Later in the decade, widening strikes by employees in the public sector (postal workers, teachers, garbage collectors) further emphasized the inability of aggregate demand policy alone to assure high employment without inflation in an economy characterized by excess income claims, particularly an affluent one in which there was broad support for raising low incomes even though such increases were demonstrably inflationary. New collective bargaining procedures for public employees marked another direct response by the government to the inflation-unemployment dilemma of aggregate demand policy.

Similar frustration over the impact of anti-inflationary monetary policy on home construction spawned another set of direct controls to harmonize tight money with stimulation of the housing market—interest rate ceilings on deposits at banks and S&Ls, plus special subsidies and additional lendable funds for S&Ls from the FHLBB. Housing proponents argued increasingly for direct government controls to force pension funds and other large institutional savers to channel more of their funds into loans for home building.

In light of the experience of the 1960s, it seems safe to predict further pressures for direct controls to help achieve simultaneously high employment, stable prices, and particular sectoral goals like stimulating home construction, when aggregate demand policy alone seems unable to do so.

30. For references to the voluminous literature on this question, see Chap. 3, note 9, and Chap. 8, note 45.

Policy Dilemmas: Domestic versus International Monetary Policies

International constraints on U.S. macroeconomic policymakers have varied widely over the past half century. Apparent conflicts between domestic and international goals have intermittently seemed a major problem to macroeconomic policymakers—especially in 1931 and in the 1960s. At home, domestic conditions called for expansion, but gold flowed out, and international payments deficits were large.

During the early 1960s, U.S. authorities turned primarily to direct measures to solve the dilemma—the interest equalization tax, a reduction in duty-free imports, American preference on military purchases, tied foreign aid, and both voluntary and mandatory controls on capital exports—rather than to general monetary-fiscal restraint. Repeated international confidence crises and runs on major currencies unsettled U.S. domestic policy and international monetary relations during the 1960s, beginning with a run on the dollar during the 1960 presidential campaign. Confidence crises for the pound, devaluation of sterling and thirteen other currencies, and a massive speculative rush to buy gold followed in quick succession in 1967–68.

Whether U.S. macro policymakers gave excessive weight to international constraints in the 1920s, 1930s, and 1960s is debatable. The international monetary system collapsed in the 1930s; but it has served the world well since the Second World War. The postwar period has seen unparalleled growth in world production, trade, and capital flows. The world economy has grown on a relatively smooth course, and inflation in the major countries has been moderate. While the Federal Reserve clearly gave excessive weight to gold outflows in 1931, statistical analyses of Federal Reserve performance since the Second World War have generally shown that the degree of unemployment and slack in economic growth and internal inflation were stronger explanatory variables for Federal Reserve action than were shifts in the international payments position.[31]

31. Economists have long emphasized that a balance-of-payments deficit of zero, especially in the liquidity balance, is not necessarily a sign of international equilibrium. But bankers, businessmen, and the news media have often not recognized this fact.

Growing international interdependence, especially because of the mobility of capital, has made the existing international fixed-exchange-rate payments system increasingly difficult to operate. Basically, the expanding economic interdependence has limited the freedom of individual nations to pursue widely divergent macroeconomic policies. Thus, U.S. officials have been increasingly circumscribed in their use of domestic monetary policy to damp internal fluctuations.

During the 1960s, the U.S. Treasury, the Council of Economic Advisers, and the Federal Reserve worked intimately with other treasuries and central banks, directly and through such international institutions as the International Monetary Fund, the Group of Ten, and the Organisation for Economic Co-operation and Development. This international cooperation has prevented major financial catastrophes. But the results have involved an uncomfortably large amount of cliff-hanging. The Washington two-tier gold agreement of 1968, the establishment of special drawing rights to augment existing international reserves, and moves toward modest exchange rate flexibility should be helpful, but they are still too new to provide much operating evidence.

Postwar experience has emphasized that, as the world moves toward more interdependent economies and capital markets, U.S. macroeconomic policy against domestic fluctuations, especially monetary policy, may be substantially constrained by the dangers of unwanted capital flows and of destabilizing international interest rate changes. Recent experience thus highlights the unfortunate need either to give up fixed exchange rates in order to improve the flexibility of the adjustment process, or to develop flexible fiscal policy as an alternative to heavy reliance on monetary policy for domestic stabilization.

Since the Second World War, U.S. international monetary policymakers have worked closely together. By both legislation and tradition, the Treasury holds major responsibility, under the President, for formulating and implementing U.S. policy on gold, exchange rate stabilization, and the like. But under Treasury and CEA leadership, policymaking has drawn on the other agencies concerned, notably the Federal Reserve, the Commerce Department, and the State Department. Moreover, it has been agreed throughout that there must be *one* U.S. policy position, not separate policy positions of the various agencies involved. Actual operations in the gold and exchange markets are conducted by the New York Federal Reserve Bank. Thus, that bank has great responsibility for actual operations, but it acts under policy directives from the Treasury and FOMC in Washington. Not infrequently its policy recommendations have been overruled. Insofar as there were mistakes in U.S. macroeconomic policy in relation to international constraints, they arose through improper judgments, not through lack of formal or informal coordination among U.S. policymakers.

Aspirations and Achievements

Aspirations for the performance of the U.S. economic system have soared since the great depression and the Second World War. By comparison with most previous history, the economy's performance over the past two decades has been good. There has been no major depression, only modest recessions. The growth rate of the economy has been higher than in any comparable previous period. Though it was substantial in some years, inflation has been moderate over all. The balance of payments, while in deficit over much of the period, was generally appropriate during the 1950s and failed to disrupt international trade and investment seriously during the 1960s, though it exerted growing pressure on U.S. economic policy.

Partly because of this good record, U.S. aspirations by 1970 may have outrun our ability to achieve them in the field of economic performance. While conscious government policy deserves some credit for this postwar performance, clearly it deserves less than full credit. Several times federal fiscal and monetary policy have been destabilizing rather than stabilizing. The record gives only limited support to the hope that it is now possible, through improved knowledge and policy instruments, to keep the economy growing stably, without substantial unemployment or inflation. But the prospect has greatly improved over the last quarter century.

The shortfalls of macroeconomic policy since the Second World War have reflected partly inadequate analysis, partly inadequacies in the policy process. On some occasions inadequate coordination among Congress, the administration, and the Federal Reserve contributed substantially to poor policy—in 1966 and 1967, for example. But most policy failures were the result of bad decisions, not inadequate discussion of those policies among the policymakers.

It is important to recognize that complete policy "coordination," in the sense of total agreement or single-agency power over final decisions, would have been desirable only if the end result were better than it was without such coordination. To assume that compulsory coordination would have yielded unified decisions that were always right is grossly to oversimplify the problem. During 1966, for example, the Federal Reserve, Congress, and the administration were moving in diverse directions. Would the result have been better if coordination had been achieved on the Federal Reserve's terms or on those of Congress or the administration? History suggests that the greatest need is to improve the flexibility of fiscal policy and the understanding of all policymakers, not to give any one part of the government more formal authority to "coordinate" macroeconomic policymaking.

On the importance of individuals in the policymaking process, history again provides no simple answer. Effective macroeconomic policy appears to have emanated from men of widely diverse backgrounds—Dillon at the Treasury, Martin at the Federal Reserve, Arthur Burns and Heller at the CEA. Clearly, incompetent officials can impede the effective formulation and implementation of macro policy. More than one observer has commented that President Kennedy was extremely fortunate in having skilled economic advisers and an economically literate and open-minded secretary of the treasury. Clearly also, for purposes of policy coordination, reasonable goodwill and working cooperation among the top officials and agencies concerned are required. With rare exceptions high policy officials have seriously tried to achieve such working cooperation—though with varying results. Men arriving with few obvious qualifications for the job sometimes did surprisingly well under the responsibilities of high positions.

Finally, the postwar period reemphasizes the importance of competent senior staff support for top officials in macroeconomic policymaking. The Federal Reserve's large and able staff of economists and statisticians has consistently provided a source of policy strength not generally matched by the other agencies. Similarly, the high level of competence of the small CEA staff in recent years has done much to improve the policy analysis and the bargaining position of the administration vis-à-vis Congress and other agencies. On the other hand, since the Roosevelt days the Treasury has traditionally not been strong in senior economic staff. It has either been run primarily by a few competent men at the top or has had to draw on other agencies for staff analysis and backup. The senior staffs of congressional committees have varied widely in quality; generally they have been small and heavily dependent on their ability to obtain needed information from agency staffs of more depth and capacity. Fortunately, the working relations among staffs of the major agencies appear to have improved substantially in recent years. To achieve the nation's aspirations for stable economic growth, this coordination needs to be continued and improved, and more economists of superior ability are needed in policymaking as well as advisory positions.

8

RECOMMENDATIONS

MOST MAJOR macroeconomic policy failures during the past quarter century have occurred because the policymakers were unwilling to use available policy instruments or because of mistakes in judgment, *not* because policymakers failed to coordinate their activities. This chapter suggests reforms in policymaking, based on recent history and on economic and political theory. It stresses the advantages of shifting emphasis from short-term fine-tuning judgments toward longer-run stable-growth patterns for both monetary and fiscal policy, while maintaining moderate flexibility for short-run ad hoc adjustments when they are clearly needed.

The thrust of the recommendations is threefold:

1. Most important is the need to reduce the possibility that macroeconomic policy will itself be seriously destabilizing. The requisite presumptions are, for fiscal policy, a moderate surplus in the high-employment budget and, for monetary policy, reasonably stable growth in the basic monetary aggregates.

2. Flexible means are needed to moderate serious disruptions to stable economic growth, should these occur from the private, public, or international sectors. For fiscal policy, this calls for built-in automatic stabilizers plus annual proposals by the President for a

(positive or negative) stabilizing income surtax;[1] for monetary policy, continued responsibility to moderate wide fluctuations in the monetary aggregates that may arise from the private sector; for international monetary policy, adoption of a wider band around exchange parities and a "sliding peg," or some comparable device, for gradually modifying exchange parities as may be required. Policy arrangements must recognize that economic developments cannot yet be reliably forecast beyond the near future and that considerable uncertainty exists as to the linkages and lags between monetary-fiscal policy actions and the levels of employment, output, and prices, which are their ultimate targets.

3. Arrangements to offset minor disturbances are also needed. For fiscal policy, this may mean giving the President power to vary the rates of federal expenditures moderately; congressional action through tax changes is not promising. For monetary policy, it means continued Federal Reserve responsibility for "defensive" open market operations to moderate financial market disruptions resulting from Treasury financing, currency drains, variations in float, and the like, though these actions should be subordinate to basic stabilization goals.

Insofar as monetary and fiscal policy cannot achieve their goals solely through control of aggregate demand, the imaginative use of new policy instruments and structural changes in the economy may be required. Some form of wage-price, or incomes, policy may be needed to help develop a consensus on noninflationary wage-price behavior and on a framework of expectations for stable economic growth. Reforms of financial institutions and of credit, labor, and commodity markets may be needed to facilitate the simultaneous achievement of high employment, a stable price level, and such sectoral social goals as more residential housing over the decade ahead. But monetary and fiscal authorities need to be sure that the pursuit of such special goals does not divert them from their primary duty—to keep aggregate demand growing roughly apace with the economy's productive capacity.

Substantial coordination among macroeconomic policy instruments and authorities will be needed. In practice, fiscal policy measures are likely often to be badly timed and to lag behind

1. Or, if this proposal is not accepted, the President should be given power to change the income surtax for six months, subject to congressional veto.

194 Making Monetary and Fiscal Policy

needs. Thus the monetary authorities will probably continue to be faced with the unwelcome problem of having to adjust not only to disruptions from the private sector but to mistaken fiscal policies as well. In general, monetary policy is likely to grow in importance, reflecting the shift from a slack to a high-employment economy.

Ultimate responsibility for the nation's economic well-being, and hence for macroeconomic policy, must lie with the President and Congress, as elected representatives of the people. In some areas, notably tax and expenditure policies, Congress has retained for itself detailed control over macroeconomic policies. In others, Congress has delegated its powers. For example, it has delegated to the Federal Reserve most of its constitutional powers to coin money and regulate the value thereof; it has similarly delegated authority to supervise financial institutions. Still other areas—for example, international economic policy—fall somewhere between. Policy procedures that effectively coordinate the actions of these various authorities across the entire range of macroeconomic issues are the objective sought.

Reform in Fiscal Policymaking

The avoidance of massively destabilizing measures and the introduction of at least some short-run flexibility are the first requisites for improved macroeconomic policymaking in Congress and the executive branch. During the Second World War, the Korean war, the late 1950s, 1963–64, and the Vietnam war, fiscal policy was under serious dispute; the President and the Treasury differed sharply with Congress, and in each of these periods the fiscal policy actually adopted was destabilizing. Moreover, several of the major failings of monetary policy reflected attempts by the monetary authorities to adjust to, or compensate for, mistaken fiscal policies.

The constitutional division of powers between Congress and the President is clear. Congress is to make the laws, and the President is to execute them. But two centuries have blurred this distinction. The President recommends, often urges, legislative measures. But Congress has jealously guarded its prerogatives to control taxes and expenditures in detail. Thus, contrary to popular belief, the President and his administration typically have little direct power over fiscal policy, beyond urging changes on Congress and bringing pressure in support of these recommendations through whatever channels the President has available.

One solution would be for Congress to give the President broad discretion over tax and/or expenditure rates. Another would be to revise radically congressional tax and expenditure decision processes. In principle, either could make fiscal policy a more flexible countercyclical tool and avoid major destabilizing actions. But as a practical matter, neither seems probable within the foreseeable future.

The practical problem is to find ways to avoid major fiscal policy errors, to focus congressional attention more sharply on the stabilization aspects of fiscal policy, and to develop a small amount of short-run flexibility for use when the need for it is clear. Three modest reforms could go far toward eliminating the danger of serious fiscal destabilization and provide modest discretionary fiscal help against disruptions originating in the private or international sectors.

1. *Substitute for the old annual budget-balance principle, now fortunately nearly defunct, a presumption that there should be a modest annual surplus in the high-employment budget.* Under this guideline, tax rates would have been substantially reduced in the 1930s. The inflationary budget deficits of the Second World War, the Korean war, and the Vietnam war would have been avoided. Instead of waiting until 1964, Congress would have cut tax rates for the entire 1958–64 period, thus avoiding the increasing drag created by the federal budget during those years. Maintaining a small surplus in the high-employment budget would protect against such major errors and would provide built-in budget flexibility to counter economic swings in the private sector.

Under this high-employment budget guideline, Congress would set tax rates each year to provide total tax receipts moderately (say 2–3 percent) above budgeted expenditures with the economy operating at approximately full employment.[2] If private incomes and

2. As was indicated above, this presumption in favor of a moderate annual budget surplus rests on the probable shortage of private savings over the decade ahead to finance needed investment, notably in home construction. By running a modest budget surplus the government would be adding correspondingly to the total of private savings being supplied to finance such investment.

spending exceeded the level conducive to high employment without inflation, tax receipts would rise automatically, producing an anti-inflationary surplus in the regular (unified) budget. Conversely, whenever the economy operated below the full-employment level, tax revenues would shrink as incomes fell, and a budget deficit would result automatically. Thus, the federal budget would automatically produce surpluses or deficits that would moderate deviations from the full-employment growth path. At the same time, the high-employment budget guideline would confront Congress with the basic need for fiscal responsibility—to enact taxes to cover government expenditures when resources are fully employed so that government expenditures necessarily would leave fewer resources for private use. The old balanced-budget rule would be followed when it should be followed—when employment is at a high level.

This guideline would not produce an "ideal" stabilization budget. Ideally, the economy should have a federal deficit or surplus just large enough, with its multiplier effects, to offset the excess or deficiency of private spending in relation to the desired full-employment level. The suggested high-employment budget guideline would often fall short of producing this ideal surplus or deficit, since tax receipts would vary by only a fraction of the fluctuations in private incomes. Moreover, given substantial inside and outside policy lags and limited ability to forecast the future, attempts to achieve the "ideal" would be as likely to produce destabilizing as stabilizing results.

Thus the pragmatic case for using the high-employment budget guideline is that it would ensure that fiscal policy moved in approximately the right direction, even though this would mean forgoing discretionary tax and spending changes aimed at short-run stabilization. Fortunately, with economic growth, Congress would be faced each year with the pleasant choice of cutting taxes or increasing spending by some $10–15 billion. Finally, a major argument for this budget policy is that it could be implemented with little lessening of the authority Congress has traditionally held over tax and expenditure rates.[3]

To facilitate this change of congressional emphasis, the Presi-

3. For a more detailed analysis, see Arthur M. Okun and Nancy H. Teeters, "The Full Employment Surplus Revisited," *Brookings Papers on Economic Activity* (1:1970), pp. 77–110.

dent in presenting his annual Economic Report and other economic messages should stress the high-employment budget, rather than the "unified" (administrative) budget, as the primary measure of the over-all stabilization impact of fiscal policy.[4]

It may reasonably be argued that the high-employment budget guideline would be so amorphous as to have little or no operational importance. Would it not be overidden by hard political realities; for example, would a President be better able than at present to persuade Congress to enact a large tax increase in time of war or major domestic need? There is no guarantee that he would. But public and congressional views do matter, especially those of leading businessmen, labor leaders, and friends and advisers of high administration officials and key congressmen. They do influence the reception that presidential proposals receive; fiscal policymaking *is* a political process, and influence can be exerted through leaders inside and outside Washington.[5]

Whatever its force, a widely shared acceptance of the high-employment budget guideline should increase, not lessen, the chances for wise legislation. The parallel with the old presumption for a balanced administrative budget is illuminating. That presumption significantly colored the reception by Congress of both depression and wartime budget recommendations, though of course it did not produce a continuous actual budget balance. The argument here is that an effort should be made to develop an alternative presumption that will build on the still-strong intuitive case for a balanced budget—one that will facilitate more rational consideration of budgetary policy than did the old balanced budget rule.[6]

4. Implementing a high-employment budget guideline would be less simple than it may appear. It would require estimates of gross national product (GNP) and tax receipts at high employment. More importantly (as will be seen in the following section), it would require Congress early each year to set a rough over-all expenditure total for the year, and tax rates would be set to match it at high employment.

5. The policy influence of those administration and congressional leaders who handle such technical matters as fiscal policy is greater than on many other less technically difficult issues. Most congressmen lack confidence in their own understanding of monetary-fiscal processes and hence depend heavily on their fellows who are thought to be experts. See Aaron B. Wildavsky, *The Politics of the Budgetary Process* (Little, Brown, 1964).

6. Some cynics argue that Congress is fundamentally irresponsible and that most congressmen will do whatever is politically expedient on spending and taxes. Under

2. *The President should routinely propose to Congress early each year a (positive, negative, or zero) proportional income surtax. This should vary from the high-employment budget guideline* when serious inflation or recession threatens. *Congress should establish a routine procedure for promptly considering this surtax proposal, exclusively in light of its stabilization implications for the economy.*

Just as annual balance was not sacrosanct under the old annual budget balance rule, it is neither likely nor desirable that the proposed high-employment budget guideline would be inviolable. Destabilizing fluctuations in private sector plant, equipment, and inventory investment are likely to continue, and international developments may dramatically destabilize private expectations and spending. In *seriously* inflationary periods (for example, in a period like 1967–69), a larger surplus in the high-employment budget would be appropriate; in *seriously* depressed years (as, for example, in 1958), a deficit. The high-employment budget guideline would not guarantee noninflationary prosperity; it would often fall short of the "ideal" budget policy outlined above.

In some years the President and his advisers would see a clear and present danger against which positive fiscal action should be taken. Then the President should propose in his annual Economic Report a one-year positive or negative stabilization surtax based on these expectations and on his proposed federal expenditure budget for the year. The House Ways and Means Committee and the Senate Finance Committee should then promptly and routinely turn to consideration of the *annual surtax proposal only— and solely on the basis of its stabilization impact.* Tax bills involving changes in tax structure would be handled separately through regular congressional procedures. If such an annual routine could be established for acting on the surtax, reasonably prompt consideration each year of the stabilization aspects of fiscal policy could be obtained.[7]

---

this view, the balanced-budget presumption had no real impact on decisions, nor would the high-employment budget guideline proposed here. I read the evidence from history differently, even though there are surely some congressmen who fit the cynics' description.

7. Similar proposals have been advanced by Herbert Stein, "Unemployment, Inflation, and Economic Stability," in Kermit Gordon (ed.), *Agenda for the Nation* (Brookings Institution, 1968), pp. 292–93; Congressman William Moorhead, "Supple-

To act on the surtax proposal, Congress would need to use, implicitly or explicitly, some budget expenditure total. Congress might, of course, have objectives that are different from the President's. It might use the tax legislation in an attempt to force the President to change the expenditure side of the budget, as it did in 1968. But in any case, both Congress and the President would routinely face the need to make an over-all fiscal decision without bogging down in the usual tax controversies.

Emphasis on attaining modest flexibility through an annual income surtax seems more hopeful than focusing the stabilization adjustment on the expenditure side. The surtax could be handled by one committee in each house and would entail one simple, over-all action. By contrast, appropriations are usually fragmented among many subcommittees, and there is no feasible, easy way of allocating fiscal-stability increases or cuts in total spending over the thousands of expenditure categories in the federal budget. Attaining agreement on even an approximate over-all spending total would be difficult enough.[8]

This proposal for more rational consideration by Congress of the over-all impact of the budget on the economy may appear modest indeed. It is. But it moves in the necessary direction. Unless stabilization issues are treated separately from tax reform,

---

mentary Views," in *1969 Joint Economic Report*, Report of the Joint Economic Committee on the January 1969 Economic Report of the President, 91 Cong. 1 sess. (1969), pp. 84–87; and Arthur M. Okun, *The Political Economy of Prosperity* (Brookings Institution, 1970), pp. 120–23. The Committee for Economic Development, originator of the high-employment budget surplus proposal, has recently endorsed the idea of supplementary annual tax rate changes if required by aggregate demand variations (*A Stabilizing Fiscal and Monetary Policy for 1970* [New York, 1969], p. 8).

8. The Legislative Reorganization Act of 1946, with a similar goal, called for a concurrent Senate-House resolution on an expenditure total in advance of actions by the Committee on Appropriations, but the attempt broke down in debate, and no limitation was integrated into the appropriations procedures. Since 1947 this provision of the act has not been given another try. The 1968 surtax controversy, in which Wilbur Mills and other congressional leaders stressed the tying of tax-level decisions to an agreed expenditure ceiling, suggests that movement toward such over-all tax expenditure consideration may be feasible.

There is an additional argument for centering the stabilization adjustment in tax rates. The level of government spending ought to be chosen to balance marginal social products between private and public goods, and that comparison should be made on the assumption of full employment. So the level of total government spending (the public-private allocation of resources) ought to be set independently of stabilization policy decisions.

there is little hope of attaining a more flexible fiscal policy. The annual surtax proposal, or some variation of it, offers a hope.

3. *If the preceding recommendation is rejected, the President should be given limited power to change tax rates for short periods, subject to congressional veto.* Many economists, and Presidents Kennedy and Johnson, frustrated by the apparent inability of Congress to move quickly on fiscal changes, have suggested that the President be given limited discretionary power to change tax rates or exemptions within prescribed limits for, say, six months, subject to congressional veto at any time. Some have suggested that he be given authority to change effective tax rates up or down by 3 to 5 percentage points. Alternatively, he could be given discretionary power to raise or lower, for up to six months, the surtax proposed above. Some, who fear that the power would be used for partisan political purposes, favor granting the President power only to *raise*, not to lower, taxes. Power to *raise* taxes is hardly likely to be an effective means of buying votes in the next election.

If Congress will not act promptly, limited presidential power to change taxes makes economic sense. Modest presidential flexibility on taxes would complement monetary policy in reacting to unexpected disturbances, such as international crises or sudden inventory swings, where action is needed to prevent snowballing effects. Monetary policy is inherently the more flexible short-run stabilization instrument, but international or domestic financial considerations sometimes constrain its use. Existing arrangements allow the President only very limited fiscal power to use against short-run instability, mainly through his ability to vary the rate of authorized expenditures. This proposal would give him more.[9]

9. McGeorge Bundy, a top assistant to both Presidents Kennedy and Johnson, has written (in *The Strength of Government* [Harvard University Press, 1968], pp. 33–37):

"The American system of government is today far too weak to do the job now assigned to it, let alone the job that it ought to be given. . . .

"The simplest demonstration of the weakness of the Executive Branch is its current lack of adequate authority in matters of appropriation and taxation. . . .

"Flexible tax rates are now quite simply indispensable to the effective management of economic policy—and so to strong and stable economic growth. The use of drastic changes in the interest rate as a total substitute is not only disturbing and wasteful in general, but especially destructive to the orderly growth of housing, which in turn is absolutely critical to the struggle against racism and poverty. Our government cannot meet its present responsibilities effectively—it cannot serve the whole economic system, public and private alike—it cannot avoid boom and bust—

These three proposals recognize the political reality of constitutional and historical forces in presidential-congressional relations in fiscal affairs. Congress is an innately inefficient body for short-run operational decisions. It can best make general laws and oversee their administration through its investigative processes. The proposals also recognize the substantial "outside" lags in the impact of fiscal policy. Pragmatically, the intermediate goal in fiscal policy processes should be to emphasize stable long-run growth, with built-in flexibility against shorter fluctuations, plus improved fiscal procedures to provide annual stabilizing tax changes where appropriate. These recommendations leave open the possibility of increased flexibility for the President to vary expenditure rates on programs already approved by Congress. Maintaining a "shelf" of public works projects, to be activated if unemployment rose, was advocated in the 1930s. This approach was unworkably rigid, but a new look at expenditure flexibility for presidential use may offer substantial promise.

Monetary Policy

In acting to meet national economic goals, the Federal Reserve cannot operate directly on aggregate demand, output, employment, and commodity prices. Monetary authorities conduct open market operations and change reserve requirements and discount rates, working through intermediate policy variables—the money stock (M_1), money plus time deposits (M_2), the monetary base, free reserves, interest rates, and money market conditions.

In principle, monetary policymakers should be able to forecast the course of aggregate demand in the absence of policy changes, and should know the lags and the impact of Federal Reserve measures operating through the intermediate policy variables. But the

---

if it cannot change basic tax rates, perhaps up to twenty per cent in either direction, with much greater speed than our system now permits. The Congress is too big and slow and varied to exercise this power on its own. It should therefore delegate that power to someone, and the President is a better agent than any one Congressman, however honorable and able. . . .

"This is a power very much smaller than that which belongs to almost every other English-speaking government in the world, as long as it has a small Parliamentary majority. . . . In tax policy the Executive Branch is not much too strong, as the disbelievers in modern government tell us, but much too weak."

links between ultimate goals, intermediate variables, and Federal Reserve actions are not completely clear; nor is it possible to forecast the economy's performance with a satisfactory degree of accuracy. Despite these uncertainties, in reaching policy decisions the monetary authorities must decide, explicitly or implicitly, which of the intermediate targets are pertinent, the probable effects on ultimate goals, and what lags to assume.

1. *Pending further clarification of the link between money and the "real" economy, the Federal Reserve should operate on the principle that there should be roughly stable growth in the monetary aggregates (the monetary base or the money stock).*

2. *Nonetheless, it should have substantial discretionary authority to adjust monetary policy to particular circumstances, which may require deviations from the stable growth rule.*

The Federal Reserve has substantial (but not complete) power to control the money stock through the monetary base; and empirical evidence shows a reasonably close, though somewhat variable, relationship between growth in the monetary aggregates and money gross national product (GNP). At least in big depressions and big inflations, changes in the monetary base and money (M_1 or M_2) clearly play an important independent causal role, an essential reinforcing role, or both. In lesser fluctuations, the evidence is less clear as to whether changes in M_1 and M_2 are the cause or the effect of changes in aggregate spending. Clearly, other intermediate variables (interest rates, free reserves, and money market conditions) are jointly affected by actions of both monetary policymakers and the private sector of the economy. They are therefore only partly controllable by monetary policymakers. In terms of monetary theory, there may be important shifts in the demand for money, which would be destabilizing in the absence of offsetting actions by the Federal Reserve, and these shifts affect the impact of any action by the Reserve authorities to change the stock of money.

Most economists argue that monetary changes affect aggregate demand through interest rates, yields on, and prices of, other assets, and changes in the availability of credit. This reasoning suggests that interest rates, multiple credit flows, and free reserves of banks are important intermediate variables for policymakers. Other economists suggest that changes in M_1 or M_2 *directly* affect consumer and business spending, though how this effect occurs is not entirely clear. This reasoning suggests that the Federal Reserve should watch primarily the monetary aggregates and focus on stabilizing their growth. Both groups agree that in periods of substantial inflation, quoted market interest rates lose a substantial part of their validity as indicators of monetary tightness, because an uncertain inflation allowance is added to the "real" rate by both borrowers and lenders.[10] Both agree, further, that it will be impossible for the monetary authorities simultaneously to stabilize interest rates *and* the growth rate of M_1 or M_2 if the public's demand for money shifts. And both agree that, while the Federal Reserve can more or less closely control the nominal money stock (M_1 or M_2), it cannot thereby necessarily control *real* output and *real* interest rates. If it issues more money than the public wants to hold at prevailing prices, increased public spending will produce inflation until the *real* purchasing power of the money stock (what economists call "real money") is at the level the public wants to hold.[11]

To choose one intermediate variable (such as stable growth in M_1 or M_2) as the *sole* guide to monetary policy, given these uncertainties, would be irresponsible. Different intermediate variables may be important at different times and under different circumstances; there is no reason to expect simple, one-channel relationships among the economic variables in a complex world. Both monetary history and theory present a strong case for at least reasonably stable growth in the monetary aggregates, roughly parallel to growth in the economy's aggregate production potential, as a protection against massive depressions or inflations. But, since the demand for money may shift for a variety of reasons, the Federal Reserve needs to be prepared to offset such shifts if they threaten to be seriously destabilizing.[12]

10. This reasoning argues against stable growth of M_1 as a policy target as well, because with inflationary expectations the public's demand for money may shift so that aggregate demand would not grow in line with M_1. However, inflation expectations are likely to have a more pronounced effect on market interest rates than on the demand for money per se.

11. A more detailed statement of the (eclectic) money–real economy linkage system generally assumed throughout this book was presented in Chap. 3, pp. 49–54.

12. In monetary theory terms, the case for stable growth of M depends on the presumption that with real growth in output the demand for money will grow roughly apace. Insofar as the demand for money varies with other factors (for ex-

Therefore, pending further theoretical and empirical clarification of monetary policy–real economy linkages, Federal Reserve officials should operate with a strong but rebuttable presumption that the monetary aggregates should be increased at a stable growth rate.[13] But they should also keep a sharp eye on other potentially important target variables and exercise their best judgment on the basis of this continuing analysis. And they should be prepared to let the money growth rate vary, if there is a convincing reason to do so, with the changing conditions.

This policy would not guarantee a stabilizing monetary policy, given the authorities' imperfect forecasting ability and uncertainty as to the lags involved. It would move monetary policy to a more stable base, however, while preserving flexibility for the authorities to act counter to the presumption of stable growth of M in case of clear need.[14]

This flexibility is essential for several reasons: (a) There is no guarantee that fiscal policy miscalculations will not require Federal Reserve counteraction to maintain over-all stability. (b) Even with good fiscal policy, international disturbances may require monetary policy offsets, as may fluctuations in spending on business plant and equipment and inventory spending in the private sector. (c) Shifts may occur in the public's demand for money that would

---

ample, interest rates or sharp changes in payments practices), a stably growing M will not maintain stable growth in spending (aggregate demand).

13. Analytically, either unborrowed reserves or the monetary base seems to me the best target, since they are most directly controlled by the Federal Reserve. But the choice among unborrowed reserves, the monetary base, M_1, and M_2 is not crucial for the rough stability needed, especially if mandatory interest rate ceilings are removed. This statement implies a generally stable relationship between the monetary base and the money stock. This has broadly been true, though there have been substantial variations, reflecting in considerable part public shifts among different liquid assets due to the effects of mandatory interest rate ceilings. Elimination of these ceilings (desirable on other grounds as well) would eliminate most of the potentially misleading differential movements between the two. Careful econometric investigations of these alternative indicators are provided by Edward Gramlich in "The Usefulness of Monetary and Fiscal Policy as Stabilization Tools," and Carl Christ in "Econometric Models of the Financial Sector," both in *Journal of Money, Credit, and Banking* (forthcoming).

14. The case for a more explicit congressional rule to govern Federal Reserve monetary policy (for example, expand the money stock by 4 percent a year) is considered in a later section. But to tie the Federal Reserve's hands completely by such a rule would be shortsighted.

destabilize spending if M were held constant. (d) Conceivably a massive liquidity crisis like that of 1929–33 could develop again, with an enormous increase in the demand for money. In such an event, the Federal Reserve should be free to, and expected to, pour into the economy whatever amount of base money (liquidity) is needed to check the contraction; this is the most important monetary lesson learned from the great depression. And (e) "defensive" Federal Reserve open market operations are often useful in offsetting temporary minor disturbances to the financial markets from Treasury financing, variations in float and international flows of funds, erratic flows in particular domestic credit markets, and the like—although the Reserve authorities have been overly concerned with financial market stability in the past.[15]

The President and Policy Coordination

Today there is wide agreement on the broad national macroeconomic goals indicated in Chapter 2, and that the macroeconomic powers of the government should be used in a coordinated way to attain these goals. Toward this end:

1. *Macroeconomic policies, including monetary policy, should be coordinated through continuing interaction among the major participants in the policy process—the White House, the Council of Economic Advisers, the Treasury, and the Federal Reserve, plus others as special needs arise.*

2. *The Federal Reserve is part of the government, and it should participate actively in these discussions while retaining the partial "independence" specified by Congress.* The stable money point of

15. For a description, see Jack M. Guttentag, "The Strategy of Open Market Operations," *Quarterly Journal of Economics*, Vol. 80 (February 1966), pp. 1–30. While a few economists have asserted that the Federal Open Market Committee (FOMC) could control the money stock precisely on a week-to-week or month-to-month basis, the evidence seems clear that in the short run, both bank reserves and the ratio between bank reserves and M are subject to strong and often unpredictable market forces—changes in float, international transactions, currency flows, and Treasury balances. Thus, even if it tried to do so, the Federal Reserve would have great difficulty in hitting a stable M target precisely. Sherman J. Maisel, a member of the Board, has spelled out these problems in detail. See "Controlling Monetary Aggregates," in *Controlling Monetary Aggregates*, Proceedings of the Monetary Conference Held on Nantucket Island, June 1969 (Federal Reserve Bank of Boston, 1969), pp. 152–74. These factors also explain why short-term fluctuations in M_1 or M_2 may not provide a useful indicator of Federal Reserve policy.

view should have a strong voice in stabilization policymaking. Complete isolation of "independent" Federal Reserve officials from administration policymaking would involve major governmental conflict and divided national economic policy. On the other hand, to merge the Federal Reserve fully into administration policymaking, were the officials to make full use of their independence, would eliminate the desirable partial independence the Reserve authorities now have to exert a drag on undesirable inflationary developments that result from the day-to-day political processes of Congress and the administration. The freedom of the Federal Reserve to differ with administration policy in extreme cases needs to be maintained.

3. *The President, as chief executive and the one official elected by all the people, must bear the central responsibility for executing government macroeconomic policy, while recognizing the important individual policy responsibilities of the various agencies within the government.*

Views may reasonably differ on the best device for bringing about this continuing consultation and coordination among major policymaking agencies. Each President must develop for himself the advisory groups and organization that best suit his style of operation. As a matter of practical government, a mechanism is needed to accomplish three purposes, whether attention is focused only on the monetary-fiscal area or on the entire sweep of the government's macroeconomic policymaking:

a. To assure full information on, and consideration of, the important interagency implications of proposed individual agency policies prior to adoption (for example, the monetary policy implications of a proposed federal deficit, or the monetary and fiscal implications of programs for new housing construction).

b. To facilitate compromise of as many differences among the agencies concerned as is practicable, resulting in informally agreed-on "operational" understandings or programs.

c. To clarify for submission to the President, and perhaps ultimately to Congress, those few major interagency policy conflicts on which no working agreement can be reached.

The President now has adequate power to establish in his executive office the officials and procedures that are needed to achieve these purposes. Some observers have proposed legislative establishment of a special advisory "National Economic Council" in the executive branch, through which the heads of the major economic agencies (including the Federal Reserve) would be required to coordinate their policies and advise the President. But there is wide agreement that the administrative arrangements that work best will vary from one President to another and that little purpose would be served by imposing a rigid format through legislation.[16]

The fruitlessness of overelaborate formal coordinating directives is adequately demonstrated by experience. Coordination is thwarted by the enormous complexity of economic, social, and political issues and interests involved in every major economic policy decision of the government and by the tendency of each participating agency to stand up for its own constituency. In this setting, to attempt to do more than is suggested in the three points above is either to invite a cabinet-level explosion in the executive branch or to encourage bypassing the machinery that has been set up. In the last analysis, cabinet officers and heads of other major agencies like the Federal Reserve generally cannot be ordered to conform to a specific policy by anyone of less authority than the President, and not always by him. Government in a democratic society must work in considerable part on a voluntary basis, in spite of the formal authority the President has over other officials of the executive branch. On the whole, major issues must be compromised voluntarily among the heads of the agencies involved or submitted to the President himself when voluntary compromise is impossible. At the extreme, dismissal of officials in the executive branch or resignation by them or by the chairman of the Federal Reserve Board are a last resort, to be used only in the most extreme cases.[17]

These facts lead some to advocate what would be in effect an

16. Of the twenty-seven high-level participants in macroeconomic policymaking in the federal government over the past two decades who were interviewed for this study, only three indicated support for congressional establishment of a formal, cabinet-level, advisory economic council to the President.

17. Richard E. Neustadt, a distinguished political scientist, writes that, even with his own cabinet officers, and certainly in dealing with members of Congress and to an intermediate extent Federal Reserve officials, a President should seek to persuade them to believe that what he wants them to do is what they would do in any case in their own best interests. But because reasonable men often hold differing views of appropriate public policy, the process of persuading these officials may be more like

"Assistant President for Economic Affairs." Such an individual might take over from the President part of the heavy burden of top-level coordination of complex economic issues.[18] In fact, most presidents have used special assistants in the White House for purposes of this sort, though most such assistants have had less prestige than is implied by the title "Assistant President." Gabriel Hauge under Eisenhower and Arthur Burns under Nixon fulfilled approximately this function. On balance, there seems to be little case for formal statutory establishment of such relationships. Each President must develop them to meet his own administrative style.[19]

Whatever the top-level machinery used by the President, close cooperation among technical staffs of the principal agencies should be assured. Senior staffs of the "troika" members have worked closely together on analysis and forecasting of economic conditions

---

collective bargaining than a reasoned argument. In Neustadt's words, "Persuasion deals in the coin of self-interest with men who have some freedom to reject what they find counterfeit." (*Presidential Power: The Politics of Leadership* [Wiley, 1960], p. 46.) See also the statement by Theodore C. Sorensen on p. 216, below.

18. The parallel to a "minister without portfolio" or "minister of economics" in parliamentary systems may be suggested. But if the analysis is sound for the handling of "economic" questions, could not an equally good case be made for three or four other "assistant presidents" or "ministers without portfolio" in other areas of major importance that cut across agency lines? Extensive use of such administrative arrangements would tend to substitute another layer of high-level officials between the President and his cabinet. Nevertheless, in 1970 President Nixon established a "Domestic Council," including most cabinet members, to advise him on all domestic policy issues. In effect, this council is interposed between the regular government agencies and the President. Strikingly, the chairman of the Council of Economic Advisers was not specified as a member by the President, and many critics predicted that in effect the council would give John Ehrlichman, as chief domestic adviser to President Nixon, supra-cabinet power over domestic economic policies.

19. Walter W. Heller, chief economic adviser to both Presidents Kennedy and Johnson, has summed up the matter well: "Almost four years of service as Council chairman kindled in me no burning desire for changes in the formal organization of economic advice in the Federal government. After a year and a half's perspective on the matter as a nonparticipant, I have not changed my view. . . . This conclusion is not a vote for no change in the economic advisory machinery, but a vote for fluidity. I do not contend that the present arrangements are the best of all worlds. Each President will recast the Council in his own image. He will probably flank it with a 'Troika' . . . or a 'Quadriad' . . . , as both Presidents Kennedy and Johnson have done. Or perhaps he will prefer a quintet or sextet. When special policy situations call for a broader view, a President can turn to a special committee like the Cabinet Committee on Growth that President Kennedy set up in August 1962." (In *New Dimensions of Political Economy* [Harvard University Press, 1966], p. 56.)

for over two decades, but parallel Federal Reserve staff work has sometimes been coordinated, sometimes completely separated. Troika chiefs may want their staffs to keep policy positions confidential, but to bar joint staff work with the Federal Reserve on basic economic analysis seems pointless. This is true especially because modern analysis increasingly merges financial flows (traditionally stressed by the Federal Reserve) with expenditure, employment, and output analysis (stressed primarily by the troika staffs). Modern macroeconomic analysis, with its explicit emphasis on linkages and detailed projections, can provide the soundest foundation for choices among goals and monetary-fiscal policy mixes only if it incorporates the economic and financial approaches developed by the staffs of all four "quadriad" members.

Federal Reserve Independence

The present degree of "independence" from the White House is about right—though the Federal Reserve should become a somewhat more active participant in top-level policymaking.[20]

The issue of Federal Reserve independence is central to the problem of macroeconomic policymaking.[21] Today it is widely agreed that Federal Reserve goals should be part of, and substantially the same as, the goals of over-all national macroeconomic policy. Moreover, the growing interdependence of monetary, fiscal, and debt policies and increasingly high performance standards for the economy require a close working relationship between the Federal Reserve and the other main arms of government economic policy—the Treasury, the Council of Economic Advisers, and the White House. Complete separation of the Federal Reserve from the President and his administration would threaten confusion and conflicts in monetary-fiscal policy. The past half century, encompassing depression, war, and inflation, has demonstrated be-

20. See also the following recommendation that the term of office of the chairman of the Federal Reserve Board should be made roughly coterminous with that of the President.

21. The analysis here is similar to that in my earlier book, *Federal Reserve Policy-Making: A Study in Government Economic Policy Formation* (Knopf, 1950), reporting a study done for the Hoover Commission (the Commission on Organization of the Executive Branch of the Government) shortly after the Second World War.

yond reasonable doubt that no modern central bank can, or should, be completely independent of, or isolated from, the executive branch of the government in times of stress. The nation cannot brook a divided, obstructionist monetary-fiscal policy in crisis periods.

Thus, the old concept of central bank independence, based on a narrow view of central bank responsibilities, has been swept away by the realities of modern, large-scale government financial operations in war and peace, and by recognition that government fiscal and monetary policies are powerful stabilization instruments. Only in periods when general economic conditions are relatively normal is it realistic to conceive of Congress and the administration acquiescing in central bank behavior that threatens the government's macroeconomic policies. Tied into macroeconomic policy as monetary policy is, proposals to keep money and monetary policy "out of politics" and "out of the government" are unrealistic, except in the narrow sense of keeping monetary policy as free as possible from narrowly partisan, day-to-day political pressures. In this sense, there is little ground for distinguishing between monetary policy and other macroeconomic policies. The real problem is how to obtain the most reasoned, deliberative judgment as to optimal policy for achieving the nation's macroeconomic goals.

THE CASE FOR INDEPENDENCE

What, then, is the case for Federal Reserve "independence"?[22] There are two powerful arguments:

First, dispersion of power is fundamental in the U.S. system of government. Control of the nation's money stock is a vital economic function. A partially independent Federal Reserve may contribute to a significant broadening of the total base of macroeconomic decision making in the federal government. The President and his aides have substantial power over other macroeconomic policies. To center more control over macroeconomic policy in the White House would further concentrate power in the hands of the President and his administration. Thus, Congress

22. This analysis rests on the premise that the costs of continuing inflation are substantial and that roughly stable prices are, over extended periods, compatible with high-level employment. The case is argued and the evidence assessed in my *Inflation: A Study in Economics, Ethics, and Politics* (Brown University Press, 1958).

chose to disperse this power by making the Federal Reserve responsible for one significant part of U.S. macroeconomic policy.[23]

Second, history warns that governments tend to err on the side of inflation when war or other factors create strong pressures for government spending. Treasuries frequently turn to money-issue through the banking system to pay their bills when taxes are inadequate. The modern world's major inflations have all come when large government deficits were covered by the issue of new money (currency or bank deposits). Although legislators vote the expenditures, treasuries must pay the bills, and they feel pressed to do so at low interest rates when they must borrow. Thus, heads of government and their treasuries have a predictable inflationary bias, however well-intentioned and generally conservative their treasury secretaries may be. Against this bias, central bankers have tended to hold stability of the monetary unit in higher esteem.

Indeed, the entire American democratic political process has an inflationary bias. It is always easier for Congress to spend money than to raise taxes; some say "politicians" are inherently irresponsible financially. Thus, an independent Federal Reserve is needed to call a halt on the overspending politicians who may respond too readily to demands for jobs and booming prosperity, even though these may generate inflation.

Stated bluntly, this second argument for Federal Reserve independence is that it allows the System to stand against inflation, providing a buffer, or temporary inertial force, against the inflationary bias of U.S. democratic political processes. The Second World War and modern fiscal policy have led to increasing expectations that the government will maintain high employment and good times. Thus, the wage, price, and income expectations of all participants (laborers, businessmen, farmers, citizens) persistently exceed the economy's real productive potential. These pressures for higher wages and prices must be validated by expansionary monetary-fiscal policy if they are not to create recession and unemployment. Elected government officials repeatedly feel compelled to give in to these excess-income claims with inflationary macroeconomic policy in order to avoid recession and unemployment. The need for a strong

---

23. It is important to recognize that giving control over monetary policy to the President would *not* guarantee coordination of monetary and fiscal policy, since the basic control over fiscal policy lies with Congress, not the White House.

"stable money" voice in government macroeconomic councils is perhaps greater now than ever before. At least, a system that ensures a thorough questioning of inflationary government policies is better than one that does not.

INDEPENDENCE FROM WHOM?

Federal Reserve independence *from Congress* makes little sense in the democratic system of government in the United States. Congress established the Federal Reserve. Congress can change it whenever it wishes or call it to account for any of its actions. Federal Reserve officials readily acknowledge their responsibility to Congress. Fortunately, however, Congress has been reluctant to intervene directly in Federal Reserve operations. Nor does the System need to go to Congress for appropriations to conduct its affairs. Thus, in practice, Federal Reserve monetary policy is substantially insulated from day-to-day congressional pressures, although there is no doubt that Congress has ultimate authority to control the System and its policies.

Domination of the Federal Reserve *by the Treasury* has repeatedly brought inflationary monetary policy (as during the 1940s), when the central bank has been called on to help assure low-interest-cost financing of the government debt. The System's independence from the Treasury, as was argued above, rests firmly on the evidence of history.

But this is not an argument for Federal Reserve isolation. The Treasury is a crucial operating branch of the government. The secretary of the treasury is inevitably in close contact with the White House; often he is a personal confidant and adviser of the President. Given these Treasury responsibilities, Federal Reserve officials feel obliged to work closely with the department, especially on debt management issues. Conflict between the Treasury and the Federal Reserve on debt management issues would threaten inefficiency and confusion. Indeed, the times when the Federal Reserve has been least effective have been when the chairman has been most isolated from the President and the Treasury, not the contrary—with the spectacular exception of 1951. The problem is to assure reasonable Federal Reserve participation in fiscal and debt-management decisions, so that it is not faced with the de facto necessity of working with administration and Treasury policies made without its participation.

In principle, the Treasury or some other administration agency like the Council of Economic Advisers could provide the strong stable-money voice needed in government stabilization councils. Indeed, in many nations the central bank is formally subservient to (or part of) the treasury and the government. Such arrangements have advantages. If all monetary-debt policy responsibility were concentrated in the Treasury, "buck passing" would be far more difficult than it is now.

But the counterarguments are stronger. Consolidation of debt and money-creating powers in the Treasury would give the powers to spend and to create money to the same agency. History warns that this would probably lead to too-easy reliance on money creation, to too-easy inflation, and to too little emphasis on sound fiscal and monetary policies when they call for heavier taxation, restricted government expenditures, and deflationary monetary management.

The central issue is should, or can, the Federal Reserve be independent from *the President?* Control over the nation's money supply is a vital governmental operating responsibility. Monetary policy is inextricably intermingled with fiscal policy and with debt management policy. The President must ultimately be responsible for recommending and executing the nation's basic macroeconomic policy. This logic leads clearly to the conclusion that the Federal Reserve must work closely with other agencies under the general responsibility of the President for carrying out national economic policy. To give an independent Federal Reserve the power to negate at will the basic policies of the federal government would be intolerable for any administration, Republican or Democratic. But independence, looked at practically, is a matter of degree. The real question, thus, concerns the *terms* on which the Federal Reserve participates in government policymaking and execution.[24]

24. A direct, radical attack on the monetary-debt policy coordination problem might be made by giving the Federal Reserve direct responsibility for all debt management. Thus, the Treasury would borrow only, or largely, from the Federal Reserve, and the Reserve would have power to raise money by issuing and dealing in its own (government-guaranteed) securities vis-à-vis the banks and the public. This approach would use simply, directly, and visibly the government's (central bank's) power to create money, while reserving open market operations for controlling the level of aggregate demand. It would concentrate responsibility for monetary-debt policy in one agency, so as to minimize simultaneously the danger that debt-management would dominate monetary policy, opportunities for buck-

Role of the Federal Reserve Chairman

To be most effective, the Federal Reserve must be in a position to work closely with the other major government agencies responsible for national economic policy—especially the White House, the Council of Economic Advisers, and the Treasury. As the main spokesman for the System, the chairman of the Federal Reserve Board must be a man respected by the President and one with whom he can work personally. Federal Reserve influence and power have waned with its increasing isolation (independence) from other top government macroeconomic officials. This was substantially the case in the much-discussed decade of the 1940s, when the Federal Reserve was most subservient to Treasury debt management needs. Secretaries Morgenthau and Snyder were close personal confidants of Presidents Roosevelt and Truman; during the 1940s, top Federal Reserve officials seldom saw either President. On the other hand, when Eccles worked closely with Roosevelt, and Martin with the administrations of Eisenhower, Kennedy, and Johnson, Federal Reserve influence was clearly greater than during the 1940s. Making the Federal Reserve completely independent of, and operationally separate from, the administration is likely to produce less, not more, Federal Reserve power. As a practical matter, complete independence is likely to mean splendid isolation from most of the decisions that matter.

The influence of the Federal Reserve for the stable-money point of view can best be assured if the Reserve is an active, continuous participant in the day-to-day processes of government economic policy formation. Cooperation is a two-way street. The Federal Reserve cannot expect to exert strong influence on policy formation unless it plays ball a good share of the time.

To implement this relationship, the term of office of the chair-

---

passing, chances of divided policy, and Treasury–Federal Reserve friction. It would result in a drastic reduction in traditional Treasury powers. One may argue that, given such combined authority, the Federal Reserve would gradually absorb the easy-money bias attributed to the Treasury, but at least it would have to face the loss of monetary restraint directly if it gave in to cheap financing. Clearly the proposal is too radical for serious consideration now, but it merits careful consideration in the event of a major overhaul of our government financial institutions and policies.

man of the Federal Reserve Board should be made roughly coterminous with that of the President.[25] This would give each President power to nominate his own chairman. To insist that a new President accept a Federal Reserve chairman to whom he seriously objects would serve little purpose and would be far more likely to reduce the effectiveness of the Federal Reserve than to increase it. It is significant that both William McChesney Martin, Jr., and Marriner Eccles, the two men who dominated the Federal Reserve for nearly forty years, vigorously support this recommendation.

But this is not to say that the Federal Reserve or its chairman should be, like the Treasury, directly subservient to the President. On the contrary, experience suggests that there is substantial benefit to be had from giving the Federal Reserve a partially independent status in the government. Realistically, this permits the Federal Reserve to serve as a buffer—to resist the pressures of excess-income-claims inflation more easily than can the President himself, Congress, or any of the regular cabinet agencies. The indirect impact of monetary policy, and its partial insulation from direct political pressures, make it a more flexible weapon against inflation than are other macroeconomic controls.

The President has great power, if he chooses to exercise it, over all agencies, including the Federal Reserve. On the other hand, even his power is limited. He does not have control over fiscal policies; this has been tightly held by Congress, on both the tax and the expenditure sides. Congress has been willing to delegate power over monetary policy only under special conditions—to a Board rather than an individual, and to a Board significantly insulated from the day-to-day pressures of partisan politics. This reflects a widespread American distrust of centralized power. Thus Allan Sproul, long-time head of the New York Federal Reserve Bank, has argued against giving the President monetary power on coordination grounds:

If you could get [fiscal policy] out of Congress and put it in the hands of the executive branch [which you can't], you wouldn't have coordination, you would have dictation by the President, directly or indirectly

25. Probably staggered by three to six months or so to avoid the need for a new President to select a new chairman in the hectic early days of his administration.

through some grouping of his subordinates. Nobody in the executive branch coordinates with the President. Occasionally it is desirable to have somebody who can hold a contrary view concerning the means of economic policy without being fired.[26]

The danger that an appropriate degree of independence for the Federal Reserve will be overridden by a President who is displeased with its monetary policies is easy to overstate. There is little doubt that Presidents have exercised informal influence over the so-called "independent agencies" throughout their existence. But here again the power of the President is far from complete. Theodore Sorensen, one of President Kennedy's chief aides, has stressed both the President's power and the limits on that power:

> Whenever any President overrules any Secretary, he runs the risk of that Secretary grumbling, privately, if not publicly, to the Congress or to the press (or to his diary), or dragging his feet on implementation, or, at the very worst, resigning with a blast at the President. It is rare, of course, for any appointee leaving office to have more public appeal than a President in office. The whirlpools he expects to stir up with his dramatic resignation and public exposés are soon lost in a tide of other events over which the President continues to ride.
>
> Nevertheless, the violent resignation of almost any Secretary of State, Secretary of Defense, or Secretary of the Treasury could cause his chief considerable trouble; and other appointees could cause trouble in their own circles. . . . Truman did not want his position on a steel settlement undermined by a public protest or resignation from Secretary of Commerce Sawyer. . . . Roosevelt could not afford politically to alienate Cordell Hull to the point of resignation. . . .[27]

Even in appointing a Federal Reserve chairman, no President is likely to exercise his power lightly. It was rumored, for example, that Presidents Kennedy and Johnson both would have liked to appoint replacements for William McChesney Martin, Jr., but Martin's high standing in domestic and international financial and business circles made this infeasible, as a practical matter. On balance, the Federal Reserve needs more independence from the Treasury than it has often had in the past (for example, during the bond-pegging period of the 1940s), but probably somewhat

26. Allan Sproul, "Coordination of Economic Policy," *Journal of Finance*, Vol. 22 (May 1967), p. 145.

27. Theodore C. Sorensen, *Decision-Making in the White House: The Olive Branch or the Arrows* (Columbia University Press, 1963), pp. 80–81.

less independence (isolation) from the presidency and basic governmental macroeconomic policymaking.[28]

Congress and the Federal Reserve

Congress's primary role in monetary policymaking should be to specify goals and general rules for the operating agencies—not to prescribe a rigid rule or detailed operating procedures.

A bicameral legislative body of 535 members, with widely diverse interests and backgrounds, and representing fifty different states, is inherently incapable of directing in detail intricate monetary policy operations like those often involved in combating private-sector or international disruptions. This conclusion rests firmly on the repeated lessons of history. Having passed governing legislation, Congress's further role properly lies in investigative surveillance of the Federal Reserve and the other agencies executing monetary policy, not in active intervention in the administrative process.

Congress has wisely chosen to delegate operating monetary stabilization responsibilities in large part to the Federal Reserve, specifying only broad goals—mainly through the Federal Reserve Act and the Employment Act of 1946. More congressional intervention in day-to-day Federal Reserve operations is not needed, nor would it be productive. Such intervention is more likely to impede than to improve the effectiveness of the Federal Reserve in carrying out the duties assigned it by Congress. Congress exerts many (often conflicting) pressures on the System in connection with individual issues, through committee hearings and other public criticism. With these powers and the always-present threat of new legislation, Congress already exercises substantial influence over the short-run operations of the Federal Reserve. It does not need more.

28. The proper degree of independence for the so-called "independent agencies" has long been a subject of dispute. Samuel Krislov and L. D. Musolf (eds.), *The Politics of Regulation: A Reader* (Houghton Mifflin, 1964), especially the papers by Musolf, R. W. Lishman, and Joe L. Evins, provides a useful survey of the issues, with historical examples. See also the perceptive analysis by Emmette Redford in "The President and the Regulatory Commissions," *Texas Law Review*, Vol. 44 (1964), pp. 288–312.

Two changes in existing congressional directives to the monetary authorities might be considered, though neither seems vital now.

1. The Employment Act of 1946 might be clarified to include specifically price level stability as one major macroeconomic policy goal. There is already widespread agreement that reasonable stability in the price level is implied in the present act, and this interpretation has been stressed repeatedly by the President and the heads of all the principal agencies concerned. However, it is possible to imagine policy dilemmas in which a clear statement by Congress of the price stability goal would reduce the danger that inflation will increasingly be accepted as a way of economic life, given pressures to assure continuing high employment. A major argument against this proposal is the danger that if congressional consideration of the long-standing language of the act were reopened, bitter controversy could result, which might in the end weaken rather than strengthen the act.

2. The argument that Congress should impose a rigid money-growth rule on the Federal Reserve has been rejected above. However, a weaker congressional directive in the same spirit merits serious consideration. As was noted in Chapter 6, the Joint Economic Committee of Congress, led by Senator William Proxmire and Representative Henry Reuss, has suggested that the annual growth rate in M_1 be maintained at between 2 and 6 percent (sometimes the committee has mentioned between 3 and 5 percent) a year, unless there are clear reasons to the contrary. If the Federal Reserve let the growth rate vary beyond these limits, it would be required to report promptly its reasons for the exception.[29]

29. *Standards for Guiding Monetary Action*, Report of the Joint Economic Committee, 90 Cong. 2 sess. (1968), and *1968 Joint Economic Report*, Report of the Joint Economic Committee on the January 1968 Economic Report of the President, 90 Cong. 2 sess. (1968), pp. 16–17. Representative Reuss appended a list of seven exceptions that would justify deviation from the 3–5 percent range, including shifts of deposits between classes, the existence of cost-push inflation or unemployment, and an excessive restriction of housing construction. Many advocates of the rule feel that such extensive exceptions would emasculate it.

House and Senate committee questioning of Federal Reserve officials on this issue suggests that at heart many congressmen would want instead a rule requiring the central bank to maintain interest rates at a constant, *low* level. The populist tradition still exists in Congress; Representative Wright Patman is perhaps its most ardent spokesman. But the inflationary dangers implicit in such a low-interest rule

Relatively stable growth in such monetary aggregates as the monetary base and the money stock is an important foundation for stable economic growth. However, until the linkages between money and output, employment, and prices in the real economy are more clearly understood, rigid prescription of stable growth in the money stock as *the* rule for Federal Reserve policy is unjustified. While M_1 is clearly important to stable growth, so apparently are interest rates and a variety of other credit flows in different situations. Holding M_1 to a stable growth path might involve wide swings in the cost and availability of credit in some markets if the demands for credit varied; these in turn could destabilize real output, employment, and prices. As was noted above, short-term money market disruptions due to international transfers, temporary currency drains, shifts among classes of deposits, and the like, may call for "defensive" open market operations to prevent them from triggering further disruption.

Moreover, advocates of the *M*-rule seem unable to agree on what definition of money should be used in policymaking—M_1, M_2, or some related magnitude. While choice among these is not crucial to the argument for *rough* stability in the growth of monetary aggregates, specification of a rigorous rule would require choice; and different monetary aggregates do diverge substantially over long periods, especially when savers shift funds among financial intermediaries and classes of deposits.[30] These issues have already been considered.

But while a rigid monetary rule would be unwise, an experimental congressional resolution (by Congress as a whole or by the appropriate committees) that the Federal Reserve should consider stable growth in the money stock as *one* presumptive guide in policymaking, along the lines of the Joint Economic Committee resolution, has much to recommend it. This would permit Federal Reserve authorities discretion to vary *M* outside the suggested range and would properly call for thorough reporting by the Federal Reserve as to the considerations underlying its actions.

---

for non-depression periods is widely recognized, and it receives no appreciable support among either high government monetary officials or economists.

30. Monetarists properly answer that differences between M_1 and M_2 for this purpose would be much smaller if all mandatory interest rate ceilings on deposits for banks and savings and loan associations were removed.

Whether or not such a resolution is adopted, continued congressional pressure on the Reserve authorities to explain their actions is appropriate. Traditionally the Federal Reserve has been cryptic in presenting the reasons for its actions. For years only a brief paragraph was released about each major open market decision, and this was in the Federal Reserve Board's *Annual Report,* issued several months after the end of the year. It is understandable that congressmen, sometimes plaintively, pressed high Federal Reserve officials to explain which variables were really the important ones for current decisions and their implementation. In recent years, these reports have become much more detailed, and they are now released approximately three months after each meeting of the FOMC—though critical congressmen still complain that they are often not very informative about the analysis underlying what is being done.[31]

31. For an extensive analysis of the issues involved, see *Compendium on Monetary Policy Guidelines and Federal Reserve Structure,* Pursuant to H.R. 11, Subcommittee on Domestic Finance of the House Committee on Banking and Currency, 90 Cong. 2 sess. (1968), especially the Federal Reserve, Treasury, and Council of Economic Advisers' statements. The following FOMC directive of May 27, 1969 (to the New York Federal Reserve Bank) is typical of recent published directives:

"The information reviewed at this meeting suggests that expansion in real economic activity is continuing to moderate slightly, but that substantial upward pressures on prices and costs are persisting. Interest rates have risen in recent weeks. Bank credit and the money supply appear to be changing little on average in May after bulging in April. The outstanding volume of large-denomination CD's has continued to decline, and the available evidence suggests only modest recovery in other time and savings deposits at banks and in savings balances at nonbank thrift institutions following the outflows of the first half of April. The U.S. balance of payments on the liquidity basis was in sizable deficit in the first 4 months of 1969 but the balance on the official settlements basis remained in surplus as a result of large inflows of Euro-dollars. However, there were substantial outflows of funds from the United States in the first half of May, during the period of intense speculation on a revaluation of the German mark, and the payments balance was in very large deficit on both bases. In light of the foregoing developments, it is the policy of the Federal Open Market Committee to foster financial conditions conducive to the reduction of inflationary pressures, with a view to encouraging a more sustainable rate of economic growth and attaining reasonable equilibrium in the country's balance of payments.

"To implement this policy, System open market operations until the next meeting of the Committee shall be conducted with a view to maintaining the prevailing pressure on money and short-term credit markets; provided, however, that operations shall be modified if bank credit appears to be deviating significantly from current projections.

"Votes for this action: Messrs. Martin, Hayes, Bopp, Brimmer, Clay, Coldwell, Daane, Maisel, Mitchell, Robertson, Scanlon, and Sherrill. Votes against this action: None." (*Federal Reserve Bulletin,* Vol. 55 [September 1969], pp. 733–34.)

Most recently, beginning in 1969, the Board has agreed to provide the Joint Economic Committee with a regular quarterly analysis of all major monetary and financial developments of the preceding calendar quarter. To fulfill this commitment, the Board releases to Congress quarterly substantially the staff reports that are prepared for FOMC meetings, which cover in detail the developments of the recent past and their implications for financial and monetary variables.

Representative Patman and others, however, contend that this is not enough—that the Board should also report its plans for the coming quarter. This demand has received little support, and properly so. Regular statements of prospective policy would involve major risks and costs.[32] As long as monetary policy responds flexibly to changing conditions, the monetary authorities should not and cannot commit themselves to *specific* policy actions beyond the very near future. It could be seriously misleading to the public for the central bank to present, at the beginning of a quarter, a detailed prospectus of future actions, when in fact the policies adopted would depend on developments during that quarter. Moreover, such statements by the Federal Reserve could generate large anticipatory swings in financial markets, which might well come to be more strongly influenced by the System's quarterly advance statements than by its actual operations.

What academic economists and congressmen search for in vain is a clear analytical statement or model of the monetary variables underlying Federal Reserve decisions and their relationships to employment, output, and prices. While the Federal Reserve has moved toward more analytical foundations for its policy decisions, it still (understandably) operates on a judgmental basis, using some formal economic analysis and a mass of information on actual economic and monetary developments. It reports honestly what it does. But critics can usefully push the authorities further toward careful analytical foundations for their decisions.

Such pressures would surely do more good than harm, since the need to justify decisions openly would help force the monetary authorities to clarify their own analysis. Fundamentally, this must depend on further basic research on money and its place in the

32. Unless a simple rule (for example, increase M by 4 percent a year) were adopted, in which case the issue of disclosing Federal Reserve plans would not arise.

modern economy (which the Board has recently begun to support generously), as well as on the wisdom Federal Reserve officials show in using the available knowledge.

3. Some congressmen and academic economists have urged that Congress direct the President to specify in his annual Economic Report the monetary policies that would be consistent with his economic program for the coming year—and that Congress require the Federal Reserve to follow this policy directive, or explain to Congress why it did not do so. This, it is argued, would guarantee coordination between Federal Reserve monetary policy and other macroeconomic policies of the administration.

However, such a congressional directive would be unwise. For the President to specify in detail each January what monetary policy should be followed for the year ahead would be shortsighted. The President and his Council of Economic Advisers already make clear in their annual Economic Reports the general implications of their program for monetary policy. Detailed specifications for monetary action over a year ahead would add little. Despite the progress that has been made in economic forecasting, projections are still often wide of the mark. Moreover, actual fiscal policy often turns out to be different from that anticipated when the budget is submitted in January. The inherent flexibility of monetary policy is an advantage in such cases. It can be used to probe new situations—to make adjustments to compensate for unanticipated fiscal, financial, or general economic developments. To tie the monetary authorities to a policy specified in detail a year in advance would limit the potential usefulness of monetary policy for short-run adjustments rather than coordinate monetary policy with the fiscal and other macroeconomic policies of the administration.[33]

Debt Management

Economic stabilization goals should override Treasury financing wishes; debt management policy should be subsidiary to (Federal

33. This opposition to such a congressional directive has consistently been supported not only by Federal Reserve authorities but also by the President, the Council of Economic Advisers, and the Treasury. See, for example, the Federal Reserve, Treasury, and CEA Replies in *Compendium on Monetary Policy Guidelines and Federal Reserve Structure*, House Committee on Banking and Currency, pp. 29–31, 56–57, and 70–72, respectively.

Reserve) monetary policy. But maintaining "orderly" financial markets is a proper subsidiary goal for both monetary and debt policymakers. Coordination of monetary and debt policy should be part of the coordinating process described above.

Debt management is at best a minor stabilization instrument. The Treasury (on new and refunding issues) and the Federal Reserve (through open market operations) can influence the term structure of interest rates, but given the huge volume of other debt in the economy, this effect is usually small and temporary.

Nonetheless, most major differences between the Federal Reserve and the Treasury have centered on the interest rates to be paid on new and refunding issues. Understandably, the Treasury hopes to minimize interest costs, while the Federal Reserve aims more broadly at stabilizing the economy. Debt management, by law and tradition, is primarily a Treasury responsibility. But assistance from the Federal Reserve has been crucial on two fronts. First, when the Treasury wants to borrow from the banks, Federal Reserve action is often needed to provide the necessary bank reserves. Second, even when no net borrowing is involved, Federal Reserve intervention (even keeling) may be helpful in providing stability for the Treasury issues against temporary money market disturbances. But the monetary authorities need to use great caution in undertaking even keeling operations, lest a series of short-term even keeling actions in essence dictate the longer-run course of monetary policy, as they have in the past.

Beyond these general recommendations, four important changes are needed in debt management practice.

1. *Interest rate ceilings on all forms of Treasury debt should be removed; given the funds to be raised, mandatory rate ceilings do little to restrain inflation and often force the Treasury into inefficient and more expensive financing practices to avoid the ceilings.* When market rates go substantially above the 4¼ percent ceiling on long-term Treasury bonds, the ceiling forces the Treasury to use short-term debt exclusively, possibly contrary to stabilization needs and involving a higher total interest cost than would occur without the ceiling.

2. *Congress should repeal the formal ceiling on the size of the national debt.* The level of the debt is determined basically by congressional tax and spending decisions, and the Treasury has no choice but to borrow to finance any deficit. Although annual con-

gressional "temporary" exceptions to the "permanent" debt ceiling allow Congress to exert some pressure against administration spending proposals, mainly they represent political record-making. More important, the ceiling sometimes disrupts orderly management of the debt, causes long delays in congressional action on appropriations, and has driven the administration to subterfuges like "agency issues," which are technically outside the budget.

3. *All direct and guaranteed U.S. government financing, plus possibly direct financing by government agencies,[34] should be centered in the Treasury, instead of allocated among numerous agencies by programmed legislation; or a new "national credit bank" should be established to concentrate all agency borrowing as one responsibility.* This would facilitate the coordination of agency financing with Treasury–Federal Reserve debt policy and would lower the effective interest cost to the government. Special agency issues of U.S.-guaranteed securities typically pay interest rates that are higher than those paid on comparable direct Treasury issues. This reflects partly the fact that they are not direct U.S. obligations, partly the small size of some of the issues, and partly a market that is usually less perfect than for U.S. Treasury obligations.

Insofar as special federal lending or guaranty programs are intended to provide federal subsidies for certain activities, there is a strong presumptive case for making the subsidy visible in the budget process. In principle, there is much to be said for the use of specific annual federal appropriations for any subsidies involved. This might, of course, be accomplished through the use of semipublic, semiprivate agencies like the Government National Mortgage Association (GNMA) in the housing field, with specific congressional appropriation of housing subsidies if they are desired —or by special subsidies through such agencies as the Federal Home Loan Bank Board (FHLBB).

4. *As was recommended above, the Federal Reserve should*

34. Debt issue by government "agencies" raises difficult problems. Insofar as the agencies are outside the regular budget mainly to circumvent the congressional debt ceiling or to avoid the appearance of swelling the federal budget, there is little economic reason for financing their debt outside the Treasury and generally thereby paying higher rates on it. Insofar as the agencies (like the Federal National Mortgage Association [FNMA]) are spun off into a quasi-private status, the case for independent financing is strengthened. Even in such cases, however, agencies should be required to obtain Treasury Department approval on interest rates.

reduce the emphasis previously placed on even keeling the market for new and refunding Treasury issues. In general, such issues should be expected to meet the test of the market. The Federal Reserve should be expected to support the market only in cases of major unforeseen difficulties, and then only temporarily.

Coordination: Credit and Financial Supervisory Agencies

In addition to monetary and fiscal policy, the government's macroeconomic arsenal includes two less important weapons—supervision of financial institutions and federal credit policy. Policy improvement is needed in both areas.

Government supervision of financial institutions is of long standing. However, what the objectives of such supervision should be, and how regulatory practices should be used and coordinated to achieve the objectives, are still unsettled questions. During the past decade, growing emphasis on the use of aggregate demand policy to attain national output, employment, growth, and price level goals has indirectly thrust financial regulatory policies back into the limelight.

As was noted in Chapters 6 and 7, tight money since 1965 has hit savings and loan associations especially hard, and through them home construction. Federal Reserve authorities have used Regulation Q to hold commercial banks' interest rates on time deposits below those paid by S&Ls on comparable deposits. The FHLBB placed slightly higher ceiling rate limits on S&Ls to prevent their engaging in "unsound" competition for funds that would endanger their basic liquidity, given the large, low-interest mortgage portfolios on which they rely for most of their income. As market rates on Treasury bills, commercial paper, and Eurodollars rose above the ceiling interest rates on deposits, savers diverted their funds to those higher-yielding assets, and construction funds became very scarce despite a widely acknowledged need for dramatic increases in home construction. These credit flows away from both S&Ls and banks then forced the Federal Reserve to raise ceiling rates payable by banks on large time certificates of deposit (CDs) to permit banks to compete for funds against the open market and Eurodollar markets. Large banks themselves developed new means of paying high rates to attract funds not subject to Federal Reserve regulations (through sales of notes and commercial paper, establishment of one-bank holding companies, and Eurodollars), to which the Reserve authorities gradually responded with new regulations. One major result was to limit interest rates paid to small savers, since bank and S&L deposits are one of only a few investment alternatives available to them, while large savers were free to obtain higher rates on less closely regulated assets.

At the same time, other special measures were devised to channel funds into the housing industry. Congress voted some direct subsidies. The FHLBB provided more reserves and eased reserve requirements on the S&Ls. FNMA, GNMA, and the FHLBB all borrowed in the open market and used the funds to finance construction loans. Congressmen and other savings and loan supporters urged that the Federal Reserve channel more funds toward construction by holding down ceiling rates on commercial bank deposits, while bankers pleaded for more freedom to compete for savers' funds. Pressures developed to require pension funds and other large institutional investors to channel some fixed percentage of their new funds into mortgages.

This proliferation of direct intervention in credit markets reflects the efforts of those hit by tight money to escape its impact. Deposit rate ceilings, technically a part of supervisory policy, have become an active tool of monetary policy and of attempts to channel credit flows away from market paths. These issues, as well as the more traditional questions of supervisory and of federal credit policy, must be viewed as they pertain to aggregate demand policy.

SUPERVISION OF PRIVATE FINANCIAL INSTITUTIONS[35]

1. *Interest rate ceilings on bank and savings and loan association deposits should be eliminated or placed on a standby basis.*

The prohibition of interest on demand deposits, imposed in 1933, was intended to reduce competition for deposits among com-

---

35. For more detailed analyses, see Commission on Money and Credit, *Money and Credit: Their Influence on Jobs, Prices and Growth* (Prentice-Hall, 1961), Chap. 6; *Report of the Committee on Financial Institutions to the President of the United States* (1963); and G. L. Bach, *Federal Reserve Policy-Making: A Study in Government Economic Policy Formation* (Knopf, 1950), Chap. 15.

mercial banks and thereby to relieve pressures for increased earnings, which might lead to imprudent loans and investments. But the insurance of bank deposits through the Federal Deposit Insurance Corporation (FDIC), plus improved supervisory and central bank liquidity arrangements, have greatly lessened the danger that was stressed in 1933.[36] More recently, as was indicated above, the financial supervisory authorities have applied interest rate ceilings that vary among classes of time deposits and institutions in order to control to some extent the direction and size of savings flows into different financial institutions, and thus indirectly into different forms of real investment.

But federal government controls over the direction of private savings flows have a dubious record in promoting the public welfare. Holding down interest rates in particular markets does little to check inflation; it merely redirects the flow of funds. Moreover, the allocative effects of rate ceilings are apt to be limited, temporary, inequitable, and inefficient, judged by usual market standards. Capital is highly fluid. If market preferences differ substantially from supervisory preferences, private investors will shift funds among financial institutions and open market securities to take advantage of changing yield differentials. For example, during 1967–69 large city banks circumvented Regulation Q as their rate-controlled CDs matured by buying Eurodollars, issuing direct promissory notes, and selling participation certificates in their loan portfolios at rates higher than the Regulation Q ceilings.

While adaptable capital markets make it possible for large savers and investors to avoid much of the intended impact of regulation, small savers often find it impossible to do so. They have few alternatives to putting their savings into savings and loan associations or banks. Limited funds and information make the risky stock market of little use to them. Government savings bonds pay no higher interest rates than do regulated time deposits. High-interest investments like Eurodollars, commercial paper, and even U.S. Treasury bills are out of the reach of the small saver. Thus, deposit rate ceilings have discriminated against the small saver, the small bank, and the housing market, even though their allocative effect has been less than is sometimes claimed. These have been

36. With tight money, banks have increasingly circumvented this regulation by providing related services (for example, check handling) at below cost for business customers.

the costs of attempts by the authorities to protect the solvency of the S&Ls and to regulate the flow of credit through rate ceilings. Few S&Ls have failed, but the costs of preventing their insolvency have been substantial.

Moreover, direct controls like rate ceilings beget further controls. Real and imagined inequities between unregulated and regulated businesses and households produce pressures to add new regulations that close loopholes and relieve inequities. The recourse to Eurodollars and the use of offshore branches by large commercial banks soon led the Federal Reserve to impose new differential reserve requirements on Eurodollars. Smaller city and country banks complained that they could not compete effectively for time deposits with S&Ls and for CD funds with lower rate ceilings than those allowed on large CDs at large banks. The large banks in turn argued for higher CD rate ceilings to compete more effectively with open market paper and overseas rates. The government authorities were kept busy plugging holes in the regulatory dike and remedying inequities.

Finally, differential deposit rate ceilings have tended to reduce the usefulness of both interest rate and money stock indicators for monetary policymakers. With a zero interest rate ceiling on demand deposits but positive and varying rate ceilings on time deposits and S&L shares, savers switch funds back and forth between the two classes of deposits and institutions as the spreads and saver preferences vary. Thus the rate of growth of the money stock (currency and demand deposits) reflects erratic shifts among classes of deposits and institutions rather than solely the effects of Federal Reserve policy. Since the reserve requirements behind demand and time deposits differ, shifting deposits between the two categories directly affects the reserve and lending position of banks. Moreover, the dispersion of power to set ceilings raises important problems of coordination among the financial supervisory agencies. A variety of considerations support the presumption that price fixing usually leads to an inefficient allocation of resources in the case of interest rate ceilings on bank deposits, as elsewhere.

Tight money must restrain someone's spending if it is to have its desired effect. Housing advocates argue that residential construction—of which we as a nation want more—should not bear the brunt of restraint. They argue that the special burden on housing reflects primarily the peculiar structure of financial markets, in which savings and loan associations lose savings as interest rates rise rapidly elsewhere in the economy. Thus, special steps should be devised to diminish the pressure on housing. During the 1960s, the monetary and financial authorities were clearly impressed by these arguments, with the consequences described above.

A reform of financial institutions to diffuse more widely the impact of tight money could indeed moderate its effects on home construction, as could direct aids to housing. But the latter would weaken the bite of monetary policy. Whether the nation prefers restriction in one area or in another is an issue that should be decided whenever economic restraint is needed.[37] But diverting the restraint from the housing industry would merely mean that it must fall more heavily somewhere else. It is by no means clear that during the 1960s the elaborate set of interest rate ceilings on deposits and related financial controls either helped to avoid inflation, held down interest rates on the average, or aided the housing industry. On the contrary, under the circumstances rate ceilings on small deposits probably reduced on balance the flow of savings into housing and held down interest returns available to small savers relative to large ones. Well-meaning efforts do not always achieve their desired effects.

The removal of deposit rate ceilings should be handled with care. Large city banks, given reasonable notice, can usually be counted on to adjust flexibly to probable changes in rates on large certificates of deposit, Eurodollars, and market instruments. But the removal of deposit rate ceilings at small banks and savings and loan associations could cause considerable disruption in a tight money period like the present. One result would surely be a rise in commercial bank time deposit interest rates. But competitive rates on S&L shares would probably rise less; S&Ls invest mainly in mortgages, and they hold large portfolios made at lower rates over the past decade or more. Their income would generally be insuffi-

37. It is important to recognize that if monetary restraint had proportionately equal impact on all sectors of the economy, it would not necessarily be optimal on grounds of either equity or efficiency.

cient to support large increases in the interest rate offered to savers. The result would almost surely be substantial shifts of funds to commercial banks.

Since S&Ls are a major source of mortgage money for home construction, their loss of funds would further depress the already depressed housing industry, even though some of the newly acquired bank time deposits might be channeled into mortgages. This situation suggests that rate ceilings should not be removed until market rates are back more nearly in line with the controlled rates, which are now clearly below free-market levels. It also stresses the urgency of broadening the lending activities of S&Ls. With or without rate ceilings, they are now potentially unstable; their liabilities are basically short-term deposits (in practice withdrawable on demand), while their assets are concentrated in long-term illiquid mortgages that often earn less than the interest rates that must be paid to hold deposits. This reform is needed quite aside from the ceiling interest rate problem. With greater diversification, S&Ls would be more like banks, presumably subject to similar supervision, and safely left to compete more freely for savers' funds.

2. *Federal supervision of banks, S&Ls, and mutual savings banks should be rationalized by reducing the present dispersion of responsibility and authority.*

At present, bank supervisory authority in the United States is divided among three federal agencies (the Federal Reserve, the FDIC, and the comptroller of the currency) and fifty state supervisory authorities. In addition, supervisory authority over S&Ls is divided between the FHLBB at the federal level and individual state authorities. Mutual savings banks have still other supervisors.

This overlapping set of responsibilities is an historical accident, the product of almost a half century during which no thorough overhaul of bank supervisory arrangements has occurred, despite a drastic change in the national monetary and banking system. A longstanding "states' rights" tradition has blocked rationalization of the system under federal supervision. Ideally, all commercial banks should be subjected to uniform federal regulation, with related supervision for other bank-type financial institutions. The creation of money, which is neither a state nor a regional industry, is what is at stake in modern bank supervision. At a minimum, all federally insured banks should be subject to Federal Reserve requirements, even though other aspects of federal and state bank supervision are kept separate. At the federal level, certainly supervision of commercial banks should be centralized in one agency—the Federal Reserve, the FDIC, or a new federal bank supervisory agency, but preferably the Federal Reserve.

History supports this conclusion. Chapter 4 outlined the policy differences among bank supervisory agencies in the 1930s, which partially thwarted the expansionary thrust of monetary policy. As late as the mid-1960s and again in 1969, there were substantial policy differences among the federal bank supervisory agencies and the FHLBB. The Financial Institutions Supervisory Act of 1966 requires consultation among all relevant federal regulatory agencies before deposit rate ceilings are changed, and regular consultation now takes place through the semimonthly meetings of the informal coordinating committee mentioned previously. But this is a purely consultative relationship, and the 1966 changes did not deal with the federal-state division of authority and responsibility.

Moreover, coordinated supervision of banks and lending agencies is likely to become more important in the future. First, specialized lending institutions like the S&Ls will diversify further, blurring the distinction between them and banks.[38] Second, as the United States moves toward the "checkless society" through the use of computer-based credit transactions, the problems of monetary policy are likely to become more closely linked to the supervisory process. For example, with a highly efficient payments mechanism, businesses and individuals will need to hold only very small demand deposit balances; time deposits and other interest-yielding assets will grow in importance as quasi-money (liquidity balances). Just how this development will affect the problem of using monetary policy for economic stabilization is not yet clear, but increased concern with quasi-money liquid assets in connection with stabilization policy seems probable.

While the arguments against consolidating supervisory authority in one federal agency are seldom stated so bluntly, in substance they amount to the following:

a. The present system, while overlapping and cumbersome,

38. Representative Henry Reuss suggests that we may soon have a new kind of financial institution, the "swank"—a combination of the savings and loan association and the bank.

works pretty well and seldom produces open clashes. So why upset it?

b. The issue is a political hot potato. While states' rights are not actually involved in a reorganization of federal supervision, any change will be viewed with suspicion by ardent states' rights advocates, who will perceive an impending encroachment on state chartering and supervision.

c. Most bankers like the present system. It inhibits the exercise of vigorous supervisory restraint by any one agency, since the regulated banks always have the option of moving to another agency's jurisdiction. Moreover, each agency views itself to an important extent as an advocate and protector of its own constituency on legislative and administrative matters.

d. Numerous checks and balances are needed in the federal government's bank-supervisory structure to prevent too much concentration of power in any one agency.

Close examination reveals little substance in these arguments, except the very important consideration of political expediency. First, while the present system works reasonably well in "normal" periods, it is inefficient even then. More important, difficulties in obtaining policy uniformity in "normal" times presage indecision and confusion in the event of another financial crisis. Second, the existence of three federal bank supervisory agencies, each of which views itself to a marked extent as protector of its banks and vies for the favor of commercial banks, can hardly be defended. Third, while checks and balances in government are commendable, the same legislative-judicial-administrative checks and balances work in bank supervision as in any other government activity. What the present supervisory structure provides is diffusion of responsibility *within* the executive branch. Few would advocate three (or fifty-three) separate Securities and Exchange Commissions, with corporations free to select the one they prefer to be regulated by. The very purpose of supervision is undermined by potential competition in laxity among the overlapping authorities.

That supervisory authority be unified is more important than the choice of agency in which that authority is lodged. A strong case can be made for the Federal Reserve System, particularly if deposit rate ceilings and/or bank supervision are to be used as significant monetary policy tools. It would be inexcusable to maintain competing monetary authorities, one having general monetary control and others control over rate ceilings. Some observers argue that the Federal Reserve is already busy with its primary monetary responsibilities, and many question the wisdom of adding over-all bank supervisory responsibility. It is important to remember that most supervisory activity involves examinations, consideration of applications for new charters, mergers, establishment of branches, and the like—matters only remotely connected with current monetary policy. But all things considered, concentrating supervisory responsibility in the Federal Reserve makes the most sense.

The case for the FDIC is that it already is responsible for supervising all insured banks (national and state), and bank supervision could be its chief operating responsibility. But as an insurance agency it would appear an improper locus for monetary policy decisions on rate ceilings, if they are maintained as policy instruments.

Alternatively, a new federal bank supervisory agency might be established to exercise all federal bank supervisory functions. The Federal Reserve could retain responsibility for monetary policy and the FDIC its insurance responsibilities. But the problem of coordination between supervisory and monetary policy agencies would then remain. Any one of the three alternatives would be superior to the present dispersion of regulatory authority and would lessen the likelihood of future federal agency conflicts and supervisory problems.

All these proposals leave savings and loan associations and mutual savings banks under separate supervision. While there is a continuous spectrum of financial institutions in terms of the "moneyness" of their liabilities, commercial bank demand deposits do not differ significantly from funds held at S&Ls and other financial intermediaries. Existing consultation between the bank and S&L supervisory agencies works reasonably well; in case of major differences, the FHLBB recognizes the ultimate strength of the Federal Reserve resulting from its ability to create and extinguish reserves for the banking system, a power that the FHLBB does not have. Most important, Congress has given the FHLBB particular responsibilities for encouraging and stabilizing the flow of funds into housing that would be inappropriate for a general monetary authority. Moreover, the long history of separate regulatory agencies for banks and other intermediaries means that there would be a major political battle if a change were proposed.

3. *To safeguard against financial crises like that of 1929–33, the Federal Reserve's power to provide liquidity for banks and other financial institutions with basically sound assets in the event of financial crisis should be converted to permanent legislation.* Some liquidity can be provided by other government lending and supervisory agencies, like the Farm Credit Administration and the FHLBB, but only the Federal Reserve has substantially unlimited power to provide new bank reserves and general liquidity by acquiring otherwise illiquid assets in times of impending crisis. The Financial Institutions Supervisory Act of 1966 clarified the central bank's legal right to acquire obligations of other government agencies (especially the FHLBB), so it now clearly can serve as a lender of last resort beyond the commercial banking system. But the power is given only temporarily, subject to annual or biennial review by Congress of the entire act.

The extent to which the Federal Reserve should provide liquidity to particular sectors like housing is a complex issue that goes far beyond the scope of this book. Chairman Martin warned strongly against construing the act as an open pipeline to the home-finance institutions.[39] Clearly, the Federal Reserve should err on the side of generosity in checking any major financial crisis. Equally clearly, it cannot and should not guarantee liquidity to all lenders under all conditions. The Federal Reserve moved in 1969 to open its discount window more widely to member banks for reasonable needs, and it has virtually unlimited power to create new

39. See his testimony on behalf of the Board in Hearings before the House Banking and Currency Committee on H.R. 13939 (*To Extend for One Year Authority for More Flexible Regulations of Maximum Rates of Interest or Dividends, Higher Reserve Requirements and Open Market Operations in Agency Issues,* 91 Cong. 1 sess. [1969]). The language of the act is somewhat ambiguous on the responsibilities of the Federal Reserve to use this power to provide funds to particular sectors through the purchase of agency securities. Martin and others have stressed the difficulty of pumping money into the sagging housing market without directly circumventing the general monetary policy goal of restraining economy-wide inflation. A number of concrete steps to avoid this dilemma have been suggested, but none promises more than modest help unless Congress simply appropriates large subsidies to homebuilding. See especially *Report of the Commission on Mortgage Interest Rates to the President of the United States and to Congress* (1969).

commercial bank reserves through open market purchases.[40] A similar assurance of help to other financial institutions in times of crisis would be generally appropriate; but it should apply only in the event of impending major-sector or economy-wide difficulties that might trigger a serious financial collapse and recession. Whatever is done about continuing federal powers to establish interest rate ceilings on deposits, the Federal Reserve's broadened powers to provide economy-wide liquidity by purchasing other agencies' liabilities in case of financial crisis should immediately be made permanent.

FEDERAL CREDIT PROGRAMS

Federal credit programs have increased greatly in size and diversity since the 1920s, and their impact on aggregate economic activity and prices has become increasingly important.[41] Large federal lending and loan-guarantee programs exist for public and private housing, community development, business, transportation, education, health, and agriculture. Currently more than seventy-five different programs scattered among various government departments and agencies either do their own borrowing, lend money borrowed from the Treasury, or lend government funds, which are then recouped through resale operations. Federal government direct and guaranteed loans outstanding, including those of government-owned and "sponsored" enterprises like FNMA, now exceed $45 billion.[42]

Most of these programs are administered primarily by agencies created by Congress for particular purposes. For example, loans

40. The new discount regulations are a step in the direction of assuring bank liquidity as long as bankers meet prescribed regulatory standards. A completely open discount window with a "penalty" rate of perhaps 0.5 or 1 percent above the Treasury bill rate would be still more conducive to financial stability and efficiency in the allocation of funds.

41. For more complete analyses of federal credit programs, see *Report of the Committee on Federal Credit Programs to the President of the United States* (1963); George F. Break, *Feder.l Lending and Economic Stability* (Brookings Institution, 1965); and two books prepared for the Commission on Money and Credit, *Federal Credit Programs*, by Stewart Johnson and others (Prentice-Hall, 1963) and *Federal Credit Agencies*, by George F. Break and others (Prentice-Hall, 1963).

42. This figure can be varied substantially by the use of different criteria for including different agencies and programs. The net debt outstanding of financial agencies grew by about $30 billion during the 1960s.

and guarantees on private housing are provided by the Department of Housing and Urban Development, the Veterans Administration, the Department of Agriculture, and the Federal Home Loan Banks. In addition, the Federal National Mortgage Association (Fannie Mae) is now privately owned but government sponsored and is widely viewed as a government agency. Similar special-purpose agencies administer other credit programs. In most cases, the primary aim of the program is to aid a particular sector or group in the economy.

Thus, it is not surprising that federal lending and loan-guarantee programs are often conducted with little concern for monetary-credit conditions and their impact on over-all economic activity. Yet their borrowing draws on private markets much as Treasury issues would, and their lending provides spendable funds to particular markets. As a result, they present special coordination problems. In slack periods special credit programs to stimulate particular sectors are generally consistent with stimulative monetary and fiscal policy, although they may compete with private borrowers for the same funds. Conflicts are even more likely when monetary-fiscal policy aims at restraint, but particular groups, often with support from their congressmen, look to federal credit programs for new loans and guarantees.

No easy solution to this problem of coordination is evident. The basic program responsibilities of each agency understandably dominate its thinking and action. And there is no rule that Congress must never enact mutually conflicting laws. But the macroeconomic implications of federal credit programs should be clearly indicated to Congress; the agencies administering credit programs should be pressed to minimize possible conflicts with macroeconomic policy; and total government borrowing should be rationalized through concentration of responsibility in the Treasury or a new national credit bank, as recommended above.

The President, who is fundamentally responsible for execution of the laws, may use standing or ad hoc interagency committees or informal groups to achieve reasonable program coordination. In fact, such interagency committees have worked effectively in coordinating housing programs. But the usefulness of federal credit programs as positive tools of macroeconomic stabilization policy is limited.

Congressional specification of interest rate ceilings for federal loans and guarantees leads to further special problems and is of dubious merit. For example, Congress has specified that FHA, VA, and student loans may be guaranteed only when the interest rate is below a specified ceiling rate. As long as this ceiling rate is above prevailing market interest rates, the ceiling creates no problems. But when market interest rates rise above the specified maximum, the effect is to shut off the flow of federally guaranteed credit.

In a somewhat haphazard way this has often resulted in counter-cyclical federal aid to private housing; the aid is automatically shut off when inflation or tight money pushes up market interest rates. But the countercyclical effect is haphazard. Moreover, it imposes on home construction a disproportionate share of the burden of restraint when interest rates rise with inflation.[43] The same over-all restraint might be more equitably spread over the economy through reliance on general macroeconomic measures.

Wage-Price ("Incomes") Policies and the Inflation-Unemployment Dilemma

Even the "correct" growth of aggregate demand along the economy's long-run real growth path will not assure high employment without inflation if prices rise before high employment is reached. And they have done so—in the mid-1930s, in the mid-1950s, and during the 1960s. This has posed a major dilemma for macroeconomic policymakers that apparently cannot be solved through monetary-fiscal policy alone. More stimulus to eliminate unemployment generates inflation; more restraint to check rising prices increases unemployment.

It is not surprising that here too, as with the resort to direct controls in monetary policy, frustration with aggregate demand policy alone has led to widespread support for direct government action to harmonize the goals of high employment and price level stability. The difficulty is magnified since simultaneously a distribution of the national income must be achieved that is compatible with the aspirations of the many economic groups whose combined income claims exceed the total output available at stable prices. The complex issues surrounding the high employment–stable price

43. But, as has been emphasized above, housing also bears a disproportionate share of the impact of restrictive monetary policy, quite apart from these federal ceilings.

level dilemma have been considered at length in Chapter 7 and are not repeated here. This section presents and supports briefly the recommendations that seem to flow from historical experience and economic analysis of the problem.

IMPROVED MARKETS, RESOURCE MOBILITY, AND INFORMATION FLOWS

If labor and product markets were all highly competitive, if resources were highly mobile, and if information on job vacancies were widely available, wage and price increases before high employment is achieved would be scattered and temporary. Imperfect markets, immobile resources, and poor information flows are fundamental causes of the unemployment-inflation dilemma. Complete elimination of these causes in the foreseeable future is beyond reasonable hope. But steps to improve labor and product markets, resource mobility, and job information flows represent the most fundamental attack on the problem.

A detailed prescription of measures to achieve these goals is outside the scope of this book. But without such measures, it will be very difficult, perhaps impossible, to avoid the unemployment-inflation dilemma in the modern American economy.[44]

WAGE-PRICE GUIDEPOSTS

One common proposal is to use wage-price guideposts—or more broadly, "incomes policies"—to provide a noninflationary wage-profit division of the national income in an excess-income-claims economy. Another proposal is for direct mandatory controls on wages and prices to achieve the same result. There are many variants of such proposals for direct government intervention to facilitate higher employment without inflation.

Both history and theory warn that stabilization authorities cannot successfully rely on wage-price guideposts or any similar form of incomes policy to restrain wages and prices for long in the face of strong inflationary aggregate demand pressures. But guideposts may help in a big-business, big-labor economy characterized by excess income claims, if demand-pull inflationary pressures are moderate. In the years 1962–66, for example, the guideposts estab-

---

44. For one relevant set of suggestions, see *Economic Report of the President, January 1969*, Chap. 3.

lished by President Kennedy's Council of Economic Advisers apparently helped modestly to slow wage and price increases. But in the inflationary excess-demand economy that followed, persuasion from Washington soon came to have little force.[45]

If all markets were perfectly competitive and resources were perfectly mobile, then rising aggregate demand would increase output and employment until full employment was reached and would only then produce inflation. But many markets are not perfectly competitive; big unions and big business are real, and they have considerable power to push up wages and prices, at least temporarily, beyond purely competitive levels. Thus, at least in key industries that are important pattern setters, some pressure to restrain inflationary wage and price behavior may be useful to complement aggregate demand policy in a high-employment economy. Above all, wage-price guideposts can educate businessmen, labor, and the public as to the conditions necessary for economic growth with high employment and stable prices, thereby helping to create an environment in which such an economy can be achieved.

Economists have long agreed on the broad outlines of wage and price behavior that should prevail if the United States is to have a high-employment economy without inflation. These are roughly the wage-price developments that would occur if highly competitive labor and product markets prevailed everywhere. The Kennedy CEA spelled out substantially these same results as guideposts for wage and price behavior where big business and labor operate in only partially competitive markets.[46]

But to expect big business and labor voluntarily to accept such constraints is asking a great deal in the highly competitive U.S. economy. One goal of guidepost policy is to make business and labor aware of the consequences of their inflationary behavior. Another important goal is to develop a public consensus on the guide-

---

45. For a sample of assessments of the effectiveness of wage-price policies in the United States, see John Sheahan, *The Wage-Price Guideposts* (Brookings Institution, 1967), who finds some positive effects from the wage-price guideposts; and George P. Shultz and Robert Z. Aliber (eds.), *Guidelines, Informal Controls, and the Market Place: Policy Choices in a Full Employment Economy* (University of Chicago Press, 1966), where the preponderance of judgments is that there are few appreciable benefits from the guideposts. Additional references are cited in Chap. 3, note 9.

46. The guideposts were initially outlined in the *Economic Report of the President, January 1962*, pp. 185–90.

posts that will exert pressure on both business and labor to abide by them in times when otherwise the inflation-unemployment dilemma would prevail. Only if businessmen and union leaders are convinced that the monetary-fiscal authorities will stand firm against inflation can noninflationary settlements be expected. Without this conviction businessmen can seldom be counted on to bear the costs of a strike resulting from refusal to grant inflationary wage settlements, or to exercise restraint in their own pricing decisions.

Critics argue that if direct government controls over individual prices and wages are ruled out, the guideposts will be little more than pious pronouncements. But the case for a noninflationary consensus based on something like the guideposts is quite different from merely saying that business and labor unions should be exhorted to behave. It rests fundamentally on the argument that a noninflationary consensus will support anti-inflationary monetary-fiscal (aggregate demand) policy—and that in a democracy the only reliable basis for preserving individual freedom in the market is widespread voluntary consensus as to what is reasonable. Public consensus can and does exert great power, for good or for ill; public attitudes do influence congressmen and government officials, including the Federal Reserve and the White House. Thus, the greatest potential of the guideposts is to help crystallize a latent, widely shared feeling that "reasonable" wage and price behavior is needed to achieve continuing prosperity without inflation.[47]

Without such a working consensus, the Federal Reserve, Congress, and the administration in power will be intermittently, or persistently, up against the dilemma of validating inflationary wage and price increases, holding the price line at the cost of accepting low employment and slack, or resorting to direct wage and price controls. With many goals but fewer workable policy instru-

47. A good case can be made for a public "wage-price commission," with representatives from labor, business, and the public, charged with investigating in public hearings wage and price actions that may be inflationary and reporting the facts to the President, Congress, and the public. Some advocate legislation requiring that all wage and price changes on major products be reported to the commission thirty or sixty days before they take effect, to assure adequate advance time for examination and reporting by the commission. Other proposals range all the way to actual wage- and price-setting power for such a commission,

ments, the macro authorities need help. The guideposts, direct wage and price controls, or reconstruction of the economy along highly competitive lines, can help monetary-fiscal (aggregate demand) policy overcome the unemployment-inflation dilemma. But wage-price guideposts are small arms in the stabilization policy arsenal. The big guns are monetary and fiscal policy, aimed directly at regulating the level of aggregate demand.[48]

MANDATORY WAGE-PRICE CONTROLS

Mandatory wage and price controls, or ceilings, represent a drastic shift from the philosophy of using monetary-fiscal (aggregate demand) policy as the main weapon against inflation and unemployment. Frustration with the apparent shortcomings of aggregate demand policy leads many persons—especially noneconomists —to favor mandatory ceilings on inflationary wage and price increases.

A detailed analysis of such direct controls is outside the scope of this study. It is no accident, however, that most economists oppose such controls in peacetime. A temporary wage-price freeze may help to break the dynamics of an inflationary spiral; Great Britain's experiment in 1969–70 is a case in point. But experience suggests that such controls produce serious inequities and misallocations of resources and have very limited, temporary effectiveness against inflation that is based on excess aggregate demand. Moreover, advocates of mandatory wage-price ceilings often end up supporting controls on the other fellow, not themselves, when specific implementation is planned. Few economists believe that direct mandatory wage and price controls can work more than temporar-

48. For an expansion of this argument, see G. L. Bach, "Inflation—Danger Ahead?" *Harvard Business Review,* Vol. 42 (July–August 1964), pp. 49–61. It is important to recognize that the case for guideposts is that, properly used, they promise to *reduce* the likelihood of direct government intervention with direct controls, not to increase it—by inducing more responsible collective bargaining and business price policies that are consistent with national goals. To some extent the guideposts had this effect in the period 1962–64. Unfortunately, they also led increasingly to direct intervention by the President and the CEA in individual wage and price decisions where it seemed important to the administration to prevent deviations from the guidepost policies, thus edging over the line into direct intervention in wage bargaining and price-setting.

ily against peacetime inflation in the United States, in the face of large excess aggregate demand.[49]

International Monetary Policy

"Equilibrium" in the balance of payments is often cited as the immediate objective of U.S. international monetary policy. But in fact, the balance of payments is merely a surrogate for a much broader set of objectives. The United States wants a healthy, stably growing international economy, with expansion in both trade and investment. And it wants international arrangements that will allow it freedom to follow domestic policies that will maintain a stable and growing U.S. economy. No single balance-of-payments statistic can provide an adequate measure of this complex set of international goals. Thus, achievement of equilbrium in the bal-ance of payments is an overly simple statement of the proper goal of U.S. international monetary policy.

Economic and political interdependence among nations has in-creased greatly since the Second World War. No country, save pos-sibly the United States, can afford to manage its domestic economy without careful attention to its international position. Especially for the smaller economies, it is impossible to remain out of step for long with inflations or deflations in the major trading nations. Conversely, healthy growth in international trade and capital flows depends importantly on a stable U.S. economy. Fortunately, significant progress has been made in recent years on the three major problems cited below.[50] Fortunately, also, no serious prob-lem of coordination exists among U.S. agencies responsible for international financial policy. The difficult issues here concern

49. If, in fact, the wage-price dilemma exists, another approach would be to accept the inevitable but to soften the blows of both unemployment and inflation by increasing the size and coverage of unemployment insurance benefits and tying more incomes (social security benefits, government salaries, and so forth) to ap-propriate cost-of-living indexes. Such policies reduce the incentive to avoid in-flation, as well as its costs. See G. L. Bach, *Inflation: A Study in Economics, Ethics, and Politics* (Brown University Press, 1958), Chap. 4.

50. See Richard N. Cooper, "The Dollar and the World Economy," in Kermit Gordon (ed.), *Agenda for the Nation* (Brookings Institution, 1968), pp. 475–508, for a balanced analysis of the implications of this growing interdependence for U.S. policy.

international relations, not the policymaking process in the United States.

1. *The liquidity problem: Growing world trade and finance require a growing total international monetary reserve base, to support normal trading relationships and to provide a buffer to give individual nations time for gradual internal adjustments when problems arise. Special drawing rights (SDRs) plus existing gold stocks and growing U.S. dollar balances should be used to provide the needed reserves.*

The establishment of SDRs through the International Monetary Fund, clarification of the (declining) role of gold, and growing recognition of the dollar as the key international reserve currency have combined to brighten hopes that the international reserve problem is on the way to being solved in the years ahead. Continued international cooperation will be required to assure smooth functioning of the system, but no further major changes appear to be required now.

2. *The adjustment mechanism: More flexibility in the international adjustment mechanism is essential, to avoid breakdowns of the international system and to preserve reasonable elbow room for domestic policymakers to maintain domestic stability here and in other countries.*

Most major nations, especially the United States, now refuse to have their domestic macroeconomic policies dominated by losses of international reserves when they are in deficit. Similarly, Germany for an extended period in the 1960s refused to let its domestic policy be dictated by reserve accumulations when they were in massive surplus. There is little reason to suppose that major nations will again be willing to permit their entire domestic economies to bear the brunt of adjustment to international reserve flows, as they were in the pre-1930s period. Given fixed exchange parities and a refusal to let international reserve flows dominate domestic monetary-fiscal policies, the standard international adjustment mechanism whereby economies are brought back into balance with one another is thwarted.

If exchange rates are fixed, balance-of-payments deficits or surpluses will lower or raise aggregate income and prices in each economy to move that country back toward equilibrium. With flexible exchange rates, this adjustment process can be concentrated in the export and import industries, by changing prices and incomes there without directly affecting the rest of the domestic economy. For the United States this is a vital distinction, since only about 5 percent of our gross national product enters international trade. To swing the entire U.S. economy toward recession or inflation in order to adjust it to international transactions would indeed be to let the tail wag the dog. This is especially true because it is far from clear that traditional fixed-exchange remedies do in fact work toward reestablishing equilibrium when highly volatile capital movements are taken into account.

Any of several moves could provide at least some flexibility for exchange rates, to aid the adjustment mechanism. Fortunately, significant support for flexibility has developed in the past few years.

a. Limited flexibility in exchange rates could be obtained by widening the range within which rates are permitted to fluctuate—now only about ¾ of 1 percent above and below parity. This band might be broadened to 3 or even 5 percent without seriously impairing the stability and certainty needed for effective international trade and investment.

b. A widened band could be combined with a "sliding" or "crawling peg." This would permit exchange rates to fluctuate within a broader band, but would also allow the parity rate at the center of the band to move automatically and gradually upward or downward when currencies were persistently near the top or bottom of their bands. For example, if the dollar were continually weak and near the bottom of its exchange band in relation to the German mark during a quarter or a half year, the dollar-mark parity would automatically move to a lower level at the beginning of the next period, say by half the distance between parity and the band limit. The band would move with the parity rate, and a similar process would be followed in each succeeding period. The sliding peg would automatically provide *gradual* and routine shifts of parities whenever changes were called for by market pressures. It could thus facilitate balance-of-payments adjustments without burdening the entire domestic economies involved, and at the same time preserve the primary virtue of a stable exchange rate system because of the slow permissible rate of crawl in parities.

c. Member countries of the International Monetary Fund

could, as was contemplated in the Bretton Woods agreement of 1945, make modest changes in their exchange parities from time to time, as might be required by differing rates of technical advance, inflation, or other domestic variations from one economy to another. Unfortunately, after Bretton Woods the tradition developed that to devalue one's currency is a sign of weakness, and most major nations have been very reluctant to do so. Conversely, and with rare exceptions, countries have been reluctant to revalue their currencies upward, as the principle would require if there were continuing surpluses. Barring the use of a sliding peg and/or widened bands, major nations should reaffirm the intent of the Bretton Woods agreement to provide moderate rate flexibility.

d. A more extreme alternative would be for the United States to cut the fixed dollar–gold price link and let the dollar move freely against other currencies and against gold. This would leave other nations free to let their currencies float or to peg them to the dollar. Given that choice, most other countries would probably tie their currencies to the dollar (or to some other major currency) to avoid the uncertainty involved in freely floating rates. The result would probably be a dollar standard, and the United States could pursue its domestic stabilization policies without major constraint from shifts in international reserves. This would increase the adjustment burden on other countries, but would achieve maximum freedom for U.S. domestic macroeconomic policies. It would, however, probably involve substantial disruption of international economic relations, at least temporarily, and it commands little support now outside academic circles.

In substance, the world has already moved far toward a dollar standard, with the dollar the world's basic reserve and transactions currency. Fortunately, installation of the two-tier gold system in 1968 has already freed participating nations from the worst dangers of destabilizing speculative runs on gold. In these circumstances, the case for severing the fixed link between the dollar and gold is substantially weakened.

3. *The confidence problem: Existing cooperative arrangements to provide reserves in the event of confidence crises should be strengthened.* Since the Second World War, major currencies have been subjected to intermittent crises of confidence—for example, the speculative raids on the pound in 1962 and 1967, and on the

franc in mid-1968. Such crises occur when uncertainty develops as to the ability of the currency in question to maintain its existing parity against gold and other currencies. Even strong currencies cannot withstand massive hot-money capital drains of this sort without large reserve buffers, or borrowing arrangements to obtain reserves needed to tide them over the crisis.

The International Monetary Fund offers substantial lending facilities for just such situations, and since the Second World War the ten leading central banks have undertaken large lending commitments to help one another withstand confidence crises. These arrangements provide a substantial buffer against crises. But so long as the world operates on fixed exchange parities, doubts will arise from time to time as to whether particular currencies will be devalued. The major protection against confidence crises of this sort lies first in a generous supply of international monetary reserves for the system as a whole, and second in adequate borrowing arrangements to tide major countries over crisis periods. Present arrangements could be strengthened further, but no major changes appear to be required, especially if more flexibility in exchange rates is achieved soon.

International reforms on these three fronts are important to the effective use of domestic stabilization policy in the United States and to a stably growing world economy. Without them, U.S. domestic policymakers will be exposed continually to the danger of international reserve drains that threaten the dollar internationally and the economic activity that is based on it. Given relatively free international trade and capital movements, even the United States cannot long expect to keep its interest rates and prices far out of line with those of other major nations. Free international capital movements in particular, desirable though they are in their own right, throw more of the domestic stabilization burden on fiscal policy—precisely the instrument that is least promising for flexible countercyclical use. This fact adds weight to the recommendations made above for substantial changes in the U.S. fiscal policymaking process.

Federal Reserve Structure and Policymaking Procedures

Changes in the internal structure and operations of the Federal Reserve System are not urgently needed, but the following suggestions deserve attention if a major reorganization is considered.[51] Most important of all, the System needs to expand further its research into the basic monetary mechanism, for monetary policy needs particularly a sounder foundation of knowledge concerning money, the monetary mechanism, and the channels through which monetary policy affects real output, employment, and prices.

1. *As was recommended above, the Board chairman's term should be made roughly coterminous with the President's. This should be done promptly.*

2. *The Federal Reserve Board should be reduced in size from seven to five members, with staggered ten-year terms.*

3. *Responsibility for monetary policy (open market operations, reserve requirements, and discount rates) should be centered in the Federal Reserve Board.* The Federal Open Market Committee (FOMC) should be abolished, but the Board should be required to consult regularly with the twelve Reserve Bank presidents in determining its policies. Changes in the discount rate should no longer be inaugurated separately at the twelve regional Reserve Banks.

4. *Special occupational and geographical qualifications for Board members should be eliminated.* Members should be selected on the basis of knowledge of, and experience in, monetary economics or finance, education, general competence, independence, and objectivity.

5. *Technical ownership of the Federal Reserve Banks by member banks should be eliminated through retirement of the present capital stock.* Instead, membership should be evidenced by a special nonearning certificate for each member.

The basic purpose of these suggestions is to centralize the policy-making functions of the Federal Reserve System in one governmental body, the Federal Reserve Board, unmistakably responsible to the public rather than to the commercial banks; to make Board membership more attractive to men of high ability; to increase the efficiency of Federal Reserve operations by streamlining the present complex organizational structure; and, with the reserve requirement and discount changes proposed in the preceding

51. A more detailed analysis along similar lines is made in Bach, *Federal Reserve Policy-Making*, based on my analysis of the System conducted for the Hoover Commission in the late 1940s. The central issues appear to have changed little over the last two decades.

section, to extend the direct impact of monetary policy to substantially all commercial banks in the country.

6. *The greatest potential for improved monetary policy lies in the establishment of an empirically validated theory (model) of money, the monetary mechanism, and the channels of monetary policy. The Federal Reserve should expand its own basic research on these subjects and further extend its contacts with monetary economists outside the System.* Disagreement among experts on these basic monetary questions lies at the root of the policy issues examined above. Federal Reserve research support for its own staff and academic economists has expanded substantially during the past decade. But more is needed, with involvement of the nation's finest minds. Failure of the Federal Reserve to do more is an inexcusable failure to face its own responsibilities to the American people.

FOCUS OF RESPONSIBILITY

The complex organization and overlapping responsibilities for major policy that exist in the Federal Reserve are hard to defend. Open market operations, reserve requirements, and discount rates —all have identical general policy goals and need to be completely coordinated. To have a different group within the System responsible for each invites delay and confusion. Monetary policy is national policy. Information on regional developments may indeed be valuable in formulating monetary policy, but this could be readily obtained without diffusing the responsibility for monetary policy.

There are counterarguments. The main one is that the present arrangement works well. Why change it? In fact, all nineteen senior Federal Reserve officials (seven Board members plus the twelve Reserve Bank presidents) consult together through the FOMC on all major policy issues and in effect make policy together. Policy responsibility is thus not as scattered as it appears to be. It can reasonably be argued that Federal Reserve policy is made in the best tradition of wide representation and careful consideration by a large group of responsible men. The regional Banks draw presidents and Reserve Bank directors of high ability into the System, which would not attract them unless it offered policy responsibility. In policy deliberations, it is thus argued, Reserve Bank presidents both reflect regional interests and bring monetary judgments and insights that add significantly to those found in the Board in Washington. Moreover, regional Banks help to provide a solid base of support throughout the business and financial communities for Federal Reserve policies that are often controversial.

What is the conclusion? Much depends on these last arguments. Federal Reserve officials, including especially former Chairman Martin, put great emphasis on them. Supporters of the present arrangements contend that regional presidents who vote on the FOMC, and regional boards of directors who back them up, provide a wide base of power and understanding for the System. On the other hand, Federal Reserve history offers little clear evidence that Reserve Bank presidents (with the exception of the New York presidents) have contributed much to policymaking. In the last decade several Reserve Bank presidents of high ability have been appointed—men whose competence in monetary economics and in practical banking compares favorably with that of the best members of the Board in Washington. It is argued that such men could not be drawn to membership on the Washington Board. In some cases, their contributions to policy decisions have been stimulating and fundamental.[52]

The evidence is not clear on this point, or on the contribution now made by the Reserve Bank presidents to policy formation or the importance of Reserve Bank directors as a link with the business and financial communities. A priori, the case for a simpler organization is strong. But the available evidence does not permit an unequivocal conclusion.

A SMALLER BOARD

If policymaking responsibility should be centered in one group, the group should be the Federal Reserve Board rather than the FOMC. And the Board should be smaller than the present FOMC.

52. For example, the St. Louis Federal Reserve Bank during the 1960s persistently prodded System policymakers to reexamine their views on the importance of the money stock per se. The special role of the New York Bank has already been noted.

Concentration of authority in a seven-man Board would be an improvement. A five-man Board, required to obtain the advice and counsel of Reserve Bank presidents, would appear to be still better. It could be more efficient, less cumbersome, and less given to delay and indecision, while maintaining the present virtues of careful investigation and deliberation on policy issues.

Few students of organization believe that a nineteen-man, or even a twelve-man, committee is small enough to do an effective job of running an organization and making day-to-day decisions on complex issues. A large decision-making group is needed when many separate interests and viewpoints must be represented. But sound monetary policy formation does not rest on a compromise of conflicting regional or occupational interests represented on the board. Regional information is needed, but those who provide it need not be policymakers. Aside from their regional positions, the twelve Reserve Bank presidents do not appear to represent markedly differing interests.

A large group may also be justified if more members would contribute significantly to the decision-making process. Both experience and a priori reasoning cast doubt on the marginal gain to be had from additional members after a committee totals a half dozen or so, unless the additional members hold views that differ substantially from those of the others. In the case of the Federal Reserve Board, there seems little reason to suppose that going beyond the half dozen or so ablest men in the System is justified on this ground.

Americans traditionally distrust concentration of power in government; we value the combined judgment of a number of men. But the case for nineteen, or even twelve, decision makers is hard to defend. Moreover, the smaller the Board, the better will be the chance of getting first-class members to serve on it. Required consultation with Reserve Bank officials could provide the needed grass-roots information on, and involvement of, the banking and business sectors of the economy—without sacrificing more effective policymaking procedures.[53]

53. Short of simple consolidation of policymaking responsibilities in the Board, a modified plan might be considered whereby all policymaking responsibilities would be transferred to the Board, but one or more Reserve Bank presidents would serve as Board members on a rotating basis. The number of bank presidents serving at any one time would depend, of course, on the size of the Board.

History suggests that in practice, System leadership has usually been highly concentrated in a few hands, notably Martin's and Eccles's for many years, and earlier those of Benjamin Strong. Given the Federal Reserve's relationship to other U.S. agencies and other central banks, it inescapably will have one or a very few members who carry most of the burden. The old judicial parallel depicting the Reserve Board as the "supreme court of finance" is not a realistic analogy. Courts apply common and statute law under an elaborate set of judicial precedents and safeguards. As was noted above, in contrast, the central bank sails on seas virtually uncharted by Congress and bears heavy day-to-day operating responsibilities for the U.S. monetary mechanism. In many respects, the Board parallels the secretary of the treasury more closely than it does the Supreme Court, though it does have some commission-type regulatory duties.

ROLE OF THE NEW YORK BANK

New York City is the financial center of the United States, and the New York Reserve Bank is in many ways the most important of the Reserve Banks. Its role in System activities and as fiscal agent for the Treasury has been described above. Thus, continuous membership of the New York Bank on the Open Market Committee has long been considered vital. Certainly it is beyond argument that consultation with the New York Bank on both domestic and international monetary issues is vitally necessary.

But responsibility for the nation's monetary policies does not devolve upon the New York district more than on any other, even though the New York banks are the country's largest, most government securities are traded on Wall Street, and international monetary transactions are centered in New York. Open market operations and international policies are national in purpose and impact, no less than changes in reserve requirements or rediscount rates. Thus, there would be little reason to give the New York Bank special *voting* representation on policy issues if the present large FOMC were eliminated.

The somewhat anomalous arrangement whereby the New York Bank serves as the chief agent of both the FOMC and the Treasury in domestic and international money market operations has frequently been criticized. There is said to be danger of conflicts of interest; and some critics contend that this key position places too much de facto operating power in the New York Bank's hands, especially in open market operations. But neither Treasury nor Federal Reserve officials support a change in the present arrangements. Someone must be responsible on a day-to-day basis for implementing domestic and international policy decisions, and the New York Bank, located in the heart of the world's financial center, does a good job.

QUALITY OF BOARD MEMBERS AND BANK PRESIDENTS

Selecting senior officials of high ability is essential to good monetary policymaking, especially in view of the gaps in our knowledge of the monetary mechanism and the effects of alternative monetary policies. The existing regional and occupational requirements for Board membership make little sense and should be eliminated. Choice of the members by the President with the advice and consent of the Senate will inevitably be to some extent "political." Few presidents could be expected to nominate Board members unsympathetic to their general economic philosophies. But increasingly, in addition to the important qualities of good judgment, integrity, and leadership, effective service as a Board member requires an understanding of the role of money in the modern economy and the complex impact of central bank policy instruments on the economy. As modern monetary economics becomes ever more technical and complex, as have the sciences and technology, it will become increasingly difficult to understand and interpret the evidence for policymaking without a reasonable working grasp of the analytical methods involved.

Contrary to popular opinion, the Board itself engages in no banking operations; these are carried out by the Reserve Banks. Thus, only secondarily will effective Board service require a detailed knowledge of commercial bank operations; this is of central importance only for bank supervisory policy.

RESERVE BANK OWNERSHIP

Technical ownership of the Federal Reserve Banks by commercial (member) banks flies in the face of the basic constitutional provision that the federal government shall "coin money [and] regulate the value thereof." Surely the Federal Reserve authorities in regulating money must be responsible not to the bankers who own Reserve Bank stock, but to the people of the United States, just as are the secretary of the treasury and other government officials. Perceptive bankers are the first to agree. Nor is there any clear justification for payment of a 6 percent annual dividend on Reserve Bank stock held by member banks.[54]

It is clear that both Board members in Washington and the presidents of the Reserve Banks, in fact, view themselves as public officials, sworn to advance the welfare of the people, rather than as representatives of the bankers. Then why bother to change the situation, even though the present arrangement is admittedly a vestige of the thinking of a half century ago? The main answer is that our national monetary authorities should, like Caesar's wife, be above suspicion. Even though commercial bank ownership of Reserve Bank stock clearly does not now mean that the banks control national monetary policy, it opens a suspicion that such improper influence might be exerted. Certainly, if Reserve Bank presidents vote on federal open market policy, they should be public officials, appointed either by the President of the United States or by the presidentially appointed Federal Reserve Board.

Full presentation of bankers' viewpoints to the Board before major credit policy decisions are reached is advantageous to both the Board and the banks. As a practical matter, there is little danger that the Reserve Bank presidents, by whomever they are selected, will fail to reflect adequately the interests of the commercial banks. Every president's day-to-day business brings him in close contact with the bankers and businessmen of his district, so that he is keenly aware of banker and business problems and attitudes.[55]

54. In effect the federal Treasury pays these dividends, since Reserve Bank earnings come almost exclusively from interest on U.S. government securities, and since nearly all Federal Reserve net earnings *after dividends* are now returned to the Treasury. Inasmuch as the Reserve Banks have no real need for the member-bank invested capital, the dividend payments might be considered in essence a federal subsidy to the banks. They may be small incentives to membership in the Federal Reserve System. However, dividends total only a relatively small sum, about $37 million in 1968, while payments of earnings to the Treasury totaled $2.5 billion in the same year.

55. President Wilson's refusal to tolerate direct banker control is reported vividly by Carter Glass in *An Adventure in Constructive Finance* (Doubleday, Page, 1927), pp. 115–16. Secretary William Gibbs McAdoo and Representative

In sum, if the Federal Reserve were being established anew today, surely the present elaborate structure should not be repeated. But whether changes now would justify the bitterness and disruption they would probably generate is open to serious question.

Conclusion: On Research

In a candid but somewhat discouraged moment, a highly placed economist of the Nixon administration recently observed, on the coordination of monetary and fiscal policy: "Much of the time they seem to me perfectly coordinated—operating together in utter darkness."

Like the farmer who wasn't farming as well as he already knew how, U.S. macroeconomic policies are not being carried out as well as they should be on the basis of experience and existing knowledge. Adoption of the proposals advanced above could help significantly to reduce still further the possibility of serious economic instability by building in safeguards against wide fluctuations in aggregate demand.

But throughout the writing of this book, and in the extensive interviews that preceded it, the Achilles' heel of stabilization policy appeared again and again. Even the experts do not have enough firm knowledge of money and monetary linkages, of fiscal policy and its impacts, of wage- and price-setting processes, of international adjustment mechanisms under alternative financial arrangements, to provide a sure foundation for policy decisions. A great deal is known about how our economy works—vastly more than a half century ago. But very little is known in relation to the complexities that are faced daily in devising macroeconomic policies. Even an all-powerful monetary-fiscal authority would often be uncertain of what action to take.

Glass had brought a group of prominent bankers to the White House to state the case for formal banker representation on the Board. After they had done so with some vigor, President Wilson inquired quietly: "Will one of you gentlemen tell me in what civilized country of the earth there are important government boards of control on which private interests are represented?" There was a moment of silence, and finally the President continued: "Which of you gentlemen thinks the railroads should select members of the Interstate Commerce Commission?" There was no reply to either question, and, in spite of desperate banker efforts in the Senate for representation, the legislation contained no such provision.

These circumstances call for policy procedures that will safeguard against major mistakes and that promise to provide reasonably satisfactory outcomes for a wide range of contingencies. Accordingly, this study has emphasized monetary and fiscal guidelines for approximately stable economic growth and built-in international liquidity and adjustment arrangements, in contrast to a policy that would rely primarily on attempts to fine-tune the domestic and international economies. But there remains the fundamental problem of modern macroeconomic policy—the inadequacy of basic macroeconomic knowledge on which to base policy judgments. Men of wisdom and integrity can help, but they cannot perform miracles. Expanded basic research on macroeconomic behavior and policies promises a very high social return for the long pull. Only sounder foundations can ensure truly effective policymaking over the years to come.

APPENDIX

THE FEDERAL RESERVE
RUNS THE POLITICAL GAUNTLET:
APRIL–NOVEMBER 1956

ON THURSDAY, April 12, 1956, the Board of Governors announced increases in discount rates at eleven Federal Reserve Banks. The increases—from 2½ percent to 3 percent at Minneapolis and San Francisco and to 2¾ percent at all other banks, except Chicago—marked the first movement of discount rates in 1956, following four successive increases during 1955. This summary of press accounts is indicative of the political reverberations that followed.

Reports of disagreement by administration officials began blossoming in print within a week, and before a month had passed the reports of "behind-the-scenes conflict" were raised, and commented upon, at two successive presidential press conferences. By that time, three of President Eisenhower's cabinet secretaries—George Humphrey of Treasury, Sinclair Weeks of Commerce, and James Mitchell of Labor—and the chairman of the President's Council of Economic Advisers, Arthur Burns, had been named in the press as critics of the Federal Reserve action.

Newsweek magazine was first in print with the story in its issue (predated April 23) that went on newsstand sale Tuesday, April 17, five days after the Federal Reserve announcement. *Newsweek* writers Hobart Rowen and Clem Morgello said in their report:

For nearly two weeks, Federal Reserve officials huddled in conferences with Treasury people and other top Administration aides, arguing whether it was time to tighten up on credit. . . .

Chairman Bill Martin and other FRB officials feared all this new money (surging credit demand, as exampled by the fact that "in February alone, commercial bank loans increased $1.3 billion, or 5 per cent") would do more to kick up prices than to boost production, since business was already at peak levels. And the price picture already looked dangerous. . . .

But a number of top Administration officials, including Treasury Secretary George Humphrey, believed that talk of inflation was being exaggerated. . . .

White House insiders also contended that consumer buying was not

256

creating a real inflationary push. . . . But the gain [in retail trade] did not seem great enough to them to force prices up. . . .

As a matter of fact, *Newsweek* learned, the President's top economic adviser Arthur F. Burns believes the increases have been surprisingly small, considering the current worldwide boom. Burns thinks the economy could absorb the pressure even if prices edged up a bit.

Humphrey's views dovetailed with these and he argued his point in conversations with the Federal Reserve's Martin. The Treasury boss—who well remembers the complaints that rolled in three years ago when money was tightened sharply—wanted to wait a few months to see if loans continued to expand rather than to act now and risk knocking the economy into a skid.

But in the end it was Martin's decision to make, and he made it. The decision: Boost the discount rate from 2½ percent to 2¾ percent (and to 3 percent in two districts). . . . So strongly did Humphrey disagree that he drafted a public statement of his views. He killed it at the last minute to avoid an open controversy. . . .

On April 23 the *New York Times,* not given to picking up items from other publications without verification on its own, said this:

It is not generally known, but the Treasury had serious reservations about the latest increase in the discount rate by the Federal Reserve. This resulted in probably the sharpest dispute between the two agencies since the Eisenhower Administration came to office.

The opposition of George M. Humphrey, Secretary of the Treasury, and his men was in part a traditional concern over the effect of over-tight money on the Government's own securities. But apparently it was based more on a different assessment of the business picture. . . .

Eisenhower States His Views

On April 25, President Eisenhower held a news conference on which the Dow-Jones newswire reported as follows:

President Eisenhower took note of reports that Treasury Secretary Humphrey and Doctor Arthur Burns, Chairman of the President's Council of Economic Advisers, disagreed with the Federal Reserve Board in its increase earlier this month in the Federal Reserve discount rate. The President said he believes, however, that since the Federal Reserve is watching the money situation closely it would move to loosen up lending terms if money gets too tight.

When asked about the report that administration financial leaders disagreed with the Federal Reserve on the discount rates, the President said that it is probably right that certain people didn't like the action. However, he noted, the Federal Reserve is set up as a separate agency of Government outside of the authority of the President. He thinks it would be a mistake if the Board should be brought under the President's power.

The Fed had unanimous agreement among 11 of its District banks before it went ahead with the boost in the discount rate, he noted. Having done so, the Board is watching the money situation from day to day and he is sure would move in the opposite direction if money gets too tight, the President said.

Criticism of the Federal Reserve's action was not confined to federal officeholders or Republicans. The *Journal of Commerce,* noting May 1 that the comptroller of New York State, Arthur Levitt, a Democrat, "has just fired a broadside on current Federal monetary policies because of their restrictive effect on New York State's school building program . . . ," commented editorially:

New York's Comptroller grudgingly admits that the current objective of Federal Reserve policy may be sound, inasmuch as too much inflationary stimulation of the economy at this particular time might easily create serious headaches for later on. Being a politician, however, obviously makes it impossible for him to accept a sound economic policy. Instead, he comes up with a typical politician's approach which is that an exception to the general rule should be made in order to facilitate the easier financing of school construction and other public works. . . . If excessive borrowing and building produce a boom and bust cycle, as well they could, Mr. Levitt's political party would be the first to criticize the present Federal Administration for not taking more aggressive steps to curb the boom. . . .

On May 3, little more than a week after President Eisenhower's initial press conference remarks, two of his cabinet officers had press conferences of their own, at which the subject came up again.

The *Washington Post* of May 4 reported these developments:

Two Cabinet members yesterday questioned credit-tightening moves by the Federal Reserve System and scouted its fears of inflation.

Labor Secretary James P. Mitchell said the Reserve Board's approval of discount rate increases last month "may have been a mistake." He told a news conference, "I see no threat of inflation at all."

At another news conference, Commerce Secretary Sinclair Weeks noted that "money is tight today and that may prove to be a handicap." He predicted that prices would be held in check.

Their views were the first open affirmation of Administration discontent with the Reserve Board's action. George M. Humphrey, Secretary of the Treasury, and Arthur F. Burns, Chairman of the Council of Economic Advisers, have also been reported as disagreeing with the System's estimate of the economic climate.

The next day, President Eisenhower held another press conference, and naturally there were more questions. Dow-Jones reported the answers this way:

President Eisenhower said today that Administration policy is to assure that there is adequate money available for the expansion of the country and that he's sure the Federal Reserve Board seeks to do the same.

He gave this view at his press conference in commenting on a question which noted that Secretary of Commerce Weeks and Labor Secretary Mitchell have been critical of the Federal Reserve's recent boost in its discount rate.

As he has commented before on this subject, President Eisenhower told his press conference that everybody has his own opinion on such an action.

But the Federal Reserve is an independent body reaching decisions and it is the duty of the Board to put its conclusions into effect, he said.

The Administration is watching the money situation all the time, Mr. Eisenhower said, and he's sure the Federal Reserve is too.

Business Week, in an editorial in its May 5 issue, introduced a new note, criticizing the Federal Reserve for playing politics. Discussing "The Politics of Tight Money," *Business Week* commented:

The prestige of the Federal Reserve System, which had fallen to a low estate during the first postwar years, has had a remarkable recovery. Under the chairmanship of William McC. Martin, the Federal Reserve Board has met skillfully and courageously the problems of a turbulent economy. At home and abroad, there is an almost alarming degree of confidence in its ability to steer our economy between the dangers of boom and bust.

The renaissance of the Fed reached a high point last week when President Eisenhower reaffirmed the complete independence of our central banking organization. He acknowledged that the policy of credit stringency now being pursued by the Federal Reserve was one that raised grave doubts on the part of his own advisers. Nevertheless, with his usual patience and breadth of view, the President defended the right of the Federal Reserve to pursue an independent course. No other President has ever spoken thus.

Yet at this moment of triumph, the Federal Reserve System, it seems to us, stands in considerable peril. No matter how secure their independence, Martin and his fellow-members of the Federal Reserve System are up to their armpits in politics. . . .

The Federal Reserve System ought to be above politics. It ought not to use its great powers for political purposes, and we are quite sure that no responsible official of the System would, under any circumstances, knowingly consent to such a course. Yet the System will not survive if it attempts to close its eyes to the political consequences of its actions. If the Federal Reserve System, by overdoing its policy of credit restraint, brings on a business recession this year, we may be certain that a new Administration of another party would not wait long to take away powers that can be used, however corrrect the motives, to accomplish such drastic political consequences.

Also on May 5, however, Chairman Martin made a speech to the Pennsylvania Bankers Association at Atlantic City that the press widely carried and characterized as reassuring. The *New York Times* noted that "Martin spoke of five 'basic considerations' that enter the making of decisions in monetary policy. In his discussion of them his emphasis was on the duty of the Federal Reserve not to let credit dry up."

Criticism from Democrats and Business Executives

The next rumbles on the political front came from Democrats. On May 12 the *Washington Post* reported that Representative Patman's

Joint Economic Subcommittee was "quietly investigating the Administration's protests against credit tightening moves by the Federal Reserve System." The *Post,* observing that "the probe could have wide political repercussions," assessed the motivation this way:

Democrats have been arguing that if the economy turns sour in the next few months, the Administration will try to blame the Federal Reserve's credit squeeze. This [Republican] argument, Democrats say, would be shattered if the [administration] protests came after the System made its move. . . . The Patman committee has sent questionnaires to the three Cabinet officers [Humphrey, Weeks, Mitchell], Burns, and Federal Reserve Chairman William McChesney Martin, Jr. asking what if anything they said or wrote each other before the credit screw was turned.

On May 18 Representative Patman confirmed that he had sent letters of inquiry to all mentioned, had gotten three answers, and was thinking of holding hearings.

Representative Rains (Democrat, Alabama), as chairman of a House Banking subcommittee on housing, issued a report that the *Washington Post* of May 14 characterized as asserting that "recent Federal Reserve Board action in tightening the money market will have 'unfavorable repercussions' on the housing industry."

Businessmen were next in the headlines with blasts against tight money. General Motors' President Harlow Curtice was quoted by the *Journal of Commerce* of May 16 as saying at a press conference in Detroit: "The restrictive money policy of the Federal Reserve Board has not only contributed to a lower trend in auto sales since April 1 but it has made questionable whether gross national product will remain at or close to the $400 billion a year level. . . ." He urged the Board to reverse itself as quickly as possible.

The National Association of Home Builders was similarly critical in testimony by its president, Joseph B. Haverstick, before Representative Rains's House Banking Subcommittee in Washington on May 16, as was the National Association of Real Estate Boards, represented before the subcommittee by Vice Chairman Robert E. Scott.

The *New York Times* reported from Hot Springs, Va., on a May 17 meeting of the Commerce Department's Business Advisory Council, "a group of more than 150 of the nation's leading manufacturing, financial and retail executives." Said the *Times* (of May 18):

Uppermost in the minds of many early arrivals was concern over the present restrictive money policy of the Federal Reserve Board. This was evidenced in comments that ranged from mild criticism to outright disapproval of the board's recent increase in the discount rate. . . . Those sharpest in their criticism said that the rise . . . had already made short-term money tight and might eventually reduce the present plentiful supply of long-term funds greatly in demand for industrial expansion. The tightness of money, it was added, might aggravate the economic situation in the third quarter, which is expected to show a softer tone primarily because of the weakness in auto and housing sales. . . .

On the same date Secretary of the Treasury Humphrey, testifying at a Senate committee hearing before leaving for Hot Springs to attend the Business Advisory Council meeting himself, finally confirmed publicly the month-long reports that he had disagreed with the Federal Reserve about the discount rate increase.

Mr. Humphrey, said Dow-Jones, commented when cornered by Senator Long (Democrat, Louisiana). At first, he "launched into a description of the Board as an agency independent of the Administration and of his own relationships with Mr. Martin," saying, "he cooperated closely with the FRB Chairman on all actions that either takes that might affect the economy. In trying to gauge future economic conditions and demands for money and credit, Mr. Humphrey said he and Mr. Martin frequently differ in their views on the meaning of various economic pressures. When Senator Long pressed for a more direct answer to his question, Mr. Humphrey replied: 'If it were my responsibility I would not have made the last move. I would have let natural conditions take their course. I agreed with all the other moves but the last one.' "

The *St. Louis Post-Dispatch,* taking note editorially on May 18 of the Humphrey, Curtice, and *Business Week* comments, observed in an editorial entitled "Ordeal of the 'Fed' ":

It will take fortitude . . . to stand up under this kind of pressure. . . . Right or wrong, however, the Board must use its own judgment if it is to act as a politically independent regulator of the economy. . . . The Board's independence, [if] sacrificed in fact, will some day be ended by law. . . . If control of credit policy becomes political, the people will have every right to insist that responsibility for it also become political.

Four days later, the National News Service's Ruth Montgomery said she was told by a "top White House official" that the White House was "putting pressure on the Federal Reserve Board to relax its tight credit policy to avert a possible deflationary trend during the fall's election campaign." Her report went on:

The White House fears the Board's recent action will cause a mild recession at the very moment that the Administration wants a booming economy. One of the GOP's favorite campaign slogans is "Everything's Booming but the Guns."

On May 23, exactly one week after Secretary Humphrey's first public confirmation of the then one-month-long round of reports, the *New York Times* said it was "revealed publicly for the first time . . ." that Presidential Economic Adviser Arthur Burns had "opposed the latest increase in interest rates by the Federal Reserve." The revelation came from Representative Patman, who made public replies to inquiries he had made about reported differences over the discount rate increase. Mr. Patman also voiced criticism of Messrs. Humphrey and Martin for "avoiding answering Mr. Patman's questions about the disagreement directly" and said he therefore would "call hearings to look into the matter."

Bankers Speak Out

Bankers were heard from next, with suggestions as well as some support of the Federal Reserve.

Allan Sproul, retiring as president of the Federal Reserve Bank of New York, made on May 24 what the *American Banker* termed a "valedictory" address before the New Jersey Bankers Association convention in Atlantic City. Mr. Sproul "answered critics of Federal Reserve credit restraint," citing economic and financial conditions, but also, in his conclusion, "voiced his belief that time is ripe for a broad national inquiry [by a presidential commission] into the banking and monetary system of the United States." He said that there was "need to know what to expect of our central banking system, of our commercial banking system, of our savings banks and building and loan associations, of our insurance companies and pension trusts. . . ." But he emphasized, the *American Banker* said, that "he did not mean 'such piece-meal inquiries as those concerning the Federal Reserve System and the Federal Open Market Committee which have marked the last few years.' "

A prominent private banker, Henry C. Alexander, board chairman of J. P. Morgan and Company, was headlined shortly afterwards as advocating an "easing of restraint." Mr. Alexander addressed the Buffalo, New York, Chamber of Commerce. The *Buffalo Evening News* account of May 26 led off with the statement that Mr. Alexander had said, "More money should be made available for the nation's expanding economy, but the dollar must not be cheapened by reducing rates of interest."

As May came to an end, Federal Reserve assurances to inquirers that seasonal needs for credit and cash would be met over the approaching Memorial Day holiday drew such headlines on May 29 as "Federal Reserve to Provide Reserves for Business Needs" (*American Banker*) and "Easier Money: Federal Reserve Begins to Relax Credit: Cites Changes in Business" (*Wall Street Journal*). But the Associated Press, on May 31, supplied more perspective: "The Federal Reserve Board, while keeping a close watch on the money supply and credit situation, thus far has given no sign of a major change in its policy."

As June began, Democrats were spotlighted. *U.S. News and World Report,* in a survey in its issue of June 1 of the month-and-a-half-long controversy, focused on the answers Representative Patman got and now planned to develop further at a public hearing. It digested the replies as follows:

From the President's chief economic adviser, Arthur F. Burns, came this pointed reply: "In view of somewhat conflicting tendencies, particularly the divergent movements that have occurred of late in retail trade and capital expenditures, I doubt the timeliness of this action."

George M. Humphrey, Secretary of the Treasury, said any important actions on money matters by his department or the Federal Reserve are always talked over in advance. He added: "It is, of course, only natural that we often have some differences of judgment arising from varying appraisals of the timing and effect of economic trends."

From the Secretary of Commerce, Sinclair Weeks, went this blunt reply to the Patman inquiry: "I did disagree with the action taken, but my disagreement was more in the realm of 'timing' than otherwise."

. . . The Secretary of Labor, James P. Mitchell, . . . wrote . . . a non-committal reply. Mr. Mitchell has said publicly that he does not see any inflationary danger and does not feel the Federal Reserve move was necessary.

. . . The Chairman of the Federal Reserve Board, William McChesney Martin, Jr., stressed the Board's "independence."

He said the Board would always consult with other agencies but that "such consultations do not, however, mean any loss of independence by the Federal Reserve in discharging the responsibilities delegated to it by Congress." Mr. Martin went on to say, "From time to time there are bound to be differences of judgment, of emphasis and of timing. It would be astonishing in a democracy if this were not so and indeed it would be reason for grave concern if precautionary action had to wait for unanimity."

On June 4 the *Journal of Commerce* saw caution in the attitude of some of Representative Patman's Democratic colleagues:

Considerable behind-the-scenes planning is going on among Congressional Democrats to make sure that the forthcoming investigation of the Federal Reserve Board's increase in the rediscount rate doesn't get out of hand. . . . The date for the hearing, which [Joint Economic Committee Chairman] Senator Douglas and others want to hold to just one day, has tentatively been set for June 12. Chairman Douglas and other members of the full committee also want to limit the scope of the investigation to the mechanics of the decision making on the rediscount rate rise. They feel it's far too early to try to assess whether or not the decision was a wise one.

On June 12 the Patman inquiry into Treasury–Federal Reserve differences opened, and the *New York Times* the next day said that it "proved mild today. Both sides answered all questions readily, conceded their disagreement in April, and said all was proceeding as before."

Witnesses Humphrey and Martin, instead of widening the area of dispute, "found themselves in agreement in principle when Mr. Patman turned to other matters [than the April disagreement]," the *Times* said. There were some good-humored passages:

Mr. Humphrey laughed off a suggestion by Mr. Patman who said he had seen it in the press, that the Administration might blame the Federal Reserve if the economy should slump later this year. Mr. Patman noted that Mr. Martin was a Democrat and asked if that were not a way to throw the blame for any slump to the Democrats. "I assure you," said Mr. Humphrey with a broad grin, "that if I found a way I'd be glad to." Everybody laughed, including Representative Patman. . . .

There was also some incidental information on the way the Federal Reserve Board chairman took the change in administrations and parties in control. The *Times* recorded it thus:

Mr. Martin revealed that he had not submitted his resignation at the beginning of the Eisenhower Administration, as Mr. Humphrey had previously asserted. Actually, said Mr. Martin, he was considering a "very attractive" private offer, and a few people knew it. But people "close to" the new Administration had told him, he said, not to be too hasty about submitting his resignation. Then after the Administration took office, both Mr. Humphrey and the President had urged him to remain as chairman. Mr. Humphrey repeated today that he still thought "Bill Martin is the best qualified man in the country for the job."

Before June had ended, however, the economy began to gather steam, and the controversy over credit began to lose it. By June 29, the New York *Herald Tribune,* surveying the scene editorially, was able to sum up developments cheerfully:

Buying demand is displaying the bounce that the Federal Reserve Board was fretting about when it made its much debated move to tighten credit in mid-April. Last month's rise in the cost of living emphasizes the fashion in which the United States is delicately balanced between inflation and recession. There can be endless debate about what would have happened if the Federal Reserve had not acted. But two things are clear—the credit squeeze did not start a recession and, in fact, most major indicators now are pointing up, not down.

The start of a steel strike brought out some subtle changes in thought in the executive branch and in Congress.

On Capitol Hill, where Representative Patman had concentrated on disagreement about past action, Senator Willis Robertson, taking note of suggestions such as former Federal Reserve Bank President Sproul's for a study of the financial system by a presidential commission, introduced a resolution for "a full and complete study and investigation of existing banking and credit needs of the nation." The study was proposed for a Senate Banking subcommittee headed by Senator Robertson.

Spotlight on Inflation

The focus of fear swung more sharply from deflation to inflation as the steel strike was settled on July 30—with an increase in steel prices as well as an increase in wages—and almost simultaneously the entire international front flared under the impact of the Suez crisis. On August 19 the *New York Times* ended a story on this note:

The Reserve System has been shown to have been right this spring and summer in recognizing inflationary trends at a time when leaders in business and government thought otherwise.

But bouquets for the Federal Reserve were neither numerous nor long-lasting.

On August 23 the "second round" of discount rate increases in 1956 was announced as under way as the rate went up from $2\frac{3}{4}$ to 3 percent at the Federal Reserve Banks of New York, Philadelphia, Richmond, and Chicago, matching the rate that had prevailed since April at Minneapolis and San Francisco.

The timing was striking. It came just one day after (1) Republicans had nominated President Eisenhower for a second term, and (2) Democratic Representative Patman's Small Business Committee had blasted Federal Reserve "credit restrictions" for causing a "high mortality rate" among small business firms.

The *New York Times* of August 25 said in an editorial, "The threat of inflation looms again as a darkening shadow upon the horizon of the American economy." But others saw different shapes in the darkness. The New York *Herald Tribune* on August 27 headlined "3 Democrats Hit Reserve Board Boost" and named them in its story as Representatives Emanuel Celler and Abraham J. Multer of New York ("they charged in a joint statement that big business can weather 'tight money' but small business cannot"), and Wright Patman of Texas. Mr. Patman threatened to hold an investigation.

Officials of the Republican party, which had just adopted a platform plank endorsing "the present policy of freedom for the Federal Reserve System to combat inflation and deflation by wise fiscal (sic) policy," endeavored with temporary success to go unquoted in the headlines. On September 17, however, Democratic presidential nominee Adlai Stevenson held a press conference in Washington that included these exchanges, according to the unedited transcript carried by the Associated Press:

Q. Would you, if elected, support and continue an independent Federal Reserve System and, particularly, the independence of the Federal Reserve System's Open Market Committee?

A. On the basis of what information I have with respect to the working of the Federal Reserve System, I would suggest no legislation to alter the present position of the Federal Reserve System with respect to the Treasury Department and also with respect to its Open Market Committee.

Republican feelings were assessed again by the *Wall Street Journal* on the following day. Said the *Journal* for September 28:

Secret feud smolders between Ike's advisers and Federal Reserve credit men.

The Administration strongly opposes, in private, any further credit tightening moves. Officials still smart over the Fed's latest discount rate boost. They shy from public disagreement to avoid recurrence of last spring's family split. . . .

On the other hand, the October 1 *Washington Post* had a somewhat different private—if not the party—line. Said the *Post*:

Treasury Secretary George M. Humphrey, hitherto dubious of the Federal Reserve Board's "tight money" policy, has recently told associates he thinks it is right. Economically, he concedes, it is the proper thing even though its political repercussions are something less than vote-catching for the Republicans.

The Election Approaches

Meanwhile, "tight money" stayed in the headlines as the campaign days ticked away and, unsurprisingly, popped up in questioning at the next press conferences held by President Eisenhower, on October 5 and again on October 11.

The thing that struck the *Washington Post* (October 6) as most emphatic about the first of these press conferences was that:

President Eisenhower yesterday disclaimed responsibility for the Federal Reserve Board's credit-tightening moves, declaring that the agency is independent. He did not comment directly on a reporter's statement that the Administration had helped lift interest rates. But he said . . . "The Federal Reserve Board is not under my control, and I think it is proper that the Congress did set it up as an independent agency. . . ." He thereby sought to blunt Democratic charges that his Administration had fostered tight money policies hurting local governments, home buyers, small business, farmers and others. . . .

At the second of these conferences, Mr. Eisenhower once more "voiced his conviction that the Federal Reserve System is properly independent of the Administration." But this time there was a new and more positive note in the lead of the *Wall Street Journal's* account and the beginning of a theme that would be heard again. Said the *Journal's* lead: "President Eisenhower declared American prosperity and strength at home depend on a 'sound dollar.' . . ." And, he told his news conference, an increasing cost of living must be dealt with intelligently.

The President's attitude toward the Federal Reserve System continued to be unshared by all members of his political party. On October 23, the *Washington Post* reported that *Business Week* publisher Elliott Bell, described by the *Post* as "an important, though unofficial White House adviser," had urged "linking the Federal Reserve System to the administration in a President-directed national economic council."

Mr. Bell, addressing the American Bankers Association convention in Los Angeles, was giving personal advocacy—and wider distribution—to the ideas advanced earlier by his magazine's editorial page. The *Post* said in its story:

Contending that the Federal Reserve should not "ignore or even go counter" to the Administration, Bell blueprinted a counterpart to the National Security Council for the economic front.

This body would "give the Administration the power to help determine basic economic and monetary policies for which it must take full political responsibilities," Bell said. . . . While President Eisenhower has publicly affirmed the Reserve's independence, Bell declared, "You can't keep the Federal Reserve out of politics."

He charged Board Chairman William McC. Martin and the Reserve governors with "resolutely ignoring the political aspects of their course." Despite the President's disclaimer that he can't control interest rates, "the public holds Mr. Eisenhower responsible for tight money," Bell said.

The Bell view was not, however, echoed in public observations of Under Secretary of the Treasury Randolph Burgess when he spoke to the same bankers' convention the next day. The *Wall Street Journal* of October 24 reported that Mr. Burgess said the administration had "assured the Federal Reserve System its freedom to exercise independent judgment in its monetary policies." He said that a Federal Economic Council, such as was suggested by Mr. Bell, "was unnecessary." (The following day, however, Mr. Bell's suggestion was "supported," according to the *New York Times,* by another speaker at the same convention: T. V. Houser, chairman of Sears, Roebuck. The *Times* reported October 25 that Mr. Houser contended that monetary policy isn't consistent in its impact and that "it operates only on the employer side of the ledger and restrains labor only through an adverse effect on the employer.")

With election day only a couple of weeks away, Representative Patman moved back into the news on October 25 with, once more, an announcement of an investigation. The *Wall Street Journal* quoted Mr. Patman as saying that his Joint Economic Committee would reopen its investigation of Federal Reserve policies with one day of hearings in December. This time, said Mr. Patman, the undertaking would be "to find out whether the trend toward higher interest rates 'had already gone too far' and whether the use of monetary devices has 'failed in its aim' as a stabilization device." The paper pointed out that Democrats had criticized the latest discount rate boost and "tight money" policies. "Administration officials were openly critical of the Federal Reserve's approval of a general increase in the discount rate last April," the *Journal* added, "but did not comment publicly on the latest hike in August. However, Administration leaders privately opposed the action."

The election was held November 6. The *Wall Street Journal* rolled out its early editions on November 7 even before the early returns began coming in. Conscious that some old controversies never die, the *Journal,* without feeling that it needed to wait for the election outcome, filled the feature space on its editorial page with a confident prediction:

The voters yesterday ended the political campaign. But the fighting over one of the main domestic issues of the campaign may have just begun.

The cause of the fighting is money. The immediate stake in the battle is the independence of the Federal Reserve Board. And the skirmishing is likely to take place at both ends of Pennsylvania Avenue, in the Congress and in the Executive Offices concerned with this highly volatile subject. . . . And certainly the invasion forces are already sending out skirmishers.

History has shown that the *Wall Street Journal* editorial staff was correct after the 1956 election. As this book goes to press, the *Journal's* page one lead story for August 28, 1970, was headlined, "Some Nixonites Fret As Their Man at the Fed Shows Independence." The story chronicles increasing strain between Arthur Burns at the Fed and some White House staff members, and the effective moves being made by Burns to strengthen uncertain relations with key congressmen. The issue of Federal Reserve independence is unlikely to vanish soon from the American monetary scene.

SELECTED BIBLIOGRAPHY

Achinstein, Asher. *Federal Reserve Policy and Economic Stability, 1951–57*. U.S. Library of Congress, Legislative Reference Service, for the Senate Committee on Banking and Currency. 85 Cong. 2 sess. Washington: Government Printing Office, 1958.

Bach, G. L. "The Economics and Politics of Money," *Harvard Business Review, Vol.* 31 (March–April 1953).

———. *Federal Reserve Policy-Making: A Study in Government Economic Policy Formation.* New York: Alfred A. Knopf, Inc., 1950.

———. "Inflation—Danger Ahead?" *Harvard Business Review,* Vol. 42 (July–August 1964).

———. *Inflation: A Study in Economics, Ethics, and Politics.* Providence: Brown University Press, 1958.

Bailey, Stephen. *Congress Makes a Law: The Story Behind the Employment Act of 1946.* New York: Columbia University Press, 1950.

Bibliography on Full Employment. Report to the Committee on Banking and Currency, Senate Committee Print, No. 2, 79 Cong. 1 sess. Washington: Government Printing Office, 1945.

Board of Governors of the Federal Reserve System. *Annual Reports,* various years.

———. *The Federal Reserve System: Purposes and Functions.* 5th ed. Washington: The Board, 1967.

——— and the U.S. Treasury Department. *The Federal Reserve and the Treasury: Answers to Questions from the Commission on Money and Credit.* Englewood Cliffs: Prentice-Hall, 1963.

Bodkin, Ronald G. *The Wage-Price-Productivity Nexus.* Philadelphia: University of Pennsylvania Press, 1966.

Braybrooke, David, and Charles E. Lindblom. *A Strategy of Decision.* New York: The Free Press, 1963.

Break, George F., and others. *Federal Credit Agencies.* Prepared for the Commission on Money and Credit. Englewood Cliffs: Prentice-Hall, 1963.

———. *Federal Lending and Economic Stability.* Washington: Brookings Institution, 1965.

Brown, E. Cary, and others. *Stabilization Policies.* Prepared for the Commission on Money and Credit. Englewood Cliffs: Prentice-Hall, 1963.

Brunner, Karl, and Allan H. Meltzer. *An Alternative Approach to the Monetary Mechanism.* Prepared for the Subcommittee on Domestic Finance of the House Committee on Banking and Currency. 88 Cong. 2 sess. Washington: Government Printing Office, 1964.

Burns, Arthur F. "Heller's 'New Dimensions of Political Economy,' " *National Banking Review,* Vol. 4 (June 1967).

Chandler, Lester V. *Benjamin Strong, Central Banker.* Washington: Brookings Institution, 1958.

Changes in the Banking and Currency System of the United States (the "Glass Report"). Report of the House Committee on Banking and Currency, 63 Cong. 1 sess. Washington: Government Printing Office, 1913.

Clifford, A. Jerome. *The Independence of the Federal Reserve System.* Philadelphia: University of Pennsylvania Press, 1965.

Commission on Money and Credit. *Money and Credit: Their Influence on Jobs, Prices and Growth.* Englewood Cliffs: Prentice-Hall, 1961.

Committee for Economic Development. *A Stabilizing Fiscal and Monetary Policy for 1970.* New York, 1969.

———. *Taxes and the Budget: A Program for Prosperity in a Free Economy.* New York, 1947.

Compendium on Monetary Policy Guidelines and Federal Reserve Structure. Pursuant to H.R. 11, Subcommittee on Domestic Finance of the House Committee on Banking and Currency, 90 Cong. 2 sess. Washington: Government Printing Office, 1968.

Controlling Monetary Aggregates. Proceedings of the Monetary Conference Held on Nantucket Island, June 1969. Federal Reserve Bank of Boston, 1969.

Cushman, Robert E. *The Independent Regulatory Commissions.* New York: Oxford University Press, 1941.

de Leeuw, Frank, and Edward M. Gramlich. "The Channels of Monetary Policy: A Further Report on the Federal Reserve-MIT Econometric Model," *Federal Reserve Bulletin,* Vol. 55 (June 1969).

Eccles, Marriner S. *Beckoning Frontiers: Public and Personal Recollections.* New York: Alfred A. Knopf, Inc., 1951.

Economic Report of the President. Washington: Government Printing Office, various years.

Federal Tax Policy for Economic Growth and Stability. Papers Submitted by Panelists Appearing before the Subcommittee on Tax Policy. 84 Cong. 1 sess. Washington: Government Printing Office, 1955.

Fisher, Irving. *Stable Money: A History of the Movement.* New York: Adelphi, 1934.

Flash, Edward S., Jr. *Economic Advice and Presidential Leadership.* New York: Columbia University Press, 1965.

Friedman, Milton. *A Program for Monetary Stability.* New York: Fordham University Press, 1960.

——, and Anna J. Schwartz. *A Monetary History of the United States, 1867–1960.* Princeton: Princeton University Press for the National Bureau of Economic Research, 1963.

—— and ——. *Monetary Statistics of the United States: Estimates, Sources, Methods.* New York: National Bureau of Economic Research, 1970.

Friend, Irwin, and others. *Private Capital Markets.* Prepared for the Commission on Money and Credit. Englewood Cliffs: Prentice-Hall, 1964.

Glass, Carter. *An Adventure in Constructive Finance.* New York: Doubleday, Page, 1927.

Gordon, Kermit (ed.). *Agenda for the Nation.* Washington: Brookings Institution, 1968. Chapters by Richard N. Cooper ("The Dollar and the World Economy") and Herbert Stein ("Unemployment, Inflation, and Economic Stability").

Harding, W. P. G. *The Formative Period of the Federal Reserve System.* Boston: Houghton Mifflin, 1925.

Hardy, Charles O. *Credit Policies of the Federal Reserve System.* Washington: Brookings Institution, 1932.

Harris, S. E. *Twenty Years of Federal Reserve Policy.* Cambridge: Harvard University Press, 1933.

Heller, Walter W. *New Dimensions of Political Economy.* Cambridge: Harvard University Press, 1966.

Jacoby, Neil H. (ed.). *United States Monetary Policy.* New York: Praeger, for the American Assembly, 1964.

Johnson, Stewart, and others. *Federal Credit Programs.* Prepared for the Commission on Money and Credit. Englewood Cliffs: Prentice-Hall, 1963.

Joint Economic Committee of Congress. *Joint Economic Report.* (The Committee's annual report on the annual *Economic Report of the President.*) Washington: Government Printing Office, various years.

——. *Standards for Guiding Monetary Action.* 90 Cong. 2 sess. Washington: Government Printing Office, 1968.

Kirschen, Etienne S., and others. *Economic Policy in Our Time,* Vol. 1. Chicago: Rand McNally, 1964.

Krislov, Samuel, and L. D. Musolf (eds.). *The Politics of Regulation: A Reader.* Boston: Houghton Mifflin, 1964.

Lewis, Wilfred, Jr. *Federal Fiscal Policy in the Postwar Recessions.* Washington: Brookings Institution, 1962.

Meigs, A. James. *Free Reserves and the Money Supply.* Chicago: University of Chicago Press, 1962.

Mints, Lloyd W. *A History of Banking Theory in Great Britain and the United States.* Chicago: University of Chicago Press, 1945.

Monetary, Credit, and Fiscal Policies. Hearings before the Subcommittee on Monetary, Credit, and Fiscal Policies of the Joint Committee on the Economic Report. 81 Cong. 1 sess. Washington: Government Printing Office, 1950.

———. Report of the Subcommittee. 81 Cong. 2 sess. Washington: Government Printing Office, 1950.

Monetary Policy and the Management of the Public Debt. Hearings before the Subcommittee on General Credit Control and Debt Management of the Joint Committee on the Economic Report. 82 Cong. 2 sess. Washington: Government Printing Office, 1952.

———. Report of the Subcommittee. Washington: Government Printing Office, 1952.

Neustadt, Richard E. *Presidential Power: The Politics of Leadership.* New York: John Wiley & Sons, Inc., 1960.

Nomination of William McChesney Martin, Jr. Hearings before the Senate Committee on Banking and Currency. 84 Cong. 2 sess. Washington: Government Printing Office, 1956.

Okun, Arthur M. *The Political Economy of Prosperity.* Washington: Brookings Institution, 1970.

———, and Nancy H. Teeters. "The Full Employment Surplus Revisited," in *Brookings Papers on Economic Activity* (1:1970).

Perry, George L. *Unemployment, Money Wage Rates, and Inflation.* Cambridge: The M.I.T. Press, 1966.

Phillips, A. W. "The Relation Between Unemployment and the Rate of Change of Money Wage Rates in the United Kingdom, 1861–1957," *Economica,* Vol. 25 (November 1958).

Policies to Combat Depression. A Conference of the Universities-National Bureau Committee for Economic Research. Princeton: Princeton University Press for National Bureau of Economic Research, 1956.

Recent Federal Reserve Action and Economic Policy Coordination. Hearings before the Joint Economic Committee. 89 Cong. 1 sess. Washington: Government Printing Office, 1966.

"The Relation Between Prices and Employment: Two Views," Federal Reserve Bank of St. Louis, *Review* (March 1969).

The Relationship of Prices to Economic Stability and Growth. Compendium of Papers Submitted by Panelists Appearing before the Joint Economic Committee. 85 Cong. 2 sess. Washington: Government Printing Office, 1958.

Report of the Commission on Mortgage Interest Rates to the President of the United States and to the Congress. Washington: Government Printing Office, 1969.

Report of the Committee on Federal Credit Programs to the President of the United States. Washington: Government Printing Office, 1963.

Report of the Committee on Financial Institutions to the President of the United States. Washington: Government Printing Office, 1963.

Robinson, Marshall A. *The National Debt Ceiling: An Experiment in Fiscal Policy.* Washington: Brookings Institution, 1959.

Schultze, Charles L. *The Politics and Economics of Public Spending.* Washington: Brookings Institution, 1968.

Sheahan, John. *The Wage-Price Guideposts.* Washington: Brookings Institution, 1967.

Shultz, George P., and Robert Z. Aliber (eds.). *Guidelines, Informal Controls, and the Market Place: Policy Choices in a Full Employment Economy.* Chicago: University of Chicago Press, 1966.

Smithies, Arthur. *The Budgetary Process in the United States.* New York: McGraw-Hill Book Company, 1955.

Sorensen, Theodore C. *Decision-Making in the White House: The Olive Branch or the Arrows.* New York: Columbia University Press, 1963.

———. *Kennedy.* New York: Harper & Row, 1965.

Staff Report on Employment, Growth, and Price Levels (the "Eckstein Report"). Prepared for consideration by the Joint Economic Committee. 86 Cong. 1 sess. Washington: Government Printing Office, 1959.

Stein, Herbert. *The Fiscal Revolution in America.* Chicago: University of Chicago Press, 1969.

Sundquist, James L. *Politics and Policy: The Eisenhower, Kennedy, and Johnson Years.* Washington: Brookings Institution, 1968. Chap. 2.

Truman, David B. *The Governmental Process.* New York: Alfred A. Knopf, Inc., 1957.

Twentieth Anniversary of the Employment Act of 1946: An Economic Symposium. Hearings before the Joint Economic Committee. 89 Cong. 2 sess. Washington: Government Printing Office, 1966.

Viner, Jacob. "Recent Legislation and the Banking Situation," *American Economic Review*, Vol. 26 (March 1936).

Warburg, Paul M. *The Federal Reserve System: Its Origin and Growth.* New York: The Macmillan Company, 1930.

Wicker, Elmus R. *Federal Reserve Monetary Policy, 1917–1933.* New York: Random House, Inc., 1966.

Wildavsky, Aaron B. *The Politics of the Budgetary Process.* Boston: Little, Brown, 1964.

Williams, John H. "The Banking Act of 1935," *American Economic Review*, Vol. 26 (March 1936).

Willes, H. Parker. *The Federal Reserve System: Legislation, Organization, and Operation.* New York: The Ronald Press Co., 1923.

INDEX